To Light a Candle

Books by Welthy Honsinger Fisher

TO LIGHT A CANDLE

HANDBOOK FOR MINISTERS' WIVES

BEYOND THE MOONGATE

A STRING OF CHINESE PEARLS

TWINS TRAVELOGUES
   KOREA, JAPAN, INDIA, CHINA

TOP OF THE WORLD

FREEDOM

WORLD CITIZEN, FRED B. FISHER

To Light a Candle

WELTHY HONSINGER FISHER

McGraw-Hill Book Company, Inc.
New York   Toronto   London

Editing and revisions
by
Suzanne Gleaves and Lael Wertenbaker

Contents

PART I

Little Sister Han

1

They say that at eighty you remember your childhood best. Perhaps, in a way, that is true of me. But it is not myself as a little girl in Rome, New York, that I recall most vividly; it is my other "childhoods," when I was reborn in the wonder and newness of strange, far places. Sometimes it seems to me as if I have had true reincarnations within one long lifetime.

The essential *me* has not changed. Good health and good humor were my God-given birthrights, never destroyed by rugged adventures. A cat's curiosity has kept me poking about in odd and sometimes dangerous corners of the world, even when I should have known better. I seem also to have been born spiritually color-blind, as others are born color-blind in fact. I never in my life could manage to make a distinction between one person and another because their skins were different shades.

My private aims, beliefs, and purposes have stayed the same, too, since they became mine so many years ago. They grew naturally in my heart. I believe in education as the means of broadening and bettering life on earth. I believe that women should be educated to take their proper part in life. And I consider, following Christ and Confucius, that all men are brothers within the four seas.

Whatever I have contributed toward these things in which I believe, I've learned more than I taught and gained more than I've given. I've had a whopping good time too, traveled all over the globe (someone suggested I should call my story *Around the World in Eighty Years*), and played my small part in many a drama.

I am writing this now in India, sitting by a smoking fire on a cold February night. The only non-Indian thing in the room (they do tease me about my avid adoption of the things around me wherever I am) is a scroll on my wall, sent me from China just before her ports were closed again to the West. "In the autumn of your life," the lettering reads in Chinese, "you are still announcing dawns!"

The place where I live and am writing is a "village," outside the city of Lucknow. It is Literacy Village, a busy settlement where we train teachers to go forth into the myriad schoolless villages of India. ("India *is* its villages," said Gandhi to my husband and me years ago.) Already five thousand teachers have left here, equipped with the materials and knowledge they need to carry literacy with them, though seven years ago Literacy Village was only the germ of an idea in my mind.

Tonight all the student-teachers and the teachers who train them have gone to bed, preferring blankets to the smoke from our one fireplace. The spirit of my dear husband seems with me saying, "Go to it, old girl! You wrote a book about me. Now write one about you."

I talk about my work many times a year in many places to groups of people who want to help. They always end up asking me questions about my life. How did I happen, at my age, to have created the village? How did I get there?

The answer takes in most of my life. And, as I think back, the best place to begin is with the young girl, born Welthy Honsinger, starting out for China in 1906.

The small Japanese steamer *Tango Maru* was sailing from Seattle across the Pacific to Yokohama and Shanghai. I remember myself well in a brown broadcloth coat lined with fur, and a rakish, high-crowned hat, coquettishly trimmed in fur, on my high-piled hair. From the tips of my high-buttoned cloth-topped shoes to the high neck of my sweeping brown charmeuse gown, I felt that I was styled by New York out of Paris.

There were two kinds of heroines dear to the fiction of that day: small blondes who smelled of violets and tall brunettes who smelled of lilacs. I was tall, firm of chin, large of mouth, deep-bosomed and straight-backed, and was sure I cut a figure that did not suggest the Methodist missionary-teacher on her way to the Chinese interior.

Chin up, I swept aboard alone. The continent I had crossed to take ship was too broad to permit friends or family to see me off, and all my farewells had been made in New York. The crew going about their duties were small, yellow-tinted men with closed faces. Other passengers nodded with the stiff formality of strangers who must soon come to know each other. The sailing was at night, and I went below to my cabin.

Instead of staying there, as the others did in theirs, I went back on deck to watch the ship move out across Puget Sound.

Resolution, growing from the night I had gone to a missionary meeting at Carnegie Hall in New York less than a year before, had carried me this far. Committed to the future, already moving toward it, I could permit myself to feel frightened, to wonder how on earth I came to be on my way. My whole past was sliding away along the moonlit wake of the ship. Staring at the majestic crest of Mount Rainier under the moon, the last sight of my native land, I felt the sensation of being reborn.

Nothing in my new life would be related to the one I was leaving behind. China was a mysterious and dangerous country. Only six years before, the Boxers had risen in rebellion and attempted to banish white men entirely from the Chinese mainland. More than one mission had been wiped out entirely. The girls at the Baldwin School, *Bao Lin* as it was called in Chinese, where I was on my way to be headmistress, spoke no English. I had as yet mastered no Chinese. I was going, against the advice of my friends and relatives, thousands of miles to be with them when they might not even want me.

The nature of the child is to accept what is, without complaints or preconceptions. The reborn me looked at the shining peak of Mount Rainier and said good-by to the person I had once been. Perhaps that peak was a symbol of true purity of purpose, of God-sent inspiration; perhaps I had changed my life merely tempted by the thought of high adventure. At the moment I did not know. Off into the unknown, all I was sure of was that I wanted to unbind the feet of Chinese girls.

What was she like, the Welthy Honsinger of my previous life who had decided to become a missionary-teacher to China instead of an opera singer? Was she reverting to the little girl who had lived in the big house in Rome, New York, where the Bible, the dictionary, and the world atlas were always open on the library table? Or was it her inheritance from ancestors who had come to the New World long before 1776 that had sent her to find her own new and far horizons?

The Honsinger family in Rome was Methodist and Republican. (Everybody up there was.) Like most descendants of prerevolutionary American settlers, they set great store by their ancestors.

The ancestral American Honsingers came from Holland, the Dunbars and Sanfords and Blakesleys on the distaff side of the family from England. (There had been three generations of Welthy Blakesleys since the first Puritan removed the *a* from Wealthy as a name.)

On the paternal, Dutch, side, most of the Honsingers had been Tories. They removed themselves, they thought, to Canada to avoid doing business with revolutionaries. But when the War of Independence was over and the new boundary between Canada and the U.S. was established, they found themselves in error and just within the United States, in Alburg, Vermont. Resigning themselves to American citizenship, they remained there and through succeeding generations left many a headstone engraved with their names beside the local church.

My father had inherited two iron foundries on Lake Champlain and did business all over New York state, but kept his home in Alburg. When the foundries failed, the Honsingers left for Plattsburg, New York. There my father's first wife died. After an interval, he married young Welthy Blakesley

Sanford, daughter of New England, whose earliest American ancestor had come over on the ship that followed the *Mayflower*. The Plattsburg business (an iron forge) also failed, and the couple moved on to Rome. My oldest brother was born there and destined by Papa from birth to be a doctor. Then came Mabel—artistic, musical, and a beauty—and then Elmina, called Mina—blonde-haired, blue-eyed, fair-skinned, and petite, very much Mother's daughter.

By the time I was born, on September 18, 1880, the children of Father's first marriage, four boys and a girl, had all grown up and gone. I was the last of the second contingent and resembled my father, a stalwart man who walked like a West Pointer. He adored this baby of his later years who looked like him. My earliest memory is of his putting me on the floor in front of company to demonstrate how smart I was at buttoning and unbuttoning my shoes. Spoiling me assiduously, he even told me playfully that Mother had not wanted me, but that *he* had, which I believed. My mother was not a spoiler of children, even her last-born, and, petted by Papa, I resented the discipline on which Mama insisted. Until Father died, I was never close to my mother.

Father's chain of blacksmith shops did not flourish, but the family was never really pinched. A red-headed maid named Cora helped in the big house where everybody in town foregathered. Sometimes the young people played croquet on the lawn, but mostly they sang around the square piano. Singing was the thing. In family quartets, brother sang bass, I tenor, while the other two girls carried the air and the alto.

Summers were spent in a cottage at Trenton Falls, where there was a Methodist camp. Each year, Papa hired a bus to take the family and Cora, all our provisions, and our summer wardrobes to the Falls for six weeks or two months. We children learned to swim in the clear-water creek, played in and under the big trees, and took long walks to pick wildflowers.

As the years passed in an orderly, leisurely routine, we went to public grade school in Rome and on to the Rome Free

Academy, the local high school. I felt myself an ugly duckling in comparison with my tiny, pretty blonde sisters, and took comfort whenever great things were prophesied for me.

My Sunday School teacher called me "Pansy" and insisted that I would be a famous writer. So, of course, I was sure I would be. When Nelly Bly's trip around the world fired my imagination in the seventh grade, I wrote an essay about my heroine and it was published in the Rome *Daily Sentinel*. I followed this with a feature on Women in the World.

I did have a naturally good voice and by the time I reached high school I had won local recognition as a singer. In church the others would stop singing to listen to me and I became a soloist with the choir.

Religion was part of our daily lives, not just on Sunday and in church. Morning prayers led by Father were as inevitable as dawn and if we were taking a 5 A.M. train to go to Camden to visit our grandfather, then breakfast and prayers took place at three-thirty. Father led Bible class meetings at the church and the neighbors claimed they could set their clocks by his departure from his house. Each child had his own Bible and read a verse from the chapter for the day. Although Mother never prayed aloud, when I became close to her I found out that she was the most deeply Christian of women.

My own piety was simple and unquestioning, but I never confused it with my pleasure in frivolity. A good enough student, I hid forbidden fiction, especially mystery stories, in my schoolbooks and perused them happily. Mabel and I conceived a secret passion for Bernarr MacFadden and his works, and went on a health binge. Out of sight in back of the house, we pored over pictures of muscular men and maidens in the Mac-Fadden publications, and did the exercises our man with the biceps prescribed. I had been born with a strong physique and my insistence, under MacFadden's influence, on drinking orange juice and eating whole-wheat bread improved on nature. Later a first-aid teacher at the Rome Academy, which had no physical-education program, introduced me to Swedish gymnastics and taught me to breathe deeply while walking rapidly forward.

In the interests of becoming an opera singer, the career upon which I now set my heart, I took elocution lessons at high school. When I was chosen one of six contestants for a prize of twenty dollars in gold, Father refused to go to the Rome Opera House where the competition took place, for fear his Welthy might not win. Win she did, reciting as her offering Will Carleton's "Negro Funeral" (which I can still declaim *in toto* if asked). The Superintendent of Schools, awarding the gold piece, said, "May the thread of gold in this coin shine in the light of your eyes as the thread of pathos did in the hearts of your hearers."

As a singer at church socials (in a favorite form of which the members of the congregation came as "poor people") I was quite likely to be the top entertainer. I was paid for singing at funerals.

Nevertheless, I agreed to go to college before studying for my operatic career. My mother wished it. Because Grandfather Blakesley had disapproved of higher education for women, Mother had left after high school to teach, and now her dearest dream was that her daughters should have degrees. Mabel, whose talent lay in playing the piano, went to the Utica Conservatory of Music, and Mina, who wanted to be a nurse, was sent to Albany Normal College. When my turn came, nothing would do but that I should graduate from Syracuse, where my brother, who wanted to be an artist but had yielded to Father's wishes, was studying medicine. I was there when Father died.

At home for a period of mourning, I soothed my sorrow with household chores, baking bread (the only thing I knew how to cook), sweeping, cleaning, and doing laundry. I had no wish to see visitors, but the minister of the church found me at the ironing board in the kitchen. Standing in the door, he remarked, "What a missionary you would make, Welthy!"

To this I responded not at all. I disliked the missionaries

who came to speak at church or college from time to time and
had even refused to go to the yearly student missionary conferences at Silver Bay, finding the student volunteers an un-
impressive lot. Ministers, I thought, knew less psychology than
they should. Never would Welthy Honsinger be a missionary.
Not for her the life of self-sacrifice in some heathen land.

Coming to know my mother at last, my admiration and
love blossomed. This small, strong-minded, realistic Christian
lady became my stalwart friend and confidante. From this
time on, I wrote my mother every day except when I was in
China; there my letters went out weekly. In one note from
college, I confessed to taking up some small frivolity. Mother's
reply was typical. "I trust you absolutely," she wrote. "I know
that you will never go too far in what you choose to do for
pleasure—and that you will never move away from your religious upbringing."

This maternal trust and faith remained mine. At twenty-
one, after college, I went to New York City alone, taking with
me my mother's blessing.

My first job was in a one-room school in Haverstraw, New
York, called Rosebud College. I had fifteen pupils to handle,
which I did with the self-assurance of the young.

An incident that occurred in this "little red schoolhouse"
was an unconscious example of my attitude toward the color
of people's skins. All God's children, as far as I was concerned,
had bright white souls, and that was what counted.

One day in late spring, after my charges were under control, I left them to study while I did an errand down the road.
When I got back, I found them all lined up outside the school
building, getting a noisy lecture from the neighboring landowner, a man whose beautiful orchards were a temptation to
all passers-by, children particularly.

Confronting the man in defense of my pupils, I demanded
to know by what right he had assembled my pupils and taken
them out of class.

"My cherries have been stolen," he told me indignantly.

"Complain to me, then, not to them," said I. "They aren't

all guilty!" Then I noticed that the one Negro student, a small, engaging fellow, was missing. "And where's Jimmy?"

The children pointed down the road, where I saw a cloud of Biblical dust in the center of which was Jimmy, running for his life.

"I dismissed the nigger and was warning these others," announced the landowner, but I scarcely heard him. I took off after Jimmy, running as if the devil himself were after me.

Spry as he was and fleeing for his life, I caught him in seconds and dropped to my knees in the dust, heedless of my thick skirts, to take him in my arms. Sobbing heartbrokenly, he denied stealing the cherries and said he would never return to the school.

"If you won't go back, then neither will I," said I, and took his hand. "You're as much part of the school as I am."

Together, both tear-streaked, we walked back to the group. When the landowner blustered and attempted to insist that Jimmy was the culprit, I said without a second thought, "If Jimmy goes, so do I," and the incident ended.

I began to study piano and then went to see Madame Canfield, a famous voice teacher at Carnegie Hall, about singing lessons. Madame Canfield was enthusiastic about my voice and my serious training began. Between walking five miles daily to Rosebud College and commuting to New York for lessons, even I found life a bit strenuous, and within two years transferred as a teacher to Englewood High School, where I could go to the school five days a week while living in the city.

A summer in Europe was the next step in my progress, and for this I had to borrow money, writing first for Mother's opinion on the propriety of this. "I am only sorry I cannot send you," Mother replied. "I am glad you are going and since you must borrow the money, I am glad you are using it where no one can ever take it from you—for your mind and your wide outlook."

Back from France, full of the sound of Paris opera and with a new fluency in French from hours of study at the Alliance Française, I got a weekly subscription for the Metropolitan

Opera season and resumed lessons with Madame Canfield.

Then I met Tom, who squired me devotedly and asked for my hand. Remembering how tempted I was to marry this charming beau, I tell young girls now: Do what you should, what you were born to do, and don't let anyone stop you. One day the right man will come along with whom you can do your work. Love must wait on the fulfillment of your destiny.

At the time, I thought what I was born to do was sing in opera. Then came the fateful missionary meeting at Carnegie Hall, and the call.

Dr. Robert Speer was speaking to a mass of eager students about the kinship of all mankind under God and the greatness of Western Christian education. To the hushed, packed hall, he said: "If every missionary around the world should die tonight, you college men and women would fill their places."

It seemed he was speaking straight to me. I could not sleep that night or the next.

I knew I could teach, keep discipline, manage children, make them learn. Other and older teachers often asked my help at Englewood High School because it seemed to come as second nature to me to handle children. I knew, too, that I longed to offer my life in some way to the service of God, to live in the "Christ way" of which my father had spoken so often.

The side of me that wanted this was the one that had kept me from marrying Tom, to whom I was so attracted and who was nearly irresistible to my luxury-loving and romantic side. He was willing enough for me to be religious, but it meant very little to him.

On the other hand, for as long as I could remember I had wanted to sing in opera, and my childhood idol had been Edythe Walker, the singer from Rome, New York. Nelly Bly, my other idol, was perhaps an influence on the side of China, but she scarcely would have undertaken to stay in any one remote spot.

I do not know now and did not know then how I made my decision. One morning it was there, unshakable, deep in my heart. God's will or my own, from that moment on nothing made me waver.

Almost everyone tried to dissuade me.

"You are throwing your life away, Welthy Honsinger," my singing teacher protested. "Grand opera is where you belong."

My colleagues on the staff of the Englewood school begged me to reconsider. "Why waste your abilities on the dirty heathen? Aren't our little Americans good enough for you?"

In upstate New York, Mother's friends were horrified. Mrs. Honsinger's youngest daughter was going into unknown, dangerous, and exotic country. But Mother, whatever trepidation she felt, only replied firmly. "Whatever Welthy does, she has my prayerful backing."

Members of my family, my half-sister and her husband in New York, took me to Chinatown with dissuasion in their minds. "Look around you," they admonished. "*These* are the people you'll be living with next year. How can you?"

Tom refused to be thrown over.

On the third finger of my right hand he put a ring—two diamonds and a deep red opal. "When," he said (not "if") and kissed me, "you change your mind, Welthy, put it on your left hand, and I will meet you in Paris. I can wait for you if I must."

In the hectic days that followed my decision, I thought of the pastor who had said in the kitchen at home, "What a missionary you would make, Welthy!" Once I knew that I would go, that neither Tom nor a glamorous future as a singer nor my career as a teacher could stop me, I wrote this man and asked for help.

Not wasting an instant, he sent me to see two women active in missions in the New York area. His choices were perfect. One was Mrs. J. M. Cornell, a generous and charming woman, who dressed exquisitely and maintained an apartment in New York and a summer home in Seabright, New Jersey. All her spare time was given to missions, and she immediately adopted me. Heroine-worshiper that I was, I promptly added Mrs. Cornell to my gallery of wonderful women.

Mrs. Stephen Baldwin, formerly a missionary to China herself, was just as attractive, though less worldly. The Baldwin Mission School in Nanchang was named for her husband. Her brilliant intellect delighted me, and she made China sound fascinating as well as dangerous. If I had the courage to go, would I be willing to take missionary training at an institute for a year? This frightened me. I feared I would meet too many of the sort of volunteer who had put me off before.

Instead of insisting on special religious training, the Mission Society offered me a job for which they felt I was already fairly well qualified: that of headmistress of the Baldwin School. I accepted happily.

From then on events moved with practical speed. I could scarcely remember, from the flurry of preparation and packing, how I had come to be actually aboard the ship, on my way, with Tom's ring on my right hand.

Taking one last look at the fading image of Rainier, I descended to the empty lounge of the *Tango Maru*. There was an open grand piano on a raised dais. To the accompaniment of throbbing engines and my own playing, I raised my operahouse voice and sang: "Thou shalt not be afraid of the terror by night nor for the arrow that flieth by day. . . ."

2

My only regret about the *Tango Maru* was that I had missed my one Chinese friend, Ilien Tang. This lovely young American-educated girl, whom I had met just once, would be a new member of my staff at Bao Lin. We had formed an immediate friendship and would have traveled together on an earlier voyage if my luggage—the massive and multiple trunks to convey a lady's five-year wardrobe—had not gone astray between New York and Seattle. Ilien Tang had gone on ahead and I would meet her somewhere up the Yangtze River, on the way to the city of Nanchang and the school. At least I had with me a library of books on China to read during the month it took to cross the Pacific.

The Japanese steward assigned me a seat at the British skipper's table. Our captain, relieved to find that I was an experienced sailor, promptly turned over to my solicitude the care of a frightened fellow passenger on her first voyage. M. was in my charge from then on. A charming, timid girl, she was on her way to Shanghai to stay with friends in order to "forget" an "unfortunate" love affair. There was no need to ask for her confidence. She told me all about it, endlessly.

Another passenger, Major V. S., was an officer on his way to the Philippines. He developed an interest in me sufficiently strong to make him refuse to leave the ship in Yokohama and accompany me as far as Shanghai. R. D., wife of a professor at Imperial University, returning to Tokyo to join her husband, did her best to encourage this one-sided romance and spoke wistfully of shipboard weddings. My favorite companion, though, was Willys Peck, China-born son of missionary parents on his way as a consular interpreter. I kept his friendship through the years of his distinguished career in our Foreign Service and bless him still because he gave me my first lessons in Mandarin.

Our days took the shape of all shipboard days, with genes, talk, and reading. I sang in the evening, accompanied by R. D., and read and studied during odd hours of the day and night. It was all most peaceful until an equinoctial gale began to blow.

Most of the passengers retired to heaving beds as the tiny steamer was forced off course toward the Aleutian Islands. Both frightened and elated, I went often on deck to watch the storm. Immense waves washed the ship up to monumental heights, tossed her down into cavernous troughs. Survival seemed impossible. The *Tango Maru* was a toy, embattled with the mighty tempest and the relentless ocean. In one terrifying moment, the wind pinned me to the wall of the deck. Blind and helpless, I clung to the inside rail with both hands as the ship dove downward and crashed as if it had hit the bottom of the sea. I heard a sound that did not match the bedlam noise of storm, straining engines, wind and sea, and caught the echo of a scream. When I made my way indoors, I learned that the sailor on lookout duty in the crow's-nest had been thrown onto the deck and picked up dead.

Silently the few passengers who were up sat in the lounge, shaken by the death of the boy. I remembered a day when my ship, returning from Europe on the northern route to Montreal, ran into icebergs and storm. Alerted, everyone spent the night in life belts. Men and women knelt in the lounge, then, and prayed aloud. One woman bargained clearly: "Oh God, if you let me live through this, I will never leave him again —I promise! Never!"

Stronger than the memory of Christians facing the danger of death well or absurdly on that other trip was my awed curiosity about the boy so shockingly thrown to the deck I had just left. What would this complete stranger have promised and prayed, if he had had time to promise or pray? What philosophies or beliefs comforted his youth, now untimely

ended? How would he be buried? Would his family mourn
and did it matter terribly to them that there would be no ashes
for them to keep?

Only the captain was English; the chief engineer, as always
in those days, was a Scot. The rest of the officers and crew,
the stewards, and the cabin boys on the *Tango Maru* were all
Japanese—silent and cat-footed, with immobile and expres-
sionless faces. They were inscrutable, I realized, because I had
no means of communicating with them. Who were the young
man's friends and who would go next into the crow's-nest at
the top of the swaying mast in the continuing storm? Would
he be fearful or fatalistic? Would he pray to Buddha to preserve his life or accept whatever happened as immutable fate?

I believed in a generous God, not one who was narrow and
tyrannous. I was not going to China to convert, but to teach
and—if so blessed—to bring Christianity with me by precept
and example, offering my heritage to others. Such reading as
I had already done gave me a sense that the spiritual ideals of
Buddhism made men seek good. Good could not be condemned because it was alien. With my whole soul I longed to
understand the boy who was dead, and his living friends. His
death had somehow shaken all my complacencies, and I never
forgot the boy I had not known.

The passengers were invited to the funeral the next morning.
On the lower deck, the boy's slight body lay on a bamboo
couch covered with a white cloth. Beside him was a bowl of
rice and chopsticks.

When the moment came, the engines were stopped in spite
of wind and waves. The silence on the tossing ship was awe-
inspiring. After the captain read part of the burial service
from the Anglican prayer book, the boy's crewmates lifted a
long Buddhist chant, strange, affecting, and impressive. Then,
in deepened silence, the bamboo bier was lifted and let gently
overboard into the sea. Even the quickly renewed roar of the
engines did not dispel my profound sense of stillness and of
wonder.

Three weeks and a day out of Seattle, the captain sent for

me to come to the bridge. Putting his powerful glasses in my
hand, he asked me to look to the east and see what I could see.

"A speck on the horizon," said I.

"Come every day and watch it grow," he invited. "Your
last sight of land was the white head of Rainier. That is the
white cone of Fujiyama." As Rainier had seemed symbol of
the land I had left, so Fuji was the Orient to which I was
coming. Somehow Rainier, for all its rough majesty, had
seemed familiar. Fuji was still utterly remote.

When the *Tango Maru* sailed into harbor at Yokohama, a
thousand tiny boats with colored sails decorated the calm
water. It was a rippling print of the East. Since a day and a
night were all I would have on the islands of Japan, I prepared
to make the most of them.

All but five of the passengers were disembarking. Willys
Peck made wagers with the others, betting on his side that
Miss Welthy Honsinger, for all her youth and gentle rearing,
would stick out her five-year contract to teach in China's interior. The others gave odds against him, all except V., who
declared he would not make up his mind until he had seen me
to Shanghai.

Mrs. D. asked me to Tokyo; there I ate my first Japanese
food, never served to foreigners on a Japanese boat. Under
Willys Peck's tutelage, I learned to manipulate chopsticks and
tuck the bowls of food under my chin. There was not much to
sightsee in Tokyo in 1906, so that evening Willys Peck and I
set out for Kamakura and the great bronze Buddha untouched
by the fire that had recently destroyed his shrine.

A Lilliputian train with a shrill popcorn-vender's whistle
ran through miniature villages, all exactly alike, and countryside cultivated in inches. From the Kamakura station, jin-
rickshas pulled by doll-like men with puppet effortlessness took
us through the velvet quiet of narrow fragrant avenues to the
Buddha that loomed over the town and the trees. A white
moon lit up the immense head. "It is living bronze," I wrote
in my diary. "He has arrived in the state called Nirvana where

the individual soul is lost in the over soul. The mouth is so tender, the eyes so deep, the head so strong and the all so filled with faith and calm that a little came down to me."

Returning to the tiny train we said nothing, hearing only the click of *getas* in the sleeping streets as some latecomer made his way home on wooden clogs. We did not speak until we were nearly back to Yokohama, and then we became so engrossed in conversation we forgot to get off. We had perforce to pay another round-trip fare and make another pilgrimage to Kamakura, and it was three o'clock in the morning before we reached the ship. Waiting for me, the remaining passengers made a cheerful mock-scandal of the episode and teased me the rest of the way to Shanghai.

Except for the slipper boats, jerked into motion with a single rear oar, and the bursts of a strange and birdlike language, Shanghai seemed from the docks like a middle-sized Western city. In the shade of European buildings, Miss M., she of the broken heart, was met by her Shanghai friends. Her American host was an expert tea-taster, a profession new to me ("Delightful," I noted). With the easy, many-servanted hospitality of the East, Mrs. Tea-Taster promptly invited Major V. S. and me to stay with them. Promising to come there later, I set out with V. to explore the hybrid city.

My trunks were sent on to the river dock in wheelbarrows and I was put into a luxurious rubber-tired ricksha drawn by the best-natured creature in the world, the Chinese ricksha coolie. My only business in Shanghai was to call at the mission home for mail before setting out for the Baldwin School in Nanchang, six hundred miles from Shanghai.

As we crossed the city to the mission, I looked for China, for camels and the caravanserai, for city walls and parapets, for Mandarins with red umbrellas and peacock feathers. There were instead Occidental shops, like those of the Rue de la Paix, with ivories and jades and embroideries to tempt my worldly pleasure in pretty things. The heavy traffic, Victorias, bicycles, sedan chairs, ponies, wheelbarrows, rickshas, and pedestrians from every country in the world moved in a tangle down streets whose buildings reminded me now of Unter den Linden, now of Fleet Street.

This international city was kept in order by statuesque figures in immaculate uniforms topped by scarlet turbans. These were the Sikhs, brought in, V. explained, by the British, who believed that one race should always police another. Immensely tall, magnificently groomed, with coal-black whiskers that rolled from chin to cheek to ear, olive-skinned and awe-inspiring, they towered over the Chinese and Europeans and controlled the traffic with sweeping discipline. I felt the truth of the saying "God never made an ugly Sikh," but where was China?

In spite of the presence of Chinese people, this was not China, and I insisted on leaving even the slow "manpower-carriage" to look for it on foot. After walking for miles, we came to a little alley under the crumbling vestige of a city wall. On the other side of a gate was my new country. It was dirty, shabby, and teeming—and it smelled. But here was the tea-house from the willow-pattern plates, and the falsetto voice of a singsong girl over a noisy Chinese orchestra floated into the air above the chuckling, singing voices of the crowding people.

"Ye gods," said Major S. "You can't spend five years in *this!* Among people like *these!* You'll leave in three months...."

I laughed at him. I was already in love with China, with China as it *was*, and I knew that I would stay—not three months, or three years, but no less than five.

When I went back through the gate and finally reached the mission home, a tall gaunt woman, dressed in black from head to foot, her hair pulled back, was speaking pidgin English to a coolie. Turning to me, she said with a poor imitation of grace, "Your mail is here, Miss Honsinger. Aren't you going to leave your money with us? And I have friends who are anxious to talk with you."

I remembered the missionaries of my churchgoing youth. It was the sight of them, grim-visaged and bedraggled, appearing before the Methodist congregation in Rome, New York, to plead modestly for pennies, that had turned me firmly from any thought of a career in missions. There was no romantic appeal in being a sad crow of a woman, and I secretly doubted if it inspired the heathen, either. I had met a charming and attractive missionary in college, a Ruth Sites from China, who was human, well-dressed and groomed and quite beautiful. By this time I was sure that opera was my metier, and perhaps it was fear of being tempted by the mission field that kept me from calling on Miss Sites before she left my college town.

Now here I was, committed to China in the role of f-o-r-e-i-g-n m-i-s-s-i-o-n-a-r-y—and I would certainly claim no kin to the likes of this dreary woman who felt, I was sure, "superior" to the Chinese and to Miss Honsinger also.

My judgments were severe in those days. I tended to believe that women who looked the way this one did made a virtue of ugliness. Detesting self-righteousness, I was sometimes guilty of it.

There were indeed too many missionaries who despised in their hearts the people they came to "save." There were those who thought salvation lay only in the narrow way of the sect to which they belonged. I was to know some of these. But I met others who were shabby and unbeautified because they thought only of the soul and never of the body. Sanctimoniousness put me off, but sanctity was a quality I worshiped in anyone.

I was, of course, also quite intolerant toward the pleasure-loving business colony. Miss M.'s Shanghai friends seemed to me unbearably frivolous and lacking in purpose. Headstrong in my own ideals, I decided to spend no more time among either Shanghai missionaries or Shanghai's foreign rich. My goal was up the Yangtze, six hundred miles from this international civilization. On the spot, I made my decision.

"No thank you," I said. "I shan't be here long enough to meet anyone. I'm taking the river boat tonight. Please forward my mail after this to Bao Lin, Nanchang!"

As Major S. and I drove back through the westernized

French Settlement and the International City—which before the Boxer Rebellion had been the British City—we passed a park. By the entrance was a sign: DOGS AND CHINESE NOT ADMITTED.

When the Shanghai residents found that I was headed for Nanchang, they protested, "Why, British missionaries were murdered there only six months ago, right before the eyes of their little child!"

"It's no use," said Major S. "She'll go and she'll stay. Nothing and nobody can stop her."

V. took me aboard the small white Yangtze steamboat that night. As I said good-by to him, I wondered wistfully when I would meet another attentive and attractive American man. The British owned the river, and the skipper of the ship was a Scot. Everyone else on board was Chinese. I was the only Occidental passenger.

The boat chugged up the wide stream through an endless flat desert of brown reeds. Now and then the reeds would part for a glimpse of villages. My attitude was already determined and loyal. When I saw the thirteen-story pagoda of the City of Peace over the horizon, I recalled that London had nothing much higher than this and that "most of our cities in the advanced United States do not boast a skyscraper higher than the pagoda—and China did it first!"

The dour Scots captain lectured me from first to last. "Mere girls," he insisted, should never go to China. "All wrong, all wrong—ignorant pigs they are, these Chinese." Then he would shout to his Number One Boy, "Two piecie man for dinner," which meant in pidgin English (a corruption of the word *business* modifying the word *English*) that he and I would eat.

"We won't pick up anyone else," he told me when I could not avoid his company by having my meals before he came down from the bridge or after he had finished. "Nobody in his right mind is going into the interior. You know about the missionaries murdered by the Chinks? And only one little white child left to remember the horror the rest of her life!

A fine healthy girl like you.... Nonsense! You go back to Shanghai with me, and don't you stay in Shanghai. You go home!"

To keep up my courage, I read the Ninety-first Psalm every morning before plunging into books about China. One written either before or after the Boxer troubles—I was never sure which—made a profound impression. The author carved up China with surgical precision. The lion's share went to Great Britain, of course, as part of Victoria's Empire (now His Majesty, King Edward the VII's domain), on which the sun never set. Germany got Shantung. The Russians and Japanese shared Manchuria. As a sop, America was offered part of South China, perhaps Canton. There would be nothing left of Great China and the only hope for the country was that the jealous foreign powers might not so easily agree on how to parcel her out among them. But, thought I, the Dowager Empress still sits on her shaky throne.

During the four days the steamer churned up the thick, fast-flowing river, the captain lectured me on my folly. Finally I made a bargain with him.

"If there is no one to meet me in Kiukiang, I'll go on with you to Hankow and wire Kiukiang. If there is no one in Kiu·kiang on the way back, I'll return with you to Shanghai. But I *shan't* stay there, and neither will I go back to the U.S.A.!"

3

On December 21, 1906, the river boat drew in toward my first port beyond Shanghai. Alongside the shore at Kiukiang a derelict hulk called *The Wandering Jew,* its decks now packed and its railings and masts festooned with coolies, served the city as wharf. The river bank was jammed with what seemed like the entire population of two hundred thousand men, women, and children—all of them dressed in blue.

The word *masses* became real to me as I stared over the railing, and I understood, too, why the Chinese were called "Celestials." It was hard to tell where blue-covered earth left off and blue sky began. As the steamboat churned and bucked toward *The Wandering Jew,* howling men by the dozen leaped across the deep swirling water, risking their lives to clamor for the passengers' luggage. First to come were paid in "cash," a unit of which twenty added up to an American penny.

As I searched for the face of Ilien Tang among the sea of faces, a woman threw herself into the torrential river. Time seemed to stop as I stared in fascinated horror. Currents seized the unresisting body, thick muddy water clutched the long garments and soaked the long black hair. Before the Yangtze could carry her away, a man plunged in and dragged her, resisting now, to the shore. The blue human sea closed in over the scene and I could see no more. Later I learned that the woman's rescuer was the husband she was trying to escape by suicide.

The captain shrugged off the incident. "Do it all the time," he said. "Stupid pigs. Now listen, you must stay aboard, you know. You simply can't go into a Chinese city."

Just then, in the midst of the yelling, elbowing people I

24

saw a head as beautiful as the Kamakura Buddha's, with wavy white hair for a halo. Blue eyes (buttermilk eyes, the Chinese called them) shone with radiance into mine and a hand was lifted in cordial greeting. It could only be Gertrude Howe, missionary to China since 1880, the year I was born, of whom I had read and heard; but no one had said how beautiful she was.

"Good-by," I said joyfully to the captain, and made my way down the gangplank into China's interior.

With Gertrude Howe was little Ilien Tang, who had been lost to sight among her milling compatriots.

"We'll tend to your trunks, and see you in half an hour," said Miss Howe, whom I promptly dubbed My Twenty-five-years-in-China-Saint, "and you shall ride in my chair to the compound. . . ."

"My Saint," I wrote in my diary, "will never know the agony of that ride!"

The covered sedan chair was carried on bamboo poles by four men. Through the glass in front I could see the crowds, so thick that passage seemed impossible. My coolie-carriers howled their way through, passing the suicide procession in which men were dragging the half-drowned and still-resisting woman along the street. The chair grazed the backs of pigs and butted against the bodies of men. Now and then my bearers stopped still, yelling angrily and arguing in a language of which I understood not a word. Men picked up the side curtains of the chair and peered at the white woman within, chattering inimically and pointing at my hat, a good-looking hat but conspicuous in a hatless country. I was irresistibly reminded that Anglo-Saxons had recently been massacred in anti-foreign riots.

Even the fur-lined coat, brought under protest to a latitude of 28 degrees, was not enough to keep me warm. Shivering and seriously frightened, I prayed, fixed my hat firmly, clutched my coat close, tried to laugh at myself, and finally—in counter-harmony to the dissonance without—sang loudly, "My Lord and I, my Lord and I, go up the road together."

The crowds dwindled as we moved farther into the city and the coolies, instead of howling, began to chant, the leader offering a phrase, the other three replying in cadence. Finally they carried the chair inside a gate and down a narrow street, soaking wet from the spilling of buckets of water hauled on coolie shoulders, and on to a walled compound. Here the bearers tipped down the chair and I stepped out, over the poles. Two ladies stood there awaiting me, and with relief and enthusiasm I rushed to them, hugging and kissing them both.

Miss Pierce and Miss Merrill, who had lived in the same house and taught school together for twenty years without calling each other anything else, disengaged themselves from my importunate embrace with shocked and chilly courtesy. After a few awkward moments, Miss Honsinger was sent on to the American hospital compound. There I would stay with Gertrude Howe and Ilien Tang until passage could be arranged to Nanchang, a hundred miles away and across formidable Lake Poyang.

My Saint became my ideal as the days went by. She embodied all I dreamed of being. This was the woman who had unbound the feet of four young adopted Chinese girls in 1880, when everyone believed it would condemn them to unthinkable spinsterhood. Radical as she was Christian, Miss Howe had two of her Chinese girls trained as doctors in the U.S., against the will of all the missionaries in China. When they were not allowed to practice, she built her own hospital for them in Kiukiang and gave it to the Chinese.

Every morning Miss Howe went down to the wharf to ask for passage to Nanchang, but the junks had all been preempted by the government for soldiers traveling to fight interior rebellions. I passed the time wrapped in wool sweaters, blankets, and my coat, studying Chinese, and at night singing at Kiukiang's English Settlement parties until I ran out of Christmas music. The day after Christmas the Saint came back radiant to announce that the three of us could go on one of a flotilla of junks carrying soldiers. "If Gertrude Howe is going to be a martyr, I shall be one, too," I thought, trying to be brave.

All our luggage and what seemed a fantastic plenitude of supplies were piled aboard a large junk made of well-oiled wood, with a single huge yellow sail. We three were in the bow. Our cabin was furnished with wooden bunks, a makeshift table, and stools, and lighted by two kerosene lamps. On a brazier the man who accompanied Miss Howe wherever she went—her *Daw Tse-fu* or head-of-her-household—prepared our meals from our own supplies. During the day we sat on deck in the shade of the sail and after sunset huddled in the chilly cabin.

With favoring winds and no storms, the trip took only five days and nights. We sailed thirty miles down the roaring Yangtze, then over the treacherous lake and up the Kan River. The sight of eight coolies, harnessed by bamboo cables, pulling the boat along the Kan inch by inch to the accompaniment of the minor-key laboring lilt they sang, almost broke my heart. "If I were a poet," I said, "I should write a sonnet to the burden-bearers of China."

Until now, I had been told only of massacres and fear. Gertrude Howe spoke of poverty and love, of Buddhist monks who lived for beauty and meditation, of friendly human beings who longed to learn and grow and break their ancient chains. By the time I arrived at the great city of Nanchang, provincial Capital City of the Flourishing South, I was more than ever in love with all China.

Five of the seven Americans living in this city of a million were there to meet us—a doctor and his wife, a mission teacher and his wife, and Miss Newby from Iowa, who was already teaching at Bao Lin. Refraining from hugging Miss Newby, I nevertheless felt her welcome warm. The old city, with its forty-five-foot-high walls of gray brick, pierced by gates wide enough for two carriages, impressed me as glorious.

The school was outside the walls and the lotus-covered moat, about two miles from the heart of the seven-hundred-year-old walled city. Its buildings were indeterminate, but flowering shrubs dotted the grounds and tall palmetto trees spread their angular fans downward in geometric patterns. Two stair-steps of girls in long, full decorous dark skirts and light, high-collared loose smocks were lined up to greet their new headmistress. Among their broad, snub-nosed faces and long black bangs I could distinguish no face from its sister any more than I could tell one long black braid down the row in back from another. But I was prepared to love them all.

Miss Newby took me at once to the biggest bedroom, reserved for the head of the school. Simply furnished, large and light, it pleased me on sight and my biggest wardrobe trunk was already there awaiting me. Attached to the room was a large bathroom.

Peering in, I saw a handsome redwood armchair. Under it was a galvanized pail, our sewage-disposal system. On a table stood a kerosene lamp, a porcelain basin and pitcher, reminiscent of up-country summers in my childhood. Then I saw the bathtub. It was gorgeous. Standing four feet high, made of brown pottery so deep in color my eyes sank into it, it was four feet wide at the top, narrowing to a foot at the bottom. Inside it was glazed a glorious turquoise blue.

"It's just like one I saw at the Metropolitan in New York," I exclaimed to Miss Newby in high delight. "Do you mean I can actually bathe in it? Are all the tubs museum pieces? Will Miss Tang have one like this in her bathroom, or do we share?"

"Good heavens!" exclaimed Miss Newby, shocked. "Miss Tang won't stay here with us. The Chinese teachers live down there, in that little house—" She pointed out the rear window to a modest building on lower ground.

I reacted instinctively. "Why I can't possibly live away from Ilien Tang," I said. "I don't even know the language yet. She's my eyes and ears. If she's to stay down there, so shall I. Please send my trunk down now, before I unpack!"

Buzzing to herself like a disturbed hornet's nest, Miss Newby disappeared. When she came back an hour later she told me that Dr. Bowen, head of the Nanchang Mission, had agreed, though reluctantly, that since there would be only the two of us in the house and since Miss Newby was going to the country in a little while, Miss Tang could stay. (What he really said, as I found out later, was, "Well, we'll have to give in to her. She's been appointed headmistress, after all, and New York would probably back her up, and I'm afraid she has a very positive character.")

That settled that. It had never occurred to me that God intended the color of their skins to separate His children one from another. By my innocent assumption, I had broken a man-made canon of behavior. For the first time in the history of Protestant missions to China, a Chinese woman came to live with Western ladies in a compound house.

4

On January 1, 1907, I wrote in my diary:

New Year, New City, New World, New Life. Here I am four hundred miles from a railroad. There is not a mechanical sound except the squeak of wheelbarrows and the watchman's bamboo clippers click-clacking on the hour. At eleven the Temple Bell sounds, a superhuman note that resounds over the whole side expanse outside the city wall. It is music that hurts like a Chopin nocturne and floats on after it stops. In New York grinding steel and horns drown out the cries of little children, but here the chorus of human agony, of human celebrations and arguments, of all life, can be clearly heard....

Heard and felt, but not yet understood.

The school of which I, at twenty-six, had sole charge was running well enough, under the watchful eye of the mission chief, Dr. Bowen, whose compound was across and down the road from Bao Lin. When Miss Newby left, the only person who spoke English besides myself was the invaluable Ilien Tang. The faculty, household staff, and the girls were all Chinese, and though we understood each other through smiles and gestures and had Ilien Tang for interpreter, it seemed to me my relations with them and with my new country would remain superficial until I knew the language.

In China, language is not only the means of communication between people, it has a special significance. Words are magic and used with circumspection, with respect. A wrong word is dangerous, a right one an incantation. Even the school, the Baldwin Institute or Bao Lin, had been christened with a second set of words to give it strength and virtue: "The School of the Protecting Spirit." I had a great deal more to learn than merely a difficult vocabulary and how to make unfamiliar sounds.

Teacher Yang, a proper *Sien Sen* ("Born Before"), master of the classics, was persuaded to instruct me in Mandarin. He was an elderly gentleman with long, brittle nails to prove that he did no manual work. Undertaking to educate his grown-up pupil in the little office from which I administered the school, he began firmly at the beginning, with the writings of Lao Tze, who lived fifty years before Confucius. He expected me to memorize the classics in the Chinese way, coming to understand them only through gradual osmosis.

Respectful as I was of the ways of ancient China, this daughter of the West intended to learn the meanings of any words at the same time she memorized them. Furthermore, I wanted to be able to ask what time it was and to give instructions to my cook even before I could quote proverbs and wise sayings.

In the ensuing battle of wits both of us preserved impeccable and impassive exteriors, but I did manage to ruffle Scholar Yang's Confucian complacency one day by depositing carrots, potatoes, onions, fish, and lettuce on his desk and demanding to know their names. "You tell me this is an educated woman," he complained indignantly to Ilien Tang. "She doesn't even know what a carrot is!"

To keep my Confucian scholar from boredom, I had to make him laugh; and to preserve his "face" I worked like a demon, six hours a day. We sat across a broad desk from each other, the Honorable Teacher in his blue gown, tight black satin cap with a button on top, and large tortoise-shell-rimmed glasses inherited from his forefathers, the American in her corseted suits and blouses with billowing jabots, with her thick, piled hair.

To capture the cadence of his language and the all-important tones, so difficult for an amateur in anything beyond the diatonic scale, I swayed with him in rhythmic harmony. Ilien Tang and the girls, passing the open door as the incongruous pair of us swayed back and forth, tittered uncontrollably and all but laughed out loud. The day I broke down my first chair and landed on the floor I drew a guffaw from *Sien Sen*, and he offered to increase the amount of time he spent with me.

When an equally "illiterate" English nurse came to the City of the Flourishing South, things picked up for me. Her teacher was a friend of my Scholar Yang's and the two, over cups of scalding Dragon Whisker Tea, met often to compare their impossible pupils. My progress became a source of pride to Yang, and by the time I broke my second chair he had taught me a number of ancient proverbs and given me a Chinese name.

China had only one hundred surnames, and among them Yang equated Honsinger with Han. Since the rest must be euphonious, after much discussion of "Welthy" I was christened *Wei-Lo Han*. Red calling cards, eight inches long and four inches wide, inscribed in elegant calligraphy, were ordered. When I went visiting, the man who preceded my sedan chair (by twenty feet as etiquette demanded) announced my arrival with the flourish of a card.

My ventures with the obstinate language of China landed me on more than the floor. I told my highly entertained cook that I loved him eight cents worth instead of owed him eight cents. Greeting a visitor, I remarked, "It is boiling water outside," and when I asked my Number One Boy for *tsai* in a low tone instead of a high, I got vegetables instead of firewood. "It is like your 'laughing magazine,'" remarked Ilien Tang, referring to the old *Life*, a journal of jokes, humorous articles, and cartoons, to which I subscribed.

Their laughter was mannerly, as were all their actions. Fortunately for me, the manners my mother believed in and taught me were like theirs. Form always gave way to consideration for others.

I rarely offended the Chinese, but I did manage to upset my fellow Anglo-Saxons. Their behavior toward the people in whose country they lived seemed to me wrong. I still think so, but at the time I allowed nothing for the entrenchment of such customs. When I was deluged with invitations from members of the foreign colony, I longed to accept. It was a relief to babble in my native tongue after struggling with Chinese. It was restful to relax among people whose habits and ways of thinking were familiar. There were enough British and American citizens in Nanchang, although it was a Chinese city and not a treaty port, to provide me with a home-away-from-home—if I wanted it. But, as I noted in my diary at the time, "I refused all invitations which did not include Miss Ilien Tang."

My intransigence reduced my social life among my own race. Of course my well-loved Saint, Miss Howe, welcomed us both whenever we could visit her in the hospital inside the city where her adopted Chinese daughter, Ida Kahn, was chief surgeon. But she never knew whether she was speaking Chinese or English, so complete was her cross-culture. Often away, she was also much too busy for social doings, and I went to her only when I needed her advice or to refresh my spirit.

No invitation ever came for Ilien Tang from her Chinese friends that did not include Miss Honsinger. Thus with her I came to know the Chinese world outside the school. It was invaluable. I had so many plans for my school—for expanding, changing, and improving it. You cannot effectively improve a part of any community unless you understand the community, its language, its customs and emotions.

Through Ilien Tang I made many friends among the poor young married couples and shared their problems, the same the world over: to live respectably in spite of an economic struggle. Later I learned that when I first came I had "smelled" to them offensively of mutton, but as I no longer ate it was no longer odiferous.

Since a majority of my forty-five pupils came from upper-class families, it also behooved me to comprehend the backgrounds from which they were emerging. There was no caste system in China (as there was in India) which separated people at birth. Aristocracy was based more, as it is in the U.S., on the possession of wealth. Anyone could become gentry, but as do the gentry everywhere, once there they clung to all prerogatives. Privilege had its strict conventions and I must admit I adored the elaborate rituals of entertaining. Besides practicing conversation among people who made an art of it, I found myself learning, in a primrose fashion, the nature of female Chinese society as it had existed for so many thousand years.

A description I wrote then of a Sunset Feast is typical of my ventures in this exotic world.

We go through the streets in a sedan chair as far as the East Lake, which is the center of the City. Here our man, Old Draw Bow, finds the servant of our hostess, Madame Vermillion, who directs him to her Pleasure Boat, sent to take us across the lake. Her sister, Madame Whisper, steps out of the boat. A faint Oriental perfume surrounds her. She is in her richest brocaded satins. The pearls about her neck and on her little hat are priceless. The sea-green jade in her rings matches the jade buttons on her gown. Her arm is heavy with richly carved gold bracelets.

After making our bows we are seated in Madame Vermillion's Flower Boat. Slowly picking his way between the large lotus leaves that lie flat on the water and the delicate blossoms beginning to close their petals at sundown, the boatman paddles with one oar. Fragrance rises from the soft pink flowers, the strident strains of a Chinese love song (better at some distance) floats across the lake. Madame Whisper offers me her water pipe of rarest cloisonné and Ilien Tang recites an old Tang poem.

We paddle across until we leave the lake at Thunder Temple. There our chairs meet us and take us to Chopstick Row.

It is as quiet as upper Fifth Avenue at the dinner hour in this residential section. The gray walls here loom up higher than those of houses of lesser fortunes. The setting sun makes the carved spirit screens cast long shadows and all we can hear is the hard breathing and soft tread of our coolies. When we reach the spirit screen of Madame Vermillion's mansion, Old Draw Bow takes in our flaming red calling cards, as large as handbills.

The great doors are opened wide. Our chair-bearers pass behind the screen, step over the high threshold and set the chairs down in the privacy of the outer court. Here are many sedan chairs with gorgeous hangings, and a handsome jinricksha which the master

of the household has not yet had the courage to use. It is an in-
novation too startling to be lightly launched.

We pass through a large room, where hollow-cheeked tailors
bend over costly material making garments for the lord and ladies
of the mansion, through Heavenly Well No. I, a large open court,
to the women's apartments.

Our hostess walks out on her tiny "golden lily" feet to meet us.
Her skin is ivory, her hair ebony, her stately poise and bearing unequalled in any European court. Her dark garment of brocaded
material, high at the neck, enhances her rare Oriental jewelry and
splendid pearls more than décolleté could do.

Lady Vermillion invites us to her boudoir, with its heavy hangings in gaudy colors. The richly carved Yun Nan teak bed, with its
red satin valence richly embroidered and its soft down comforter,
holds the center of the room. Her chests are of rarest carved wood
inlaid with pearl, and she has special silver vanity cases for those
of us who have not brought our own rouge and powder. Waiting
for the other guests, we sip hot Paradise tea and eat the ever-
offered watermelon seeds.

Dinner is from five to seven, and one arrives at any time between.
As a foreign guest, I ask to see the house, and am taken to every
one of its sixty rooms where a hundred and fifty people, half of
them servants, make their home.

A private open theatre lies across the Lotus pond beyond the
boudoirs of the daughters, and farther on is the Treasure room.
Here are the jewels and art treasures—a trunk of pearls, a dozen
chests of jades, coral under glass, carved crystal, Chien Lung porcelains and Tang Dynasty bronzes inlaid with gold. . . .

In another room scholars are working on manuscripts, the yearly
reprinting of the Vermillion family genealogy, which has reached
the seventieth generation. Then the "Little Dolls" are brought
out of their fragrant apartments—such delicately dressed girls
(Madame V. buys their clothes), chosen for their beauty and to
enhance the reputation of the Vermillion concubines.

At last we are ushered in to dinner, and seated with time-consuming etiquette and many bows. Then what chattering takes
place over sixteen varieties of *hors d'oeuvre*, Bird's Nest Soup,
shark's fins, chicken savories, fried duck, pigeon's eggs, almond tea
and dumplings, and dozens of other things, ending with Ba Bao,
or "Pudding of Eight Precious Things."

When toasts are drunk, I lift my cup of Paradise tea, instead of wine, which they accept, saying "It is her custom."

"Drink to the health of Madame Earnest," says Madame Whisper, in what sounds like a tone of sarcasm. "Drink to her health as our instructor. May she teach us how to hold the keys of our husbands' hearts and their purses as she does hers."

We drink, and I remember that Madame Whisper's husband had just taken a new concubine, even though she has four sons. I knew this concubine had the keys to the heart and purse of her husband and that Madame Whisper was a lonely woman.

"At any rate," says Madame Repose, "some of us do not take home the gossip of our feasts to our husbands, even though we admit we cannot manage them!"

Madame Repose had drunk too much wine at a feast some time before, and lost her self-control. Madame Earnest related an amusing incident about Madame Repose's drunkenness to her husband, and Mr. Earnest, thinking it funny, teased Mr. Repose next day. Mr. Repose, much displeased, had, with great ceremony, reprimanded his wife and refused to pay her gambling debts.

After the long feast is over, Madame Repose turns to me and puts her finger to her lips. "I pray thee," she said, "do not take the silly gossip of our feasts across the ocean to thine honorable countrymen." And Madame Earnest whispers in my ear, "Little Sister Han, I may say to thee that I am willing that they should tease me as they like. Of all the twelve women at that table, I am the only one whose husband has no concubine. I alone am a happy woman."

Much as I enjoyed such high-style goings-on and however much they contributed to my fast-growing knowledge of China, I by no means confined my ventures to the upper strata. I visited the straw huts of the starving squatters and even the lairs where the "flower" beggars lived, so called because their rags were as tattered as the petals of chrysanthemums.

The more I knew and the more I saw, the more I felt that the education of the women of China was of paramount importance. Old China, fascinating and other-worldly, was changing. A new China must emerge, important to the whole world of which it was inescapably a part. As long as the redoubtable "Old Buddha," Dowager Empress of the Imperial Kingdom, lived, Old China would survive, held together somehow by an elaborate tissue of tradition and the web worn by thousands of years of remote, mystical Imperial rule. But when the Old Buddha died, Young China would be born. The best of the West must be brought into the East so that transition would not mean anarchy and foreign conquest, but a strong nation which would preserve its arts and beauties and abolish its slaveries, the terrible poverty of its masses, and the subjection of its women.

The School of the Protecting Spirit was the only educational institution for girls in its province of forty-five million people. I determined that before I left China I would not only expand Bao Lin, but would also inspire other schools to be built. Whenever I could, I would travel through the interior and preach my own gospel, talking to the women, talking to the men about their wives and daughters.

My first personal venture into written Chinese was a careful translation of the words: "Ye shall know the truth, and the truth shall make you free." In spite of Scholar Yang's protest that this was revolutionary and not a suitable sentiment to teach young women, I had a mammoth sign painted—with the words in bright red. It would go over the main gate of my school.

5

No amount of reading could really have prepared me for China. That the descendants of the foreign Manchu conquerors who took Peking in the 1600s still ruled I knew—but I never saw a Manchu in Nanchang, and most people there had never seen one. Their Chinese representatives, yes. I had come to know many of them, and many of Nanchang's rich and powerful people—but never a Manchu.

I knew the mass of the Chinese people were poor, but nothing had prepared me for the lines in front of the rice kitchen during times of food shortages. The murmuring of the thousands gathered before dawn to collect the bowl of rice, offered by the organized charity of the rich, woke me often with the birds.

I knew that Chinese superstitions and beliefs were different from ours—but *how* different I had scarcely begun to measure.

When it came to running a school, I was better prepared. The administration of Bao Lin was not so different from home that I could not manage. When I took over, it had only forty-five pupils and four teachers and extended only to the eighth grade. The standards were fairly high. I did approve the fact that (unlike in other countries) the mission schools almost always taught history and the classics from the Chinese, not the Western, viewpoint. We began with the history of China in history class and the country of China in geography. The literature we offered was Chinese, and so were the ethics. Our curriculum was much the same as that in America, but it added up to a Chinese education. I started immediately to

38

plan for added grades and more teachers and pupils, but this was expansion rather than essential change.

It was in the housekeeping—a responsibility I had sedulously avoided at home—that I ran into problems. For one thing, in keeping my institutional house I was not dealing with people educated as were the members of my staff but with shrewd Chinese peasants harder-headed than any Yankee farmer, for all their gentle ways. Their minds were closed books to me until I slowly came to know them.

I was also responsible for the health of all my charges—and I knew very little of American diseases, let alone the form they took in China. *And* I was expected to keep the parents of my pupils happy. This is always a problem, and it became mountainous when I ran into traditions I did not understand. Oh my! My first year there was a cram course on China.

"One day drama and tragedy, the next comedy!" I commented in my diary. "And the more I learn, the more there is to learn." Unrelated though the crises that confronted me were, each cut a facet in the rough block of my ignorance until, by year's end, I had begun to learn to learn.

China in working terms was represented by my Number One Boy, Hsiung, and Cook, a merry and efficient old man, my head amah who, having borne nineteen children of her own, was ideally suited to be chief nurse and mother-substitute for the girls.

I found I had plenty of American practicality and enough organizing ability; but how was I to organize what was not there, had never been there? Garbage disposal, for instance. There was none unless, as I remarked, "one can call pigs a system." I found that I was fattening porkers as part of my routine.

One day Hsiung came into the office to announce that a pig was sick. Before I could find out whether there was a veterinarian to consult, Hsiung returned and reported that the animal was dead. I told him to remove the carcass and to bury it, outside, away from the school, and went on with my work. That evening when I settled accounts with him—scrupulously, for the Chinese were apt to be careless—Hsiung proudly presented a credit for the dead pig. He had sold it for a fine price.

Horrified, I ordered him to get the pig back at once.

"Too late," sighed Hsiung happily. "Already cut up and eaten. Many places in city."

Haunted and unable to sleep that night, my sympathy went out to the medical missionaries faced with the Augean magnitude of trying to save lives in China. Even the most elementary precautions, such as destroying diseased animals, were cavalierly disregarded.

Cheeriest member of the school staff was the amah, a hearty middle-aged woman of whose nineteen children only two sons were living. She embraced my Westernism with delight. Despised all her life for her natural feet, she promptly claimed kinship with us Americans. Of the other teetering women servants and housemothers, she said, "They laugh at me, Little Sister Han, and say my husband makes mistakes mornings and sticks his feet into my shoes. Bad jokes, Ocean Teacher, bad jokes!"

"And what do you answer?" I asked her once.

" 'Our Great Teacher,' I say, 'Little Sister Han, has GIGANTIC feet, like boats,' " she replied, and ran giggling out of the room.

Then came three days when no smile or giggle was forthcoming. Nothing I could say penetrated the amah's quiet gloom. Finally one evening she confessed that her youngest son, the darling of her heart, had been kidnaped for the Army. There was little chance she would ever see him again. She had not wanted to tell anyone until she had wept all the tears out of her body. All her life she had prayed to Kwan Yin, the goddess of mercy, to give her sons, and now only one was left to her in her old age, and that one was no comfort.

I had little comfort to offer, either. Because it was my own greatest solace, I sang to the woman, and because it was what she wanted most, gave her gifts of soap. The amah did not understand the Western music but was thrilled and grateful for the soap.

Cook came in his turn to tell me that he had a most terrible pain in his arm and must go home. After he had gone and before I could get the American mission doctor over to his house, relatives and friends appeared at the school and excitedly told Ilien Tang that the old man had hydrophobia.

Taking Ilien Tang, I set out immediately for Cook's home, unable to believe that this horror, to me no more than a word in the dictionary until now, could be real. Within a simple, well-kept courtyard, we were met by Cook's wife, who said her husband wished to see us.

In his spotless room, he lay in agony. The sight of water or food sent him into spasms, yet he was wild with hunger and thirst. Apparently sane, he could only say over and over, "It was the mad cat at the School of the Protecting Spirit. It was the mad cat . . . and now no water and no food can pass my lips and I shall die."

The mission doctor, to whom this disease was also only a theory, arrived and told us that in all probability it was just neurasthenia, but that if it was indeed hydrophobia, Cook would die within seventy-two hours. Seventy-two hours later he was dead.

One of the teachers, Little Sister Cloud, remembered now that she had been bitten a month before by a pretty stray cat in the compound. Old Wang, a manservant, reluctantly confessed that he had been scratched. Amah, too, had been clawed before the cat was evicted.

Shanghai was six hundred miles away, and the trip had to be made by water. I packed the three of them off, praying with Ilien Tang, "May favoring winds of heaven attend them" until they reached the Pasteur Institute in Shanghai and serum. "If I could have been anybody but Little Sister Han," I wrote in this hour, "I should like to have been Pasteur."

During the long days while I waited for news of them, I was too busy to brood. Already the school was growing like bamboo. Within a few months enrollment had increased to eighty, and more pupils applied daily. We took in as many from Nanchang as the classrooms would hold, stuffing beds in every corner of the dormitories.

Regularly I wrote home, cheery letters that omitted distressing details. Mail took a month in or out, so there was no use discussing a problem that would be solved by the time anyone could answer. So far away from my old home and my family and Mother, I waited for the packets arriving for me with an intensity that only people in places as remote as the interior of China come to feel. The "paddy-field telegraph" quivered with rumors of far events in China, but the outside world was a myth beyond the walls until the mail came.

When the south wind blew, Lake Poyang could not be crossed by the junks with their tiny motors and single sails. It blew, that late spring, for a month and a half. No word came through from home or from the three who had left the school. Every night I sang for the north wind, just as the sailors on the junks did, singing *Dalila* while they chanted to their gods.

Then Jasmine Purity, one of the loveliest of the pupils, fell ill. When the doctor came, he diagnosed smallpox. The scourge called by the Chinese "Heavenly Flowers" was, he told me, endemic in the Oriental city.

Promptly isolating Jasmine Purity, I moved with her into a house in the rear and sent word to her family that I was nursing their daughter myself. For forty-eight hours I was alone with the girl in fear and suspense. To the Chinese, my precautions seemed excessive. Perhaps it was the euphonious name by which the dreadful disease was called as well as fatalism that kept them indifferently calm.

On the third day, Jasmine Purity's father, an old-fashioned Chinese medicine man, arrived at the compound, as unworried and unconcerned as the rest. Examining his child, he laughed and pronounced her ailment not Heavenly Flowers at all, but Water Flowers—chicken pox—and cheerfully took her home with him.

Then I went to work on the eighty-seven other pupils. Sending for the doctor to vaccinate the lot, I firmly administered eighty-seven large spoonfuls of castor oil.

"Eighty-seven squirmings," I recorded, "and tears enough to overflow the Yangtze. But no more cases of any Flowers, Water or Heavenly."

The weather changed at last, and the north wind began to blow. Word came that Little Sister Cloud, Old Wang, and the amah were in Kiukiang, well, and waiting for a junk to bring them home. On the night I could expect them and my mail, I went every few minutes to the window to catch the first glimpse of the red light that meant a boat was coming in and to listen for the sailors' song as they hauled down the huge single sail of a Poyang junk.

Instead, I saw the light of bamboo torches carried through the narrow, black street and heard a weird, wild sound. As the procession came nearer, I made out eight men shouldering an open sedan chair with a huge seated idol in spangled garments. The soloist leader cried incessantly, *"Lien-when-whei-lai-o"* and the followers replied in chorus, *"Lien-when-whei-lai-o,"* the last tone held in a long diminuendo.

The words meant "Precious spirit, come back," and the procession was making its way to the cemetery on the hill near the Temple of Dragon Light next to the school. There, resting the idol among the graves, they burned silver paper as a symbol of money, beseeching without pause the precious spirit to return.

I watched them from my window as they started back toward the school, apparently dissatisfied, soloist and chorus still wailing antiphonally. Then, to my surprise, they stopped at our gate. Old Willow, the gatekeeper, came running to my office with Ilien Tang. The wife of a Mr. Lee was sick and out of her mind, but not dead. Looking for her lost spirit, the procession was retracing the steps she had taken before she grew ill. They hoped to find her wandering spirit, to bring it back, restore her sanity, and prevent her death. She had visited the school two weeks before, so might they now enter? Ilien Tang urged me to give permission, assuring me that there was nothing to fear.

Leaving the idol standing outside, the men entered the building and went into each room, wailing. Respecting their customs and their intensity I saw that there was no use suggesting a visit by the mission doctor instead of the idol.

After the last *"lai-o"* faded into the night, trailing the

jiggling idol on the shoulders of the men, I made a final entry in my diary. "Eleven P.M. The Temple Bell sounds and calls my neighbor Buddhist priests and me to prayer."

Along with the missing members of my staff, a bundle of letters arrived next day. One of them was from Tom. China must be deadly dull and monotonous as well as horrible, he said. Was his Welthy not ready to give it up and marry him?

Welthy was not. Even my diary was reduced to hasty notes like "Terribly busy—" to which one day I added, "Adopted a baby. I couldn't resist it."

The child had been left on Gertrude Howe's doorstep. Big, black saucer eyes peered out from the torn rug in which she was wrapped. Tiny ears bore the tattoo marks of a government orphanage. Someone had loved the girl-child enough to steal her from the medieval orphanage, attach a tag with her name and birth date, and leave her where My Saint might find her.

Gertrude Howe's adopted children had already grown up, two of them to be doctors. Looking at the emaciated button-nosed face of this one, I claimed it as my own.

"You can't adopt her legally," said Miss Howe, "unless you marry. The Mission Board won't let you."

"Never mind the formalities," I said, and took the endearing three-month-old back to school.

A wet nurse with natural feet was found for her in the hills. Like any excited new mother, I began to read about bringing up children. The new amah and I came to blows almost immediately on the subject of swaddling. Since the days of the Mings, Chinese babies had been sewed into their winter clothes, with an outer wrapping of carpet, and the amah was sure that loose blankets would kill the baby. I had to check every night to be sure a carpet had not been surreptitiously stitched around the little body of Precious Pearl.

In many other ways I gave in to the amah's traditional notions on how to bring up baby. Only where I was sure that I was right did I insist on my own opinions. And between us Precious Pearl grew and flourished.

Now that I had a Chinese daughter of my own, I felt more than ever close to my adopted country. I suppose I am as American as pumpkin pie or the Fourth of July, but I have never felt that one splendid heritage should keep anyone from expanding to include another. It was with satisfaction that I made a diary note: "I am becoming more and more Chinesey."

Chinesey enough, and sufficiently fluent in the language, so that Ilien Tang decided she could leave me to cope with Bao Lin. She had not visited her ancestors and the living members of her family in the far interior since her return to China.

Just after she left, an older pupil, Fragrant Water, confessed to me that she was in love with a fine, young university graduate of excellent family. This seemed most suitable. There was a catch, however. Fragrant Water's parents were arriving at the school for the purpose of committing suicide on the grounds.

"Heavens above," said I, and in the absence of Ilien Tang sought the advice of my Honorable Teacher.

Scholar Yang was no help whatever. So far as he was concerned, the parents were behaving with great correctness, although it was unfortunate for the school. The young man, it was true, was an impeccable suitor—but he had not been selected by Fragrant Water's father and he had not bargained for her with him, in accordance with custom. Yang's own son was, of course, marrying a girl whom he would not see until he lifted her bridal veil.

Custom—honored, intricate custom, so much of which was wise and good and worthy of respect.... How firmly should I stand against its ramifications? Modern China was coming into being amidst Old China, but it would be different from Modern America or Modern Europe. I wanted only to help my girls be the best they could. In this case, I examined my own feelings and convictions in the light of Fragrant Water's and decided that I could take only one stand.

Bitterly I argued with Yang, insisting that young men and women in the twentieth century should choose their own mates.

"Absurd," said my Old Born Before testily. "We tried that centuries ago in China. It did not work."

Fragrant Water's father formally protested to his daughter's headmistress. If his daughter persisted in saying that she was in love and refusing to marry the man he would choose for her in due course, he could only go to the river and drown himself. This would, in effect, make Little Sister Han his murderer, for it was the influence of the school that had ruined his child.

At the end of the interview, during which I staunchly defended Fragrant Water, he did indeed stalk to the water and throw himself in.

However, he chose a populous spot on the bank and I had already made sure that men were on hand to haul him out.

The mother refused to speak to me, but took up her stand on the school grounds. She would, she announced, producing a dagger, kill herself there so that her spirit would remain on the spot to torment Little Sister Han. I rallied a few ladies to hold her hands and prevent her, and eventually succeeded in rounding up both parents, their daughter, and the fiancé himself in adjoining rooms at the school. Running between them like a labor mediator, I succeeded in affecting a compromise. The young man would yield his principles to the extent of providing his in-laws with all the feasts and all the trousseau and whatever jewelry his Fragrant Flower wished in return for parental consent to the wedding. In the end, the young people were wed with all due ceremony—and a reluctant blessing from both parents.

My girls had, of course, followed the course of true love with romantic interest. They approved of my role in the affair and began to think of me as their champion. This brought me closer to them and, partly for my own pleasure and partly to solidify my position with them, I began to take my noon meal with my pupils, using chopsticks until my hand ached. The girls were emboldened by my constitutional insensitivity to teasing and made fun of my Chinese, but did not venture to defy my intuitive knowledge of just how far to let them go. I needed to retain their respect for their young American head-mistress. Though I was shaky in the vernacular, little girls with black bangs and dark eyes and yellow-tinted skin were little girls just the same—and I did understand them.

Feeling secure in the world of the school, I began to venture outside it. I went regularly to town with the gatekeeper, Old Willow, to test my ability to shop and to cope for myself. Happily, I adapted to Chinese manners. I learned never to look toward a chair in which anyone I knew was carried. If I did, the gentleman would have to descend and make the prescribed three low bows. It was far politer to ignore his presence. In the shops, I was learning to bargain Chinese style and was pretty pleased with myself altogether. But pride, as ever, went before a tumble.

Old Willow usually followed me, which was easy since I towered, pagodalike, among the short Celestials, and I was aware that he spent a good deal of time explaining me to people. One day I lost him and a crowd began to gather. The noise they made and the argument they appeared to be having grew so alarming that I was sure there was about to be an anti-foreign riot. These were by no means so much a matter of the past that an ugly one could not occur, and in fear and trembling I ran into a shop. Forty or more people pushed in after me. Frightened clerks finally managed to shove them out and lock the door. I waited inside until dusk, then went back home in a sedan chair, curtained as tight as a bride.

When Ilien Tang returned, the two of us went off to town together. The same jostling crowds began to gather. After listening to the rising decibels, Ilien Tang made a speech which magically dispersed the threatening throng.

Then she turned to me, her face crimson with suppressed laughter. "It's the feather on your hat," she explained. "Feathers are only for officials. They wanted to know what kind you were and what that particular feather signified. Some of them thought you must be masquerading, and this made them furious."

Putting it away in a box that night, I regretted the hat,

bought with extravagant care to match a favorite suit. "Good-by pretty hat and memorable feather," I mourned. "I hate to lose you, but you were almost my undoing."

Ilien Tang's return was a relief in every way. To catch up with administrative matters and correspondence, I turned the student body back over to her entirely.

Most of the girls came from Christian Chinese homes, some from vast distances. Their expenses, in many cases including that of the trip across the interior, were paid by Methodist missions, although many of them came from well-off families. One of my plans was to increase the fees to those who could afford them and to institute a system of scholarships for those who could not. Among the new pupils, I had already made some such arrangements.

For a week or two I scarcely saw the girls, so busy and absorbed was I in general matters which would improve the School of the Protecting Spirit. Then one night Ilien Tang reported a fresh problem. There had been mutiny.

That evening at dinner one of the Christian students, Sui Ling, whose boat fare and all expenses had been paid, stood up and threw her bowl of rice on the floor.

"Is this the best the church can do?" she shouted at Ilien Tang. "I shan't eat this filthy food, and *you* can't make me!"

Several other girls had gleefully joined the protest. No one had ever complained of the food before, but spoiled and assured, this rebellious group was waiting to see what would happen.

I promptly sailed into the fray.

"Sui Ling, you may pack your trunk and go home tomorrow," I told the ringleader. "And anyone else who feels as you do may go at the same time."

This was a bombshell. It was not the Christian behavior to which they had been accustomed. They expected the missionary teacher to take them into her office, to kneel with them and pray for their immortal souls and plead for their repentance. Then compromises would be made, forgiveness asked for and received, and all would proceed as before. In

their experience, missionaries leaned heavily on the efficacy
of prayer and a few tears. I had no intention of letting them
get away with such easy penance and then to take them per-
suasively back to my bosom.

Sui Ling, expecting me to yield, boastfully packed her bags.
A contingent of noisy girls joined her.

Ilien Tang was distressed and afraid for the school. If I
would remove from her some of the authority I had given
her, she suggested, all would be well. She was the source of
the trouble.

"Nonsense," I said.

"You must remember how deep the prejudice against
women is in this country," Ilien Tang explained. "Perhaps
the more liberal parents will send their daughters to learn to
read and write, will let them walk on free feet, will even
allow them into the professions. That is different from taking
orders. You are different. You are Western. But it is very
hard for Chinese women even to take orders from each other.
It's not my teaching here, but my authority that's in question."

I would have none of this. "As soon as the girls are in
order, I'm going to name you Assistant Principal," I said.
"One day this school will be *yours*, as it should be, not mine
or any other foreigner's!"

Up to the moment of their mass departure, the defiant
group of pupils expected to be asked to remain. They taunted
the girls who stayed outside the strike and refused to join the
exodus as the Chinese equivalent of "squares." Then, un-
begged and unforgiven, they left.

Gertrude Howe was all on my side. She and Dr. Bowen
stood by me staunchly, although he was worried about the
development and afraid it might reflect on the mission as a
whole. All the Chinese, the girls and their families and the
interested onlookers, who were everybody, watched and waited.
Most of them thought Little Sister Han would give in.

"The school will have no students," ran the gossip. "By
and by they will beg them to come back."

"Our tears run upward," is what the Chinese say for "keeping a stiff upper lip." I meant to enforce discipline, to keep Ilien Tang in authority, and to reinstate or take in only pupils who wanted an education and were willing to be taught and guided as we saw fit.

Several Chinese pastors whose children had departed arrived to plead and exhort me as to my proper behavior. Gertrude Howe sat in on a conference with one angry man whose two daughters had both left.

"Do you expect the children to take orders from a *Chinese woman*," he asked, "and a young one at that?"

"That's exactly what I do expect," I replied. "Now and from now on. When Miss Tang makes a decision, I follow it and so will the school. When I make one, she and the school will follow. We two are one, and of the two of us, Ilien Tang is the more important. *She* is the one who provides their model, the one they should want to be like. I can't be their ideal. I'm from a different country!"

When Dr. Bowen wondered whether I was wise to continue so adamant, I told him as firmly, "I'd rather have ten serious pupils here to learn than fifty who have to be petted into behaving themselves!"

One by one the girls came back, capitulating wholly, and new pupils entering the school found a wholesome change in the atmosphere. I never did take offenders into my office to pray with them. To me prayer is a spiritual exercise, not a means of moral suasion. If they did not want to follow the ideals and ideas represented by the school, they could leave and make room for others who did. As for the individual badnesses and small infractions of normal discipline which come up like hiccups whenever youngsters are together, I could handle these with laughter, tolerance, or firmness. Or turn them over to Ilien Tang.

Furthermore, Ilien Tang was made Assistant Principal and was able to operate effectively and without any further question as to her authority. And so, for the first time, a Chinese woman became a central force and power in a mission school.

6

China and I adapted to each other (by no means always a one-way process) with a readiness that surprises me now. I suppose it was partly because the Chinese put such a premium on courtesy. While it may be necessary to be firm on principle, it never seemed to me worth offending anyone when it came to form. This attitude brought me many happy relationships.

It worked with my teaching staff, among whom were women from different parts of China and one Moslem woman of enormous erudition who taught Chinese literature. Respecting their customs, I asked them to respect each other and me. Friction was diminished by consideration all around. The pupils, too, brought with them some odd peculiarities, and so long as the ways of one did not infringe on the ways of others or on the school, I gave them considerable leeway.

Even in music we exchanged courtesies. Though it was strange to their ears, they soon learned to love Western music. In a very short time I had a middle-school chorus of girls which rivaled any glee club back home. As for me, I set about not only learning to tolerate but to like the sounds, so unlike our harmonies, which make music to Chinese ears. I even took lessons from a singing teacher in Nanchang, though I must admit that I had trouble adapting my robust, scale-trained Western soprano to the eerie nasal slides.

My own adaptations entailed a few personal sacrifices, one of them in the matter of my giddy wardrobe.

I had brought along with me a selection of décolleté evening dresses, for instance, suitable for singing at concerts or wearing to evening parties. I did love them. It was a shock to discover how I might look to the Chinese, who invariably wore high-necked gowns with narrow standing collars.

One of my pupils saw the cover on a *Ladies' Home Journal*, sent to me from home. In the painting a lady with fine shoulders and bust was seated at a dinner, leaning toward a male companion in white tie and tails.

"Is the woman," asked the child, titillated and upset, "naked *under* the table, too?"

From then on I tore off any magazine covers that displayed women in evening clothes—and modified my own wardrobe. For a while I considered wearing Chinese robes, which I found enormously chic, but was deterred by meeting some foreign men and women who had "gone Chinese" to the extent that the men even let their hair grow and plaited it in queues. (Pretty ludicrous, I thought, especially when the alien hair was red.) These same people would not permit the Chinese, whose clothes they aped and whom they believed should be Christianized, to sit with them at table or to come in through the front door, sending even Chinese clergymen to the back entrance.

When I broached the subject of my own attire to a Chinese friend in Nanchang, Madame Ho replied, "Ah, but Little Sister Han, we think we look better in ours and you look better in yours."

That solution suited me and was in keeping with my own instinct: to remain me while trying to expand that me.

As its staff got used to me and Ilien Tang took more and more direct responsibility, Bao Lin was running so well I felt the time had come to branch out a bit. Since I intended to speak a good deal on behalf of my dreams for Chinese women's education, I decided to make a maiden effort near home. Choosing a village which had not previously been visited by any white woman, a little settlement named Wu, across the Kan River from Nanchang, I had myself and my servant, Fleet Foot, rowed across in a little boat I had bought for my amusement.

My idea was to persuade the villagers to visit Bao Lin.

Perhaps I should gain a pupil or two—who would graduate from the school and return to change the ways of the village.

I still dissolve in laughter when I recall this first venture into public speaking in Chinese.

As was proper, as soon as we landed I sent Fleet Foot with my calling card to the house of the local patriarch, then followed the card to his gateway.

In the living room across the flagged court, I bowed deeply to the old gentleman and then to his wife, and properly insisted on the smallest seat nearest the door. Urged, indeed dragged, to the highest seat farthest from the door, I duly left my tea untouched and took the inevitable social lubricators, watermelon seeds, when they were offered. Practice in the skill of cracking the seeds with my front teeth, sucking out the meat and then spewing the shucks across the floor stood me in good stead. I noticed with self-satisfaction that I could spit them almost as far as the elderly patriarch. This time-consuming operation was accompanied by elegantly ambiguous conversation.

Curiosity in time brought the elder to direct questions.

"Ocean Teacher come Bao Lin School other side river?"

"Yes, Elder Teacher. I crossed in a small boat, hoping to meet the women of your honorable village."

"How many years have you and how long in Middle Kingdom?"

"Thirty years, Elder Wu," I claimed mendaciously. Thirty was quite young enough for the head of a school. "Many moons in Middle Kingdom."

"And where is your husband?"

"I have no husband, Elder."

"You are concubine, then?"

"No, Elder Wu, I am a servant of the Christian Church and come here because we follow Christ. Like your Confucius, He believed that within four seas all men are brothers. I am little sister of the world's honorable family, though I crossed the ocean to come here."

"Then you are nun of this God-Father-Family religion?"

Before I could answer, he commented to his wife, "She not look like Buddhist nun, no shaved head. Have on false hair under hat, yes?"

"No. I am not a nun. I am head of a school where almost one hundred of your Chinese girls study. The governor honors us with his visits and his approval."

"Will Ocean Teacher speak to our women and children, then?"

"With pleasure," said I. Now I had what I had come for.

Elder Wu gave orders. Word was sent to every house. Soon I stood in the courtyard which had filled with the feminine population of the hamlet. Rich and poor alike crowded as close to me as possible.

A very old lady, nearly bald, demanded of Fleet Foot, "Is he a woman?" Assured that he was, she asked how many children he had. "Not married!" exclaimed the crone at the answer. "A concubine, then."

In my spanking-new Chinese, I told them who I was and why I had come to China, that I wanted to be a sister to them, big sister to the children, little sister to the older women, their friend.

Some women, feeling my silk stockings, interrupted to ask if I knotted them. They felt my dress. "Sheeps?" they asked, and then one turned to another and said in admiration, "She doesn't bind her breast—look, she must be nursing twins."

Talking against the hubbub, I felt that at least the children were listening. They stared at me with open-mouthed attention. Urgently I invited them to visit my school.

One of them ran across the courtyard and screamed through the portals. "Grandmother, Uncle, Aunts, everybody, come quick. Hurry!"

I paused, delighted that I was making such an impression.

"What does Ocean Teacher have to say?" called back a voice from outside the entrance.

"I don't know," yelled the child. "But come quick while he still opens his mouth to talk. He has TWO gold teeth in his head!"

Deflated, I resolved to get more coaching from Honorable Teacher before making more addresses.

To have my parting sip of tea, Elder Wu took me into an inner court. There, to my horror, I was confronted by a great black shining lacquered coffin. If a funeral was to take place, the polite Chinese had not mentioned it. Madame Wu went over to the coffin and lifted the lid while I watched, paralyzed. Then the lady extracted a warm jacket to put on one of the grandchildren, allowed out of bed with fever in order to see the Ocean Teacher.

"The coffin," explained Elder Wu, doubtless amused by my audible sigh of relief, "was the gift of my sons and grandsons when I reached sixty years. Good sons. Good grandsons. Good coffin—made of eternal ironwood."

Nanchang was not a treaty port and no foreigner was supposed to do business in the city. Such few as were there— Gertrude Howe, Dr. Bowen, a ubiquitous Standard Oil man or two—came under the protection of "extraterritoriality." No Chinese law could touch any of them, including me. The United States enveloped the ground on which I stood, and whatever I did I was subject only to American justice.

Perhaps this was one reason Chinese officialdom in our province of Kiangsi was slow to recognize my existence. The excitement was all the greater when a messenger arrived one dawn to announce that the governor of the province "West of the River" was coming. There was no question of my convenience. He would arrive at "four o'clock" that afternoon, which meant any time between three and five.

Everyone turned to. Sweetmeats poured from a frantic kitchen. Girls and servants swept and garnished the houses. Scholar Yang spent the morning coaching me in suitable phrases and the etiquette for receiving high officials.

"And don't begin to sip tea before the governor lifts his cup!" warned Yang repeatedly.

From two o'clock on the staff sat in nervous state, while the schoolgirls formed a rigid avenue of welcome.

At three another messenger came with His Excellency's large red calling card. The gates of the lodge were flung wide. His personal bodyguard preceded men carrying a huge red umbrella on a twenty-foot bamboo pole, symbol of power which cleared the streets for the governor's passing. Bearers in uniform conveyed His Excellency's person in a befringed chair.

When the chair was dipped, the governor emerged, an immense and impressive man. His hat, badge of his office, was round, with a turned-up black velvet brim. Its crown was red, covered with black fringe, and in the center was a crystal ball. Hanging down from the brim was a long, iridescent peacock feather. A sable coat, the sleeves a yard long, came down to his knees and as he walked the turquoise satin lining flickered into view. Over his chest, sewn to the coat, was an emblem embroidered with a bird, signifying that he was a civilian official. (An animal denoted the military.)

Entering my living room, he dropped to his knees, put his hands together and touched his forehead to his fingertips nine times. On my side of the room, I likewise knelt and did the same.

Then after an exchange between us of three low bows and three deep drawings-in of breath, the great man seated himself in the smallest chair—for which he was dangerously too large. Well-coached, his hostess entreated him to remove himself from so lowly a seat and to take the largest chair, farthest from the door. After a display of formal reluctance, he changed his place to the seat of honor.

Scalding tea was brought, in porcelain cups with silver saucers, and duly ignored. In spite of my impulse to urge him to drink the hot tea on this cold day, I refrained and discussed the affairs of the world with him.

Graciously descending to homelier topics, the governor said he had heard that ours was a wonderful school. Half-standing and bowing in response to this, I insisted somewhat insincerely that I was unworthy, the school humble. Half-standing and bowing in response to me, the governor pressed on with compliments and then asked me to show him around.

Every threshold was a problem. The governor asked that I precede him. I urged His Excellency to go first. Each time I won the game, as he knew I would and I knew he knew I knew he would, but no ploy in the ceremony was omitted.

After the tour, he returned briefly to the drawing room, sat down and began to sip his tea. His bodyguard, who had stood at the doors listening to every word, as had a dozen others in the vestibule, immediately ordered his bearers. After a hundred bows by everyone concerned, the visit was over.

"I adored," I confessed to my diary, "every second of those thirty minutes. When the red umbrella moved off down the street, emptied for His Excellency, the School of the Protecting Spirit was recognized, socially and politically. Little Sister Han is radiant."

Three weeks later I had a letter from a missionary I had never met.

"Dear Miss Honsinger," ran the letter in spidery script. "We here in Nanking hear of some of the things you are doing down there in old Nanchang. You are young and new to China, while I have been here over twenty-five years. I am speaking for all of my colleagues when I tell you that an American *never* bows the knee to *any* man. . . ."

After thought and prayer and discussions with Gertrude Howe and Ilien Tang, I composed an answer to this woman, who might well cause trouble back in the United States if she tried.

Dear Miss S——,

I received your letter with a good deal of surprise and I have prayed about it thoughtfully and quietly. I must reply that my mother brought me up well, and I would be unable to face her were I to report that I had stood or sat while a Governor of 45 million people knelt before me. I am in China, deep in its heart, and I believe I should follow its etiquette.

Thank you for your interest in my welfare.

I had no further communication from the missionary, but I did have the governor's daughter in my school the next year, along with the daughter of my dead cook.

The truth must be told that, with notable exceptions—among whom were a bishop, Gertrude Howe, and an ambassador—I got along better with the Chinese than I did with my own compatriots in China.

My first visitor from home was a woman I called Tourist-Lady-Interested-in-Missions. We had met at the Tea-Taster's in Shanghai. Not even my warning letter that interior China was nothing like the comfortable, modern city on the coast deterred Tourist-Lady from New England when she decided to invade Nanchang.

As a proper hostess, I made the rough trip across Poyang to meet my self-invited guest. When the two of us climbed down into the miniscule cabin on the dirty junk, Tourist-Lady professed to be thrilled.

"How picturesque!" she exclaimed. "What fun I shall have describing it to my party. None of them have done anything exciting like this."

Before the craft entered the lake, it began to rain in torrents. The Chinese passengers crowded every nook and cranny of the boat and for four days Tourist-Lady and I were stuck in the tiny cabin, unable to budge or to go on deck. One small window over the upper bunk provided a bit of light, but no view of the beautiful hills tipped with picturesque Buddhist temples that fringed the lake. We could stand and stare at the rain or read the books we perched on the upper berth, or could take turns on the one stool or lie in the bunks. At night, we lit a smoky lantern and read a while before sleeping if we could. By the end of four days, my visitor was at least cured of the theory that mission life was wholly luxurious.

At the School of the Protecting Spirit, she insisted on inspecting everything. The dormitory bedrooms, spotless and curtained and counterpaned in white, brought the comment, "But you are making Americans of them! Why should Chinese girls sleep on beds?"

For centuries the Chinese had always slept on beds, I told her, if they could afford them.

Tourist-Lady's next unfortunate remark was made in the class where Ilien Tang was teaching the girls English. "But of course there's one thing you can't teach them," she remarked loudly, apparently unconvinced that they knew enough English to understand her; "that is music. They just can't get it."

That night I displayed my middle-school chorus. Selections from *Elijah* and "The Holy City" in harmony were followed by Gaul's trio, "It shall come to pass that at eventide it shall be light. . . ."

Tourist-Lady streamed tears. "It *has* come to pass," she admitted. "It is a miracle. I have never seen such light in any faces or heard such singing. I wish I could take them all to America!"

From then on she loved the girls, but I suspected she had a good deal more to learn about love.

By the time she left, I was heartily glad to see her go. It was easier for me to be tolerant of strangers whose customs were wholly different from my own than to exercise the blessed virtue of charity toward such as she.

After she had gone I went back with relief to my absorption in the school and the country which had come to mean so much to me. I felt strongly that Napoleon had been prophetic when he pointed to the map in Fontainebleau and called China a sleeping giant. "Let her sleep. When she wakes, she will change the world." I felt her waking, and I felt the restlessness of the nightmares that were part of her long sleep.

The weather turned warm and bright, heralding the long, hot summer to come. The only visitors were preceded by the large red cards inscribed with one of the hundred surnames. At the gatehouse in the six-foot walls, the loyal gateman, Old Willow, who could not read but who knew the surnames as he knew the flowers around his little house, never made a single mistake in announcing the honorable guests.

I was devoted to this man whose devotion to the school

was unqualified. When his wife asked permission to go home with their boy for a visit, I inquired solicitously whether Yan Tse-fu would be quite contented without her. Given this assurance, accompanied by many shy bows, I sent the woman and the son off in a wheelbarrow, the common means of locomotion in the region, where there were no horses or bullocks. With them went a strong "pusher" to shove them to their destination, along the paths among the paddy fields, days away.

Ilien Tang and I were sitting over tiffin on the veranda the next day in the hushed heat of noon, with a punkah waving over our heads. A boatman glided up to us, crying in loud tones, "Have save life. Your man drown in river. Now he out. I pull him shore. Where is my reward? I save life."

Telling the man to get money from the cook and then to go for the doctor, we ran to the river. Old Willow was lying stretched on a board and surrounded by a gathering crowd.

"His soul has gone, the gods of the river have taken it," a bystander told us.

Ilien Tang, trained in first aid, ordered the people away and told two men to turn Old Willow just so. The American doctor arrived in time to resuscitate the old man while the lingering crowd watched in awe.

"The miracle man," intoned one of them, "has brought back the soul of Old Willow, which had gone away."

I discovered then that he had been acting strangely for several weeks and that this was why his wife had taken their son and left. It was apparent that his soul had indeed gone on a journey and that when he threw himself into the river he had been out of his mind. "I thought a dragon was after me," he apologized.

Hoping for the best, I kept him on at the gatehouse and sent out a message to his wife to come back. He had been at the school much longer than I had and was as much part of the place as the gate itself.

A week or so later at dusk, Major-Domo—as I had titled him for his pleasure—Yang Tse-fu came stealing into my office.

The lamps were not yet lighted and I thought the soft steps in the room were those of Precious Pearl's amah until I looked up to see Old Willow, in a new blue gown, kneeling on the floor.

"Honorable Little Sister Han," he whispered loudly. "They wish my life. Out there in the lodge they go back and forth, back and forth, back and forth, trying to take my life. The long-haired Boxers are after me!"

For twenty minutes I soothed and quieted him as I would have a child. As soon as he rose and left, I sent servants to follow him and see that he was safe while I hastily fetched the doctor.

"No matter what it costs," I told him, "Old Willow must go to an asylum."

"There is only one hospital for the insane in all China, for four hundred million people," the doctor informed me drily. "And that's in Canton."

The old gateman, the other servants told me, had been through flood and famine and rebellion in his life, and this was not his first breakdown. All I could do was to keep the demented fellow under observation until he could be sent to the country, to the home of his ancestors. From then on the school would send him remittances until he died.

"Oh suffering China," I demanded bitterly in my diary, "when will you be able to take care of tens of thousands like poor, good, dear Yang Tse-fu?"

7

My own character and sense of mission were gradually crystalizing. Whether I had come to China guided by the Divine Will or more humanly influenced by lively curiosity, impulsive energy, and a longing to stretch my wings, I felt I had come to belong there. I was not inclined to excavate in my unconscious for psychological explanations. Once my "heaven feet" were set on a road, energy carried me briskly wherever it led.

Along my Chinese highway three signposts gave me final bearings.

The first was the never-forgotten sign in Shanghai: DOGS AND CHINESE NOT ADMITTED. Unless it was obliterated in spirit and in fact, the white people would lose all right to China's friendship and hospitality forever.

The second sign was inscribed over the lintel of a small mud house in a village near Nanchang. IN THIS FAMILY, read the large gold Chinese characters on bright red paper, THERE IS A PH.D. Learning, to which such respect and importance were accorded, could bring salvation to the illiterate millions, living still as they had lived for four thousand years. Women, bound and chatteled, must learn, too, and take over their own destinies.

The third signpost was a question. "Do you," the Moslem woman who taught Chinese literature at Bao Lin, asked me casually one day, "have the moon in America?" How very little even literate China, behind its Great Wall and tens of thousands of small walls, knew of the world—even less than the world knew of China.

Inspiration leads to action with me. (Sometimes far too precipitously!) This time I acted not to spread the news in China that the moon shone over the Rockies but to inform myself. I found an Englishman in Nanchang who had made a study of astronomy and persuaded him to hold a course of study for the English-speaking colony. All the rest of my life I would recognize the constellations wherever I was and remember how they shape the sky over different parts of the world.

Looking back, I think the main reason I could take a great deal from any environment was not a childlike willingness to learn, but the fact that I did not incline to doubt myself and my roots, who and what I was. We did not question our souls so interminably in my early days. I accepted myself. I admired my Puritan ancestors, respected my strict, small-town American upbringing, believed in my old-time Methodist religious teaching. My contradictory worldliness, ambition, and love of pretty things seemed natural to me. Modern concern with equality and freedom for women, with education, with the expansion of the religious spirit through all and any sincere worship, did not conflict in me with inherited or older conceptions. I could also love all of China without conflict, the old and the new, the faults and the virtues. Of such was mankind. And if there was so much tragedy in China, it was also true that they faced tragedy with extraordinary endurance and humor.

Since large contradictions seemed to me in the order of things, I could take small contrarinesses in stride. I might be momentarily shocked, but not deeply disturbed at a feast where my hostess yielded first place to her husband's new and favorite concubine and I did admire, unstintingly, the grace and discipline with which she made this gesture. In a coolie hut, I sank to my sufficient haunches and flattered the authority of the male while coaxing a timorous wife to speak with me. When the U.S. Standard Oil men in Nanchang nicknamed me "Maxine" for a fancied resemblance to their favorite actress, the glamorous Maxine Elliott, I was delighted, perhaps even coquettish—but not too diverted to lose sight of my purpose in life. With, I believe, all due respect, I argued with the bishops and the mission chiefs and the Chinese fathers of my girls in favor of views that opposed theirs. But in doing so, the manners my mother had instilled in me helped me to get away with more than many a brash bearer of larger torches.

Once I had settled the matter of Ilien Tang's authority, I was free to leave Bao Lin whenever I chose. I had a little money of my own, enough to take trips without spending mission funds. Insatiable for experience, and with roaring good health to withstand the rigors of primitive travel, I was always ready to hie myself about my vast new domain.

Although I took a good deal of frivolous pleasure in my appearance, this did not lead to folly. I donned big blue goggles and a bulky pith helmet to protect myself from the deadly China sun or bundled myself into the "seven layers of coats" that kept out China's piercing cold. I knew I looked odd, but the Chinese scarcely judged me by Western standards: I was startling enough to them anyway. In contrast to most missionaries, even bundled or helmeted I looked all too chic, but when I visited the fashionable in Shanghai or elsewhere I never failed to do myself up in proper style.

My first trek back to Shanghai was for the 1907 National Conference of Missions. The wind was favorable. We made it to Kiukiang in four days by junk and in three more days arrived downriver at the "Paris of the East." As soon as the steamer dropped anchor there, sampans and slipper boats, barges and tenders swarmed alongside. Aboard them and on shore the crowd of supplicants and salesmen massed as thickly and pled as noisily as if the tatty river boat were a ship from across the ocean. Even the penny patronage of such passengers as arrived from the interior might make the difference between life and death for one more day in the marginal existence of the blue-clad Celestials.

"Change money, Missie," one called, flourishing Mexican dollars. "Good money, Missie, better than Bund."

Many things were for sale in the melee, offered with out-thrust hands, touted in liquid triple-tones grace-noted with laughter.

One little sampan was packed with garments, all beautifully embroidered. The boatman held up a pair of elegant soft slippers. "Just fit Missie," he called. "Belong fat lady." By this time I knew that fat was a symbol of prosperity and that the laughing boatman was flattering, not insulting, me.

It was hard to believe, surrounded by smiling, sunny faces, that these people lived so precariously close to death from undernourishment, that however many died many more would be born in the same hour. Poverty and overpopulation were so overwhelming that one had to learn to take them for granted in China, as a dweller by the seashore takes for granted the limitless ocean.

The good-humored masses of China seemed complacent and passive in their acceptance of the will of heaven. They scarcely cared who ruled over them and took what was wrong as their birthright. Yet they could be aroused to violence and revolution.

Only a half-century earlier a man, Hunh Shiu-chuan, had come to personify their deeply buried hopes of a better life. He gave leadership to the slumbering desire to throw off their terrible poverty, to end the tyranny of their rulers. Under him, the Taiping Rebellion grew and spread like a Yangtze flood.

Hunh Shiu-chuan worshiped the cross. From Christianity he had learned to believe in the dignity of the individual man. Starting with only a handful of followers, within three years the armies he commanded swept through the South and he was enthroned in Nanking as the "Peace Emperor."

His regime was to have made of China a kingdom of peace and heaven, with all men equal. He forbade the buying and selling of slaves, outlawed concubinage, and proclaimed a new system of land ownership.

To destroy this dream, it was estimated that between fifty and a hundred million Chinese were slaughtered and historians have been diligent to blacken his memory. But the defeat of his ideals at the hands of Chinese scholars and the English General Gordon who helped suppress the Taiping Rebellion had not killed them. The dream lingered. As a boy, Sun Yat-sen heard the true history from the lips of an old soldier who had served Hunh Shiu-chuan. Now Sun Yat-sen was becoming a revolutionary force in China. Revolt against the Imperial throne and against centuries of Manchu rule was in the air once more. No one knew when, where, or how it would break out.

Even the absolutist Dowager Empress, the "Old Buddha" herself, had recognized the inevitability of change. Perhaps she saw herself, in her old age, as a cautious Chinese Victoria reluctantly leading her nation toward moderate constitutional reforms under the Manchu monarchy. But would she leave an heir strong enough to hold the throne? North China was monarchist-minded, but in the South, *republic* was the word, Sun Yat-sen the name, and the U.S.A. the model.

I was never a political person. To me there was virtue and grace in "Old China" and virtue and hope in "Young China." Proud of my own rich inheritance of freedom, I was trying to teach my southern Chinese children to "know the truth." My charges, ranging from babies to teen-agers, were the women of "Young China's" future. In the happy assurance of my Christianity, my belief in Western progress and the emergence of women, I was sure that moral good could only beget good. When I was accused of encouraging young revolutionaries—a word I associated with 1776 and not with the ferment in Russia or the writings of Karl Marx—I agreed that indeed I was.

In Shanghai, I listened to the incessant political talk, rarely attempting to contribute. There were as many opinions as there were men and kinds of men to hold them.

"Every European knows the necessity for keeping Russia out of China," pontificated my American friend the Tea-Taster, in his living room. "But American businessmen are meeting right now in Peking to put through a deal that will weaken some of the necessary Japanese control. Nevertheless, Japan's going right ahead to snatch her rights in this huge, rich land. Far better the Japanese than the Russians. . . . The British know that."

"Why not China for the *Chinese?*" I asked.

"China's helpless," snorted the Tea-Taster, dismissing the idea.

Among the Sinologue missionaries, there was much discussion of a world-wide peace meeting to be held at the Hague. They talked about who should go from England, America, France, Germany, Japan. . . .

"And who will be there from China?" I asked one evening.

"China won't have a representative," said one man authoritatively. "After all, she can't go to a peace conference—she has no army or navy!"

Like the Chinese, I have a long memory and, after more than fifty years, I am still angered by such reasoning. "You reap what you sow," is my proverb.

All too seldom did I find my own people talking of China as a nation that belonged, essentially, to itself. Diplomats spoke of control, extraterritorial rights, partition, and "influence." Too often my missionary friends seemed to consider China a "field" in which to expand the Kingdom of God (each according to his own definition of God's kingdom). The foreigners were pleased that the heathen Empress Dowager had changed her reclusive habits and now received their delegations, especially the ladies, but they rarely acknowledged what limited sanction from her had meant to the Westerners. She had approved decrees aiding and regulating the introduction of Western civilization in China. Mission institutions as a result were no longer shunned as centers of alien learning, but were thronged with students in a burgeoning cross-culture.

Even mild reforms contributed to deep unrest throughout the country. News of Sun Yat-sen, touring the world to raise money and propagandize his cause, circulated by paddy-field and street-corner telegraph. In Tokyo a close-shaven youngster named Chiang Kai-shek was among thousands of Chinese students eager to discover the secret of Japan's westernized progress. Branches of Kwang-Fu (The Returning Light) were springing up all over the Chinese Empire and unsuccessful attempts to overthrow the Manchu dynasty were suppressed during the year in Kwantung and Wai Chow and elsewhere.

The country was becoming closer knit, with railroads and postal service and newspapers printed so that all literates, not just the scholars, could read them. With the abolition in 1906 of the ancient classical examinations as the only means of entering China's civil service, the powerful system of central control began to crumble. How much longer would Chinese passivity and traditionalism resist upheaval which could change the entire country?

In the cities, everyone spoke of change and revolution except those too poor to think of anything but their bloated and empty bellies. Sun Yat-sen's words echoed in teahouse and on street corner, "Power is with the people and we are the people." To me, the greatest mistake my international friends made was their failure to acknowledge that power in the future lay with the Chinese themselves. China *was* the Chinese, not the American businessmen or the missionaries or the British, policing the city with awesome Sikhs in brilliantined whiskers and vivid turbans, or the Japanese who resembled the Chinese not at all, except to blind Western eyes.

At the Shanghai conference, missionaries from all over met together. The one who impressed me most was the Chinese Reverend Mr. Liu. He opened one meeting with the simple statement: "We are here together. We have agreed to differ, but are resolved to love."

While I was in Shanghai, I heard a lot about the famous woman revolutionary Chiu-Chin (Gem of Autumn), who edited a woman's magazine called *Chung Kuo Nu Bao* (Middle Country Women's Publication). The flaming editorials she wrote herself.

"In our language are two miserable, pitiable, hazardous, dangerous words," said Chiu-Chin in one. "Black Darkness.

They mean a failure to comprehend reality, not to have sight or hearing. . . .

"If I can awaken women from their deep drunkenness of ignorance and startle them with ten thousand terrors then they themselves will evolve plans. . . .

"In the past ten years the winds of custom have slowly veered. Slowly, how slowly, the thread of light is piercing the black darkness of women's realm, which has been shut in on all sides for four times one thousand years!"

Ringing and sympathetic words. No wonder she was a heroine to some of the teen-agers at Bao Lin. That my children stirred and whispered, awakening from this sleep of centuries, I knew and approved. It was their future amaking.

One of the girls, a lively young lady named Chang Tren, had even refused to take her place in the receiving line when the governor came to call. Although this seemed to me confusing rebellion with discourtesy to an official visitor, I had allowed Chang Tren to go to bed as if sick.

Too busy to pay attention to the child and sympathetic to her attitude that China should be ruled by Chinese, not Manchus, I demanded no apology, and the incident was closed. The whole school was my concern and I could not single out particular girls to talk with lest it be taken for preference. Not for a headmistress were the pleasures and pains of confidences. My intimacies with the youngsters in my charge were limited.

Chang Tren was a dutiful daughter. Recently she had taken several trips to Kiukiang to "call back the soul of her dying grandfather" in her country village near the river city. The letters which she said asked for her presence at home came across my desk, important-looking and carefully sealed. Each time she received one the short, impatient southern girl asked permission to leave at once and hurried away.

When I heard in Shanghai that the fiery Chiu-Chin also supervised the manufacture of bombs in her house nearby, bombs which were sent to the interior and distributed by students, I did not connect "students" with my eighth- and

ninth-grade girls. I was, I suppose, still too American to think
of Bao Lin's moppets as mature, disregarding the fact that in
China early teen-agers might be already married and bearing
children if they had not been sent to me. Thus I was not prepared for the dramatic turn Young China's rebellions would
take at the School of the Protecting Spirit.

To return to Nanchang was already like coming home. The
interior city, with its own rich, terrifying mixture of old and
new, belonged to me and I to the city. At the school, staff and
girls welcomed me with a concert, surest way to please the
person who had taught them choral singing. Only two pupils
disdained to take part. These two were Chang Tren and her
best friend, Yen-sien, both brilliant students. My intention to
ask them why they would not sing was lost in the many dis-
tractions. There was my Precious Pearl to hug and coo over.
There were housekeeping matters to attend to, and my volu-
minous correspondence on behalf of the school to catch up on.

As I was writing letters one evening, Ilien Tang came into
the office and drew a chair close to my desk. I looked up from
the circle of lamplight and smiled at the snub-nosed, slender
girl who was my eyes and ears and good right arm. How much
the two of us had given and received in the bright attachment
of mutual admiration and respect!

From me Ilien Tang had learned, I knew, to stiffen her
gentleness with determination, to handle the pupils with authority as well as warmth. From Ilien Tang I had learned to
temper my impatience, to deal with circumlocution and not to
confuse it with deception, to accept the drip of the water clock
as the measure of passing time in China rather than the rapid
ticking of my American wristwatch.

"Well, dear?" I asked, leaning back and thinking how
charmingly Ilien Tang matched the room, which was now entirely Chinese.

"The girls are organizing, Welthy," said Ilien Tang in a
voice so soft I could scarcely hear her.

"Organizing? For what?"

"Shh. Cracks have ears," said Ilien Tang.

"The ears not hear English, Ocean Teacher's tongue," said I, still lightly.

"We only need to hear one or two words, we Chinese, to guess the rest," said Ilien Tang, deadly serious. "Or to think we do. They are organizing for revolution. In the town they say I am a young revolutionary and that you are aiding and abetting me."

"It's true, absolutely true," said I stoutly. "Sun Yat-sen is lighting the candle and our Bao Lin girls will certainly take their part in Kwang-Fu when the time comes." Before I could launch into my sermon about freedom, Ilien Tang interrupted.

"Many patriots will die before Sun Yat-sen comes home," she said. "It's not going to be easy to overthrow the Manchus, even when the Old Buddha dies. Men only curse and spit in the streets here now, but later.... And even now. You know of the woman leader, Chiu-Chin...."

"Of course," said I.

"You've heard, too, about the bombs that come from her house and are sent to the interior. I think our little Chang Tren is one of the distributors."

"That must be terribly dangerous," I exclaimed.

"She's the leader of a group here. She came to me this morning, as spokesman, to ask for a daily newspaper for them. They want to study the Imperial decrees and the notices of the democratic societies. It isn't enough to read *Liang Chi-Ch'ao* and *Kang Yu-wei*—even Scholar Yang reads them; they want to prepare themselves as women citizens of New China. Can't you hear yourself saying this to them, Welthy?"

"Yes," said I. "But bombs...."

"Do you want to forbid Chang Tren to go the next time her 'grandfather is dying'? How much do you want to interfere?"

"I don't know," I said. "Find out all you can, and help me protect the children."

All that night I paced and prayed. I was an out-country woman and these were young patriots in their own country.

As a free spirit myself who could never be shackled, I could not keep them from doing their duty as they saw it. I did not dream then that Sun Yat-sen himself would ride a white horse out to Bao Lin School one day, but I knew that some of my girls idolized his name. To them he stood for a republic like the U.S.A., rich, free, progressive, powerful, and un-dominated by foreigners. One of my own ancestors had been that Tory who fled to Canada rather than have anything to do with the ragtag and bobtail revolutionaries under George Washington. I had always been ashamed of him. Now could I draw a line and say to my young Chinese: You may do this and think this but not do that or think that?

I was no more than a girl myself, barely twenty-seven, and I was foolhardy. When the next sealed, important-looking letter came for Chang Tren I knew that it meant another trip across the lake for my charge. Fear and responsibility, pride and sympathy, struggled in my mind as I sent for the girl.

The closed face told me nothing, but the tension of the small body betrayed her eagerness. I am afraid I glared at her.

"Why don't you join in the singing, Chang Tren?" I asked her, stalling for time.

"What will music do for my country or for women?" countered Chang Tren.

"Mass choral singing will help a people to stand united for a better life," I argued. "That's why I teach you to sing to-gether, in harmony, in unison."

"I will sing next time," said Chang Tren. "Now may I have my letter?"

Slowly, reluctantly, I handed it over. In my silence was consent.

News seemed to reach the railroadless interior faster than ships could steam upriver or across the lake. Within a few days of its happening, it was known in Nanchang that a cousin of Chiu-Chin, one Hsu Hsi-lin, had shot the governor of An Hwei during an inspection of the police. At the same time Im-perial soldiers were moving relentlessly to squash revolution in

With my colleagues in Nanchang: Ilien Tang, Gertrude Howe, Little Sister Han (in the hat with the feather that caused a crisis in the city), and behind us Dr. Ida Kahn, Estelle Paddock of the YWCA in China, and Julia Cheng.

Ilien Tang and I

The red Mandarin robe was the only treasure I saved from the fire when Baldwin burned. In it I sang to my future husband that the world was dying for a little bit of love.

American generosity rebuilt Imperial China's Baldwin School for Girls after it burned to the ground.

The new Baldwin grew bigger every year. Expanding at top and bottom, we had a kindergarten as well as a high school.

Little Sister Han with the graduating class of 1917.

The good-humored masses of the Chinese people dealt with their desperate poverty as best they could. Competing for largesse, this "flower beggar" turned his rags into an artful costume. To add to their meagre food supply these men on the Kan River fished with cormorants.

every province, including Kiangsi. "I glory in belonging to the Revolutionary party," Hsu Hsi-lin was quoted as shouting on his way to the judge, who sentenced him to die, his heart to be removed from his living body.

Under the Wu Tung trees in the east corner of the school grounds, beside the wall that gave on the Temple of Last Prayer outside, Chang Tren called the first open revolutionary meeting at Bao Lin.

Speaking to a small group of serious girls, she said: "We live in a city of walls and most of our women have golden lily feet. Until women enter the revolutionary movement no Kwang-Fu will come. Sun Yat-sen has written so and we will follow him like wild geese high in the heavens. He is like the first bird that leads the formation."

Ilien Tang mingled in the group and heard one of the girls whisper to Chang Tren, "Where are the bombs?"

"Under the shelf in the cart of the traveling barber, Lao. Take Chiu Min with you and take them to Hwa Tze at the South City Gate at the Hour of the Snake. Must get there before sundown. Hwa Tze will take them into the city. After that, forget all."

As I had done, Ilien Tang said nothing. She was also committed to a new China, although she questioned such hothead methods.

In low tones, to be sure that girls who disapproved of them could not overhear, the revolutionary group discussed what Hsu Hsi-lin's death might mean to their heroine-leader, Chiu-Chin. "The time has come," said Chiu Min, who was proud that her given name was the same as the great woman's, "and a woman will lead us."

The same girls gathered under the Wu Tung trees a few weeks later when news was flashed by bamboo telegraph of Chiu-Chin's execution. Over and over they told each other the story:

Chiu-Chin had been arrested in her room, at daybreak, on the sixth day of June. From then on she spoke no word, only wrote her last message— "Autumn rain, Autumn wind, Autumn heart, grief, slay." Led out in the red robes of a criminal to have her head chopped from her body, she had asked that she not be stripped to the waist. The police were Chinese, not Manchu, and they left her body covered. As she knelt, they took hold of her hair, short like a man's, and bared her neck to the axe. Even her son and daughter did not dare to claim her head or her body for burial and her remains were thrown in a criminal's grave.

"Her deeds were carried even to the Dragon Throne of Old Buddha," said Chang Tren. "Yes, and even Old Buddha shed tears at her death."

The meeting under the trees ended. As the group dispersed, a hush brooded over the whole school. That night, in Chang Tren's room, four of the girls wept and wailed all night long. Neither Ilien Tang nor I interfered. With Chiu-Chin's passing the women's movement, lacking leadership, might not function actively for a while. The girls at Bao Lin would have more time to grow and develop, to prepare for college, to get ready for the future—whatever it was.

The school returned to normal. Black heads bent over lesson books, dragging long black braids with each movement. The grounds echoed in recreation periods to the scoring of games and the normal exchange of chatter. The groups that formed and re-formed seemed no longer political, but based on the sudden whimsical affections that girls come to feel for one or another of what we call "leaders"—the ones who attract and dominate others. A distraction was provided by the arrival of the governor's niece, a girl of great charm and chic who promptly gathered her own satellites.

Having hiked the fees for rich girls, I now started a workshop where the poor ones could make things for sale outside. I taught them to cross-stitch patterns on the beautiful "grass" linen made in Nanchang from Kiangsi flax. Bedspreads, curtains, tablecloths, napkins were soon ready. When the moneyed young ladies felt cheated and demanded to cross-stitch also, I expanded the workshop. The scholarship fund mounted rapidly as institutions, even as far away as Shanghai, began ordering sets of table linen decorated with our favorite blue-bird design.

About a month after the night Chang Tren and her three closest cohorts had mourned the execution of Chiu-Chin, the school was briefly rocked by another political crisis. It was discovered that the four had done more than weep. Chiu Min had brought with her a pair of scissors, borrowed from the school tailor, and during the course of the night they had chopped off each others' hair. In the morning they concealed the dramatic gesture with hair ribbons tied around the black yarn they used to fasten their long braids back onto their shorn heads.

Bobbed hair was a shocking thing at that time, anywhere. When other girls discovered the cropped heads in their midst, some of them, led by the governor's niece, protested against such outrageous revolutionaries remaining in the school. Ilien Tang and I held a conference with the four in my office.

"Why did you cut your hair, young women?" I asked.

"Chiu-Chin wore hers like a man," said Chiu Min.

"That was only a rumor," said Ilien Tang.

"Because the queue is the symbol of Manchu slavery," said Chang Tren.

"Only for men," said Ilien Tang. "Women have always had long hair. Long before the Manchus."

"For us," said Chang Tren stoutly, "it is like when Old Buddha was sick and her head eunuch cut off flesh from his thigh in devotion to make medicine that would cure her. We did it the night our woman leader died. We each one cut our fingers, too, and pledged in our own blood to keep alive the memory of our leader. We show our devotion to Sun Yat-sen and the freedom of our country by cutting our hair. Now we shall never even tie on the braids again. That was cowardly."

"Do you think you should stay in this school, Chang Tren?" I asked, looking only for understanding.

"You, Teacher Principal Han, put over the Moon Door 'Ye shall know the truth, and truth shall make you free.' You believe this, Ocean Teacher, yes or not yes?"

"Yes," I said. I could argue with their reasoning perhaps, but not with the emotion behind it. "But you must never lose all the wonderful things that come from your forefathers, either, in new freedom."

The four girls kept their short hair and remained at Bao Lin. Since I was firm against dismissing them, protest died down and after a while even the most conservative forgot to taunt them and even forgot, in familiarity with it, that their hair was short at all.

As summer crushed the city and the school and all the flat countryside around the lake under the weight of 120 degrees in the shade, most of the girls went home for vacations and—sturdy though I am—I began to wilt. (I was never slight!) I decided that both Ilien Tang and I should go up into the Li Mountains for a respite, to the mountaintop town of Kuling.

Before we left, a young woman sent by the mission center from Indiana to Nanchang to do evangelical work in the outlying cities and villages, came to stay a few days. When she heard that we were going to Kuling for a rest, she retired to her room and bawled.

"What is the matter?" I asked, trekking after my weeping guest.

"I'm so disappointed," sniffled the woman, who was slightly older than I. "I thought you were a saint."

"Whatever gave you that idea?" I was appalled.

"I thought all missionaries were saints," sobbed the newcomer. "And all they did in Shanghai was quarrel with each other and be jealous and the women talked about the men and the men about the women. And here you are going off to *enjoy* yourself. I thought you'd be a dedicated, holy person."

"You don't become a saint by crossing the ocean," I remonstrated. "You bring yourself along."

"I want to be a saint and there aren't any," said Miss Indiana.

"You have to work to become a saint," I said. "Gertrude Howe is a saint."

"Oh, no, she's not," protested Indiana. "She believes in *Confucius!*"

"Of course she does," I said indignantly. "He thought all men were brothers, just as Christ did. If she can quote his proverbs to a coolie and leave him smiling, he's more likely to believe in her Christ than otherwise. It's the Christian example of her life that counts."

"Well, there's one sure thing," said the disappointed idealist. "*You'll* never be a saint."

"No," I agreed, "I shall never be a saint."

8

The trek across the plain behind Kiukiang to the foothills took hot and dusty hours. Every time Ilien Tang and I came to a cluster of houses along the road, the coolies set down the chairs to rest, have a cup of tea, and smoke. Immediately their unusual passengers were surrounded by every live object not at work in the paddy fields, including babies, pigs, and dogs. Each pause was a lively party.

When the time came to transfer to mountain chairs of light bamboo for the long climb, there was a crisis. The eight waiting mountain coolies sized up the ninety-pound Chinese girl and the helmeted Ocean Teacher at a glance and made a concerted dash for Ilien Tang's chair. Before they could come to blows, I hired two additional coolies to heft my chair.

Stone steps and worn paths made the trail safe for the sure-footed men, and as they trotted up above the bamboo groves and trees into the treeless heights, around sharp corners and along the edge of a ravine, a relief map of the province spread out below. I saw the Yangtze, curling in sunlight, and understood why it was called the "golden thread." Pagodas, a temple, villas, farmhouses, and the vivid green steps of terraced rice fields on the sides of the slopes decorated the brown vistas. "The Chinese rice farmer," I thought, "is the best landscape gardener in the world."

Kuling was an international settlement. Only Europeans used the paths that served as streets and took advantage of the clear, sweet mountain air in the hot season. The Americans and British who predominated, the French and Italian priests,

78

the Swedish and Norwegian missionaries, the German businessmen made their own laws, collected taxes, administered the summer city. Except for coolies who bore the chairs which were the only means of getting about except on foot, the only Chinese people in the locality worked in nearby quarries, singing a mournful labor-lilt that sounded from sunrise to sunset and mingled with the liquid song of flocks of bulbul birds.

Ilien Tang took no part in the strenuous Western life of the town. She thought the white ladies quite mad to walk twelve miles to picnic on sandwiches by waterfalls and then to walk the same distance home again. "The coolies could carry you," she protested to me as I went off daily with jolly crowds my own age.

Indefatigably I explored the region on foot, discovering how beautiful China can be. There was the Emerald Grotto, with a natural swimming pool, and another filled with huge bats, considered good omens in China, and a trail that led to a mill where incense sticks were made, filling the air for miles around with fragrance.

I went to the Methodist bishop's party, at White Deer Grotto, site of the oldest university in China, founded by Chu Fu Tsz hundreds of years before Columbus discovered America. Only a few elderly classical scholars still wandered under the stately pines with a few pupils, teaching them a philosophy as old as the crags.

The bishop spoke to me of recent famine conditions in the area, but firmly refused my offer to raise a family of orphans from the district. He did not, I felt, quite approve of me.

Word had gone out that Miss Honsinger would help with the summer program of concerts, including the oratorio *Elijah*. In Kuling a Scotch musician, not a missionary, had a piano, hauled up the mountain by thirty coolies. With her as accompanist, I rehearsed with the choir for hours.

Just before the performance of *Elijah*, two women arrived; they were battered, shabby, and very much alike. The music had brought these missionaries a month's journey by junk from an interior station. It was their first vacation in three years, during which they had heard not even a Victrola or a harmonium.

The church was packed, with an overflow audience on window sills and the grass outside. When the concert was over, Ilien Tang was crying and the audience was wonderfully demonstrative, but it was the tears and gratitude of the missionary sisters Dill that most moved me.

As I jogged home in my chair by the light of a lantern, I felt I would rather satisfy the music hunger of hearts like theirs than to sing on any opera stage in the world. "I sang my heart out," I wrote that night, "for those women, starved for music. Underneath their old-fashioned clothes and hats made seven years ago, they have the minds of poets and the hearts of heroines."

On my last Sunday morning, I sang "Is it nothing to you, all ye that pass by . . . ," and in my mind was the Chinese walled city to which I would be descending next day. Hundreds of children burning up with fever. Bamboo beds lining the streets where cadaverous men lay through the sultry nights waving palm-leaf fans. Behind heavy curtains lay the women and girls, racked with coughing and caring for emaciated babies, without condensed or malted milk in a town whose cows numbered less than ten. Without sanitation, without ice, sewage, a water system, with no vaccinations, and only the one hospital run by Gertrude Howe with her Chinese daughter-doctor, the city of a million sweltered.

Back in Nanchang, I eyed the lower western hills across the river with new eyes. They should be the natural sanatorium of the City of the Flourishing South. So far, through the centuries, only Buddhist priests had gone up into them for beauty and for health.

Occasional moods of deep melancholy came over me. Bright new brooms scarcely stirred the timeless apathy of China. Ignorance older than Western thought defied all attempts to alleviate it, and the sages of the country had a wisdom beyond the reach of Western minds. For a moment I would feel lost, helpless, and forlorn.

I turned to music, then, played on my piano the upbeat chords of Protestantism's optimistic faith or sang arias to the north wind, which brought good weather, a calm lake, and mail. These private concerts at dusk were for myself alone, but I had an audience.

The Chinese gardener stayed in the light, high basement below my living room. A man far from his home, he was incurably sad. I knew that he listened to me from below, and when I would pause, he took up his violin, a one-stringed instrument from which he drew sounds that wailed of Oriental sorrow. Listening to him in my turn, I knew that he was also playing out his heart.

Nanchang missionaries thought I was wrong to allow him to play where I had to hear. "How can you stand it, even if you let him?" one of them asked me.

Enjoy was not the word for my pleasure in listening to the weird, unwestern sounds. I could not explain what I felt—that China had become the real world to me, America and Europe so distant as to seem unreal. Four thousand years of written history was continuing as he played. Whatever my mood, melancholy or distressed, it was never mingled with regret over coming to China.

The contribution I hoped I was making to my adopted country lay in the field of women's education, in which I passionately believed. In this I was sustained by the period and the place from which I had come. Many in turn-of-the-century America were sure that when women, properly prepared, took their places alongside men in all the professions, when they had the vote and a place in the government, a miracle would occur. Such long-suppressed energy, brains, and virtue would raise the rate of human progress as a number is raised to the second power: squared, not merely doubled.

In that first fall, to carry my message I made trips by sailing junk to different cities, taking along a member of the staff and a few students.

In one town I was invited to participate in a meeting with other Christians. I spoke fervently of education and then a

Chinese woman read from the New Testament about the people who came in flocks to be healed by Jesus.

A mother came up the aisle with a very sick baby in her arms. "If you believe in such a wonderful religion," she challenged me, "cure my baby."

"I can't do it. I don't know enough, and I am not a saint," I said unhappily. "But if you will let me take him to your own Chinese woman doctor, Dr. Miss Kahn, in Nanchang, she will try...."

At the mention of a doctor, the woman turned away and left, her dying son clutched firmly to her breast.

Back in my own bailiwick, I managed to get on at every level of society. However much I outraged some of their traditions, the wives of Nanchang's officials seemed to love to have me and Ilien Tang as guests at their relentless feasts. These ladies came from everywhere, Szechuan, An Hwei, Fukien, Kwangtung—like British police, sent always from somewhere else. (It diminished nepotism and the ancient uses of blackmail practiced where a man had been known all his life.)

Ritual was always strictly observed in these sheltered official palaces. At the round table used in that section of China, a group numbered eight. More than eight for luncheon meant that the hostess must increase the number to sixteen and set up a second table. On each table there were sixteen varieties of *hors d'oeuvre* to start the meal, and eight teacups into which tea was poured as each lady was seated. Someone told my friends that I was in the habit of making a prayer of gratitude before eating, and from then on I was asked to say a grace whenever I was guest of honor.

Shark's Fin or Bird's Nest feasts were the lengthiest and most expensive, but Sea Cucumber (or Sea Slug) pleased me equally well. All conversation was in Mandarin, the lingua franca of officialdom. Gossip and chitchat took up most of the time, but even in these sanctuaries politics was fearfully discussed. When the Old Dowager died, there would be such a time of trouble! How could they totter out of harm's way in lovely four-inch embroidered slippers? How awful it was when anything changed at all!

"Ah, yes," said Gertrude Howe to me when we discussed these things. "When I have complained to Chinese gentlemen about the slavery of bound feet, they have said 'Tell the women—they are the ones who keep it going. We would welcome a change!'"

Having enjoyed myself immensely with the charming women, I would go home more than ever determined that my girls should never live behind bars. With special vigor I would take my turn massaging the arches and toes of those of my children hospitalized and in splints while their bound feet were straightened out as best they could be. Not for them the oddly provocative sway, the stiltlike movements on knobbed points encased in embroidered bags.

A group of officials' wives tottered over to see the school one day, and I showed them about. Tennis was a fashionable game among New China's girls, and the visitors were taken to the courts to watch a game.

The two best players were matched for their entertainment, one of them the pupil from the gubernatorial mansion. When the game began, the governor's niece dashed vigorously onto the court. In her wake came two other undergraduates, less privileged students, short of pocket money. One of them chased after the player waving a palm-leaf fan to keep her cool; the other retrieved her balls.

The visiting ladies saw nothing odd in this and I thought it best to take it in stride.

The sixtieth birthday of the man of a Chinese family was a time for elaborate celebration. Families who had money sent to Shanghai for actors, and the feasting and entertainment would last a week. In the fall of 1908, I was invited to several of these.

On one such occasion, I took two housemothers, two teachers, and Ilien Tang with me in my rowboat down the Kan River, ten miles away. We reached the estate of the sixty-year-old gentleman in time for the evening feast and the play. It was from the period of San Gwa, or the Three Kingdoms, and a classic which had come down through the centuries intact.

I sat next to my hostess, Nien Si-mo, who spoke exquisite Mandarin and could tell me about the play. Nien Si-mo could not only unravel the intricate plot but knew all the allusions, the symbols, and the legends involved. In her exquisite voice, she repeated passages to make them clear to me.

When it was over, I demanded, "Where can I get the book, Nien Si-mo, that will give me such things as you've told me about these plays? I want to study them."

"Oh, Little Sister Han," admitted Nien Si-mo sadly and quietly, "I do not now. I have never learned to read and write."

I was aghast. Here was a cultured woman who stumped on tiny bound feet and could not read. The future must be different, the younger generation taught—and yet how sad if such ancient culture should be lost in progress.

To preserve for myself some of the beauties of old China, I began to buy small treasures. A YWCA friend, met in Kuling, sent me a book on Chinese art which I studied assiduously. Every Saturday I would take time off to walk in Nanchang, with my new man Friday along and my book on art.

You could always tell where to find what things. There was Porcelain Street, Grass Linen Street, Silk Street, Basket Street, Furniture Street, but the two-mile-long Chop Stick Row, where art curios were for sale in little shop after little shop, was my special joy. Every week I brought home a Tang vase or a Sung painting or a bit of silver or bronze. Later I started a collection of musical instruments. The most precious acquisition was a very old one called a Ch'in. It was a tiny handful of pipes in different lengths tipped with ivory. I learned to blow on them and make the scale with my fingers on the little vents.

I had a wide shelf built in the dining room for my exquisite objects d'art. Others went into the rooms at the school. Estelle Paddock, National Secretary of the YWCA, who became a close friend of mine, traveled a good deal and bought the furniture I ordered. Redwood tables and chairs came from Canton, rugs from Peking.

One day in Nanchang I found a stunning Chinese bridal skirt, red and embroidered in strips. It was so decorative I tossed it like a shawl over my piano. Chinese friends came in and looked askance without saying a word. I realized that I had offended their sense of propriety, and removed the skirt from sight.

With the reaction of other visitors, missionaries from the North, I had less sympathy. Taking a look about my handsome new possessions, one of them said, "Well, Welthy, one of these days you'll throw out all this Chinese junk."

Reveling in my own pleasure in China, I continued to build my collection, watching especially to find out when an official from Nanchang returned home after having lost his post. In order to buy a new and lucrative one elsewhere, the unemployed official would sell his treasures—paintings, bronzes, cloisonnés and porcelains. Whenever I saw one that matched the illustrations in my art book, I bought it.

Before the end of my first year, I rejoiced that everything around me was good Chinese, and had begun to really enjoy my Chinese singing lessons. Now I could join the girls in their traditional music just as enthusiastically as I led them in Stainer, Handel, or Bach.

One day in late November I was on my way with Ilien Tang to call on one Madame Wang. The gatekeeper told us that he had just heard from the teashop, receiving station for the bamboo or paddy-field telegraph, that big news had reached the city. Tszhi Toanyu Kangi Chuang Cheng Shokung Chinbien Chungsih, the Empress of China, was dead.

When I had completed all the polite gestures of a visit down to the last bow, and was thinking with satisfaction that I now ate watermelon seeds as if my tongue was native to the art, my hostess turned to me. "But Little Sister Han," she said, chiding, "You tell me Old Buddha is dead and yet you are wearing red. I thought we could not wear red as long as her body lies unburied in the Forbidden Palace."

Disregarding what her foreign friends or her young revolutionaries might think, Little Sister Han went home and took off her favorite Peter Thompson dress. This middy blouse and skirt, with the sweeping back, were piped in red. Indeed red was my favorite color, but for the required twenty-seven days, Miss Welthy Honsinger from Rome, New York, went into mourning for the hard-hearted old Dowager Empress of all China.

9

The death of the Old Buddha brought about no immediate revolution, but only added to political tension. Life went on with the same almost insurmountable problems for the country as a whole as ever before. An incurable optimist, I never doubted that someday, somehow, China's manifold ills would be cured. Old China hands took a gloomier view.

One historian, J. O. B. Bland, published in 1912 a book which discussed the period of history through which I was living. In a pessimistic summary, he wrote:

A nation which implicitly believes and unanimously acts on the belief that a man's first duty in life is to provide as many male heirs as possible for the comfort of himself and his ancestors, inevitably condemns vast masses of its people to the lowest depths of poverty, condemns the body politic to regularly recurring cataclysms. The chronic condition of China, except in those districts where plague or famine or civil war have temporarily relieved the pressure, is a struggle for life unequalled in any other part of the world. . . .

. . . herein lies the great and remote cause of China's intolerable afflictions—a cause not to be removed by any political shibboleths or panaceas of philanthropy. Even supposing that, by good government, the conditions of life were to be alleviated for the masses, that by economic reforms and applied science the resources of the country might be materially increased, it is clear that, for a people which rears four generations while Europe is rearing three, with whom the absence of posterity is a crime, and concubinage the reward of success, any relief would be temporary—the fundamental problem deferred, not solved. The immediate results would be a decrease in infant mortality which, at present, reaches terrible, almost incredible, proportions. (In Hongkong, under British administration, the death-rate of Chinese children, under one year of age, was eighty-seven per cent of all births reported in 1909.) A certain percentage of the vagrants and outlaws who infest the outskirts of every city might be reclaimed for the space of one generation; but the insoluble problem of filling three stomachs with one bowl of rice would speedily have to be faced anew.

Even if we assume, with the optimists and financiers [elsewhere Bland added Christian missionaries to the deluded] that a modus vivendi can be found between North and South, Monarchists and Republicans, between civilians and soldiers, between the haves and the have-nots, there must remain those persistent causes of disorganization which lie in the mental state and social structure of the masses—causes removable only by slow educative process. Of these the chief is the procreative recklessness of the race, that blind frenzy of man-making born of battle, murder and sudden death, which persistently swells the numbers of the population up to, and beyond, the visible means of subsistence.

As for me, I clung sturdily to my belief in the "slow educative process" as I listened night after night for the temple bell to clarion the hour of eleven, the sound hovering in the air so long after the bell was stilled.

There was repetition without sameness in my years as they flew by. My second and third New Years exploded in a glory of fireworks, kites, music, and din. The School of the Protecting Spirit in the City of the Flourishing South expanded as fast as room could be found for more pupils. High school was soon added to the eight grades and a few of my older girls were graduating in an accelerated program to go on with honors to colleges in Peking or Nanking, to Japan to study or, those from the one or two families who could afford it, overseas to America.

I never lost hope that when the people of China knew how to read and write they would learn how to cope with living and would find out how to water their desert of poverty.

Philanthropy should be expanded, too, I felt, and our girls must learn to think in these terms. To bring our poor neighbors, the village of squatters who hunkered in huts constructed of boxes and bits nearby, closer to us, I instituted a new kind of Christmas party.

These men, who lived from one bowl of charity soup to another, were invited to visit us on Christmas morning.

By ten o'clock several hundred had assembled near the gates. Within the compound, the girls prepared the food themselves. When the big gate was opened, the cheerful, ragged derelicts, young and old, came decorously inside. A few of the girls stood guard to protect tender young trees, others acted as guides to take the lame, halt, and blind to places at the long picnic tables.

Each guest was royally fed, with steaming bowls of rice, meat, and vegetables. As a kind of grace, the brightest of the pupils made the annual announcement: "We worship God, the Great Spirit, at Bao Lin. On this day a Babe was born in Bethlehem who loved all men, and in His name, we want to share our food with you, our neighbors."

Once Chinese New Year holidays began, nothing was done unless you did it yourself. If I wanted a box made or a wall repaired, I was told that the carpenter had returned to the home of his fathers, to pay his respects to his ancestors. If I asked for a chair coolie, he was in a teahouse, feasting, and I must go on foot. All of patient and industrious China took the holiday, making it last as long as each man could possibly afford. Even the squeaking wheelbarrows were silent. At night, when I went within the city walls to visit Gertrude Howe or to one of the incessant feasts given by the Chinese, I heard only the cries of gamblers in the shuttered teahouses as I passed along empty, dark streets.

On the river one stormy night, the cries of men rang out, "Chou Min, Chou Min (Save life, save life)," but before rescuers could be dragooned from feasting to man the lifeboats, two hundred aboard the foundering junk were drowned. So filled with tragedy was ordinary life in the City of the Flourishing South this disaster caused only a momentary sigh of distress.

It was not long after my third New Year that Gertrude

Howe came to me with another child. Gertrude had been aroused at night by a woman's cry, "Take my baby girl, take my baby girl!" This mother had refused to throw her fourth girl away, and her husband would not, indeed could not, feed her.

So I took in a little sister for Precious Pearl, and this time the amah did not even try to sew the dark-eyed creature into a carpet.

Active little Precious Pearl chose the moment, perhaps in jealousy, to fall from a window and break her collarbone. The doctor said she must go to the hospital to have it set, and I walked beside the sedan chair, regardless of etiquette, speaking to the child in English and attending her baby replies in Chinese.

When I got home with Precious Pearl after midnight, there was a cablegram on my desk:

LEAVING ON TENYO MARU FOR CHINA TO FETCH YOU. TOM.

My reply was definitive: IMPOSSIBLE TO SEE YOU. BUSY AND HAPPY. YOUR COMING UTTERLY FUTILE. DON'T COME.

That night I slept to dream of little yellow faces with black beads of eyes filled with tears that ran down strained faces. Within the year, I took in two more discarded girl children, and my nursery was full of happy tots. If I ever regretted Tom, my life was too full for pining.

The political tensions and outbreaks prevented me from revisiting Peking, but I did go to other places in the North, one of them Bei Teh Ho, a seaside resort where I gave concerts.

I found a British woman in the North making speeches on Christian doctrine. At least she had learned Chinese, but she used this skill to tell desperately hard-working women that if they believed the things she told them about the Saviour they would be saved, but if they did not, they would go to the Christian hell.

"Look here," I told her bluntly, "before you threaten the women of China with our hell, do you know the Buddhist temple hells? They've got special punishments for each of eighteen crimes—like lust, greed, anger, murder, stealing, and so forth—that make Dante's inferno seem like a picnic. I think the Chinese women might prefer our heaven, but when it comes to scaring them with our damnation, we can't compete."

Such brushes with my cohorts created an occasional prickly situation. Now and then Methodist Bishop Bashford would chide Miss Honsinger for her outspokenness, but surprising proof came one winter of his evaluation of her. He and Mrs. Bashford came to Nanchang to see me, and Mrs. Bashford took me aside for a long confidential conversation. Two of the missionaries under the bishop's charge were not getting on with the others. Would I take them to work with me at the school for a while? I hesitated, but the bishop himself undertook to persuade me.

"I believe you'll know how to handle them," he said, and then twinkled at me. "Somehow you do seem to get on with people."

I doubted my ability to make good missionaries of poor ones but, never one to refuse a request or a challenge, installed the two as teachers in the mission house on the grounds. I was busy at the time, living in the dormitory, and was only at the mission house with them for meals. The two women were older than I and since, I readily admit, I myself am something of a chatterbox, I did not notice that they were refusing to speak to each other until one of the Chinese teachers asked me what was the matter.

The next morning at breakfast when the chapel bell rang, I said, "Friends, we aren't going to chapel. We're going to stay here and do something more important. We've come six thousand miles to be an example of love and are behaving without a bit of it."

There was a long silence. The women sat rigid and offended.

I went on. "I don't care what's the matter. That's none of my business. But if we all can't at least *act* as if we loved each other, how can we justify being here?"

At the end of an hour chapel was over, tears had been shed, and speaking terms reestablished. "I think we prayed," I wrote afterwards, "the best way possible."

Because they were honest and generous, I retained the friendship of the older women whose heads I had knocked together in the name of love.

There were men friends among the Standard Oil representatives, who kept me "human" with their compliments and affection, considered most unsuitable by the critical group in Kiukiang. Even more unsuitable, among my many Chinese friends was the Mother Superior of a Buddhist nunnery.

The nunnery was at the other end of Nanchang, just outside the Gate of Eternal Light. It was a large, rambling old house with a garden where the Mother Superior, an expert botanist, supervised the raising of rare orchids and other exquisite flowers. The house itself was kept spotless and I found the worship room beautiful.

In a shack apart on the grounds a water buffalo ambled blindfolded around and around a tiny room, turning the stone that ground rice, beans, and wheat to flour. In my diary, I wrote about it:

Ancestors of this animal, I suppose, have walked in this same groove for centuries as the predecessors of these nuns have knelt for ages on the bamboo mats in the prayer room.

My friend is enormously interested in us. "Are you, then, a Christian nun?" she asked me. It was hard to say what I was—an unmarried woman who had left her friends and her country to help other girls and women find a new "tao" or Way of Life. What am I, anyway?

She is not at all interested in the English language, she says, but she wants to know what we think and how we think it. And she and I have decided to be mutual interpreters of each other's country and customs and philosophy and religion.

Her feet, of course, have never been bound. She wears a yellow garment exactly like that of the priests. Her head is shaven and she has nine round scars on the top which were burned in when she took her life vow of celibacy. Her father was a high official of the old day, and as she had the same tutor as her brother, she is educated beyond most of her friends.

"Why do you wear a hat on your head?" inquires my Buddhist nun of the shaven head and "Why are your shoes shaped so unlike your feet? Is the foreigner's foot that shape?" I had to admit I didn't know why—that there was no satisfactory explanation for either hats or the shapes of shoes.

She likes my watch, thinks it is pretty, but does not see why when there is a sundial in the garden, one needs to carry the time about. "One couldn't go faster for seeing the time," she says.

The Chinese will, some day, I suppose, buy watches because they are beautiful, and they will some day be the *fashion*, but carrying the time will never save it in China.

I had learned to live by Chinese time, but still the time fled. Triumph and tragedy, comedy and calamity. Intense heat and a cholera epidemic one summer in Nanchang, when nine hundred people a day died in the city and I walked among them heartsick. A growing procession of criminals brought out in the topless sedan chair to the Buddhist temple near the school—the Temple of Last Prayer from which rang out nightly the glorious bell. (I could hear their last cries before they were hung or crucified and afterwards I would sing for them in my own way "There is a green hill far away/Beside a city wall/Where the dear Lord was crucified/Who died to save us all," though I never knew whether they were murderers, thieves, or political men who were defying the regime in Peking.) And more and more girls, and more and more graduates of Bao Lin, went forth into the turbulence of China.

My delicious group of orphans grew like flowers and I continued to refuse advice that I raise them as charity children. I decorated them with ribbons and dressed them prettily and taught them manners and gave them all my love. Ruin was their fate, prophesied the conservatives, until the day when a high official sent a formal request for the hand of Precious Pearl for his only son. "A child whom you have raised will make a proper wife for my first-born," said the rich and prominent father. Though I flatly refused to betroth my adopted child, to the added distress of my critics, I was none-theless pleased with this tribute.

On December 8, 1910, I remember feeling that almost everything was satisfactory. Far from seeming too long, the five years I had contracted to "bury" myself in China's interior were going to be too short. Perhaps I would return to the U.S.A. in 1911, but only long enough to interest more people in Chinese education and pick up a better piano. My fifth year began the next month, and I had plans ahead for a decade.

It was fearfully cold, and the water in the basin had been frozen that morning. More than making up for any discomfort, my houseboy had come bursting in to make a delighted announcement. "Little Sister Han, you like the frozen cream. Last night, big cold, so this morning many icicles hang from gargoyles on the Dragon Temple. I get them, bring them home, make frozen cream for Little Sister Han's dinner. Other people say my master big fool, eat ice cold, I say my master *like*—I get!" So I had gargoyle ice cream for dinner and sat by the fireplace in my den that night in the highest of spirits.

It was a wild and frozen night, moonless and black. When I put out my lamp and turned over to sleep, I recall thinking how bleak it was outside, how far away the school was from the American compound, even from the city. But the bitter north wind would bring the sailboats in across the lake with a cargo of mail from home and, with this thought in mind, I slept.

Han Sciao Chieh, Scio Tan fa Ho! "Little Sister Han, the school is on fire!"

I recognized the voice of the new gateman. Leaping to my feet, I grabbed my warm red bathrobe and screamed to Ilien Tang, who slept across the hall. Hearing a reply, I dashed down the stairs and through the hall, which was already filling with smoke. Unable to get directly from my apartment to the dormitory, I ran outside to see the whole compound aglow with lurid light.

The gateman was arousing the school, but I found Kanmendi, the lodgekeeper, stupefied with fear. Crying to him to run for the American compound, to let the city officials know, I ran myself to the big school gong and sounded it, then rushed to the dormitories. Teachers and students were pouring into the courtyard in their night clothes. "Take the children across the street! Bring me a lamp!" I ordered, and then took two teachers with me to pick up the rest of the orphans, rolling three of them in blankets and depositing them in the arms of the teachers. Twice I made the rounds of all the sleeping rooms, as smoke poured through the buildings, to make sure no one was left behind. Blinded by smoke, I smashed the chimney of my lamp against a door and made my way down the stairs for the last time. A man's voice spoke to me in English. The Americans were here.

Later they told me that I replied to every question in Chinese and asked in Chinese, "Where is Ilien Tang?"

"Safe," someone told me. "All your people are safe. What things are most valuable?"

The rugs, priceless porcelains, bronzes, and music were gone. My living quarters were in flames, but four men did drag out the piano. Though the bricks were falling, the old cook went in to bring out valueless pots and pans, but I yanked him away and sent him across the street.

Even then officials in their chairs were arriving at the compound. The city's magistrate arrived and the police commissioner and a representative of the governor offering whatever assistance could be provided. A company of soldiers, I was told, was on the way.

"I haven't heard the fire department!" said I.

"No, no, you couldn't hear it, but it's here," they told me, and it was—the fire department of the City of the Flourishing South—in force.

Their twenty iron carts the size of children's express wagons were lined up and a sparse line of men was forming a bucket brigade to the river. Buckets had to be borrowed, one at a time, from neighbors, and spaces in the brigade to be filled with volunteers from among the onlookers, who by this time numbered thousands. The light from the fire raging in the three-story central building had shone over the city and surrounding country, they said later, as no other blaze in two thousand years had done.

Finally buckets and men were in operation and the express wagons, or "water dragons," filled. A fireman stood by each cart with a hand pump attached to a little hose. Tiny streams were then played on the roaring blaze.

"The straw huts! The squatters' huts!" I insisted. "Stop this and go there! You can save them!" And they moved on to protect structures for which their toys were quite adequate.

Bricks tumbled like leaves now, and I led a military procession of those who belonged to the school but were still in the compound along the road to the hospital, where the American doctor had turned over an empty ward to us.

"Where is Ilien Tang?" I demanded, shivering in my dressing gown.

"Resting," I was told.

This was so astonishing that I knew she was injured. And so she had been, during her own escape from the holocaust. Roused by me, she had tried to follow me down the steps, but found the smoke too thick. Instead she ran out on the veranda, found the rope which held the bamboo awnings and let herself down. The rope was too short and she found herself hanging in midair over the glass which enclosed the veranda below. No one heard her cry out, so she broke the glass with her shoes, making a space large enough to crawl through onto the veranda, cutting herself badly but not fatally.

In the cruel, cold light of dawn, I saw the ashes of my school. The soldiers dispersed the crowd and remained to protect the few things that had been saved and were strewn about the grounds. The governor sent congratulations that in such a catastrophe no lives had been lost, for the first time in a history of disastrous local fires. Even the safe had burned as it dropped into the flames of the winter's woodpile and the school's deeds were burned, but the human beings were safe.

There was no insurance on buildings, equipment, or treasures; the teachers, students, and I were bereft of everything we owned.

"Everything is gone," I wrote in my journal. "I am without a hairpin, a fountain pen, a toothbrush or a bar of soap. A British nurse gave me a comb, but no hairpins and nothing can be bought here—and there's not a pair of shoes in town. I wear borrowed slippers and have arrayed myself in a man's overcoat, cap and gloves and a dress from my friend the nurse. The treasures of my life are gone. The mail came this morning, and in it was my first Christmas present—a string of red beads from my sister! And a letter describing a friend's wedding, telling of orchestras, caterers, presents, laces, silver, flowers. But what are my losses compared to my girls'? Their little all, clothing, bedding, everything, is destroyed."

The students who lived in Nanchang were sent for by their families, but the others were stranded. Ilien Tang and I decided immediately that the school must, would, be kept going, no matter on what basis. In the hospital ward, the cook fixed a good breakfast with his rescued pots and pans, and one of the Chinese Christian teachers led us in prayer. She quoted loosely from Paul: "I have learned how to live in abundance and in want. I am content to live in whatever state I am!"

Together we laughed and cried and prayed, and then began to plan.

I wired the bishop and wired church headquarters in New York—that cable arriving the afternoon before the night of the fire, according to the calendar, as it traveled backward in time around the world. From Nanking the bishop sent his blessing and said that he and Bishop Bashford concurred in my plan to go back to the U.S.A. immediately to collect money. Later they amended their blessing to insist that I sign a statement that when I got home I would not raise money enough also to start a college in Nanchang. It was quite sufficient that I had added a high school at Bao Lin, the first high school with music and science and girl students from all classes of society, and the other missionaries were afraid I would take too much on myself. I must stop in Nanking on the way to Shanghai to sign my promise not to go too far.

Ilien Tang would run the school in my absence. We rented a little house and bought enough books and clothes to carry on. Then, as if catastrophe must always bring more in its train, the students that were left came down with chicken pox. With my Chinese staff and the children, I was quarantined for Christmas. As soon as I was decontaminated, I set out for home in borrowed clothes and the bright red beads.

"I wouldn't fail my children now for anything," I wrote. "Not for anything the world has to offer. I am going home, but not to Tom and not to stay. No power on earth can tempt me—I'm theirs for better or worse. I've got to see them through. So beware, America. I'm coming for your money and your goods!"

10

In a borrowed dress of deep purple satin, Mabel's beads, and a large brimmed hat of black velour to which I added a smashing red silk rose, I returned to the United States. My luggage consisted of one carryall in which I crammed going-away presents from my Chinese friends, a lighter dress hastily run up in Nanchang grass linen, a sweeping red Manchu robe that had somehow escaped the fire, changes of underthings, and a second pair of slippers, since no shoes to fit me could be found among my friends and there were none on sale in all China. The difference between the girl who had left in 1906 and the woman coming back in 1911 was underlined by my odd appearance.

During the long journey I thought of little except my mission. How could I explain the utterly different world of China to my home folks? I was returning as a stranger. How would I be received? I knew that one of the missionaries in Shanghai had cabled New York to complain that Miss Honsinger had been wrongheaded and highhanded to appoint a Chinese girl headmistress of Bao Lin even temporarily and the woman had suggested she herself take Ilien Tang's place. I did not yet know that Bishop Lewis, with whom I had not always seen eye to eye, had written a letter to the same home office expressing his own opinion. Welthy Honsinger and Gertrude Howe, he said, were both trying to develop Chinese leadership, which was the right thing to do. In fact he suggested that if the New York organization planned to send other missionaries to Nanchang, Miss Honsinger should approve them. Her mission station was doing things no other had succeeded in accomplishing.

Had I known of it, the bishop's report might have comforted me as I worried about the future. Collecting funds was a chore I'd never tried. Was I capable of raising a single dollar?

Before I left Nanchang, I overheard the children at the American mission telling each other about the fire. "Did you know the lady let herself down by a rope from upstairs with her piano and two babies?" I would have to perform a different kind of Bunyanesque feat to raise my school phoenix from its ashes, to be twice as glorious as before. My Chinese girls, my darling Precious Pearl and the other babies left in Ilien Tang's loving care, who had lost everything in the fire, depended on me. I must keep faith with them and in myself.

San Francisco was the port of my return. Going straight to a good hotel, relieved that no one met me, I found myself, as newcomers from the East always have, astonished and somewhat shocked by the extravagant wealth of my country. The lowliest porters were dressed in material fit for high officials. In my soft slippers, I tripped on the deep-piled hall carpets. My bedroom was thick with appointments and furniture. ("Stuffy," I thought.) The bellboy was so handsome, well-fed, and expensively dressed that I hesitated to tip him, but sensed his expectancy and remembered home customs in time to produce from my borrowed purse a shining dime. ("Equals three hundred 'cash,'" I translated to myself, "Enough to pay four chair-bearers for a week. Surely generous.") The boy gave me an indignant look and slammed the door on his way out.

It took me a moment of thought to recall that I could drink water from the spigots and did not have to have a bottle of boiled in which to brush my teeth. Sinking into a tub of hot water, I found myself homesick for my glorious museum-piece tub in Nanchang, the Soochow pottery glazed such a brilliant turquoise. I had learned to sit in its narrow base, on folded legs, to get the greatest benefit from the two buckets of hot water in the bottom. Now I found myself wondering if I would be charged for extra water and could scarcely luxuriate for fear of extravagance.

Homesickness for my family took hold of me for the first time, and I could scarcely wait for the train to leave. There was time to buy shoes next morning, and then I was on the way across the green expanse of the United States. Treating myself to steak, after living so long on chicken and fish, I was horrified to find that my first dining-car meal cost over three Mexican-Chinese dollars. Enough to support one student at Bao Lin for a month eaten up in an hour!

When the train, belching smoke and steam, pulled in to New York, the first face I saw was Mother's and I was truly home at last. Tears, the first I had permitted myself to shed in four years, ran down my cheeks.

My oldest and closest sister, Mabel, who now taught kindergarten in New York, and my sister Elmina, who was married to a Presbyterian minister, were with Mother to meet me. For three days I wallowed in the pleasure of reunion. My future task would take everything I had, and I needed to refresh myself at my own sources before embarking upon it.

Horrified at my shabby appearance, Mother and my sisters took me shopping for a new wardrobe, and between times we all laughed and cried together and mingled our news with a thousand reminiscences. For a few hours, Little Sister Han of Nanchang, China, could relax and be just her mother's little Welthy. That wonderful woman had believed in me and backed me up in everything. How good it was to be with her.

As for the mission society, they might lack Mother's total enthusiasm and pride in my accomplishments, but they seemed impressed with the record and Bishop Lewis's report as well as horrified by the catastrophe which had sent me back. Seeing me thin and worn, the society insisted that I go to Clifton Springs Sanitorium for three months' recuperation. I stuck it out dutifully for two weeks, and then departed. I wasn't ill and I couldn't sleep until I started raising money.

My salary as a missionary at home was four hundred fifty

dollars a year (in the field it was six hundred dollars). In addition to this I was to receive two dollars and a half a lecture, as well as expenses while on the road. I was thankful that I had a little to add to this and that my family had lavished clothes on my back.

"Well, hmmmm," said one of the officers of the society, who was arranging my tour. "You are thin enough, I must say, but you really should look more *pathetic* when you've just come in from the field!"

Part of my problem was still the mixture that was me. I was still a girl, pleased that I was not homely, loving pretty things, and taking pleasure in looking my best. My piety was my own, private like my mother's, and not part of my surface. The world to me was a wonderful place, to enjoy as well as do one's best in. It seemed to me that God's creatures did their best by being themselves and not by pretending to be someone else.

My first assignments were in northern New York, and my first lecture softened hearts to the tune of a basket overflowing with bills. I was delighted until afterward, when the president of the group under whose local auspices I spoke brought me the basket. Retaining her grip on the handle, Madame President gave a meaning look at the new and dashing clothes in which "Miss Honsinger" was dressed. "Why should we pay you $2.50 in addition?" she asked. "The mission society pays your salary."

"Oh, please don't, then," I said, wanting to weep.

That night, I struggled once more with the problem of being both myself and a missionary. I knew I didn't look right, not like a deaconess—no straggly hair, old-fashioned hat, and clothes well out of fashion. The last thing I wanted was pity; like Lucifer the fallen angel, "I prefer this ruin, if ruin they think it." In the name of what I did want, money for my school, should I be bedraggled in appearance and pretend to be poor in spirit?

Like Gideon, I asked God for a token. Would He somehow let me know if I was right to do His will my own way?

In Syracuse for two days with my doctor brother, I had a respite with people who loved me as I was and did not wish to change me. My brother fed me lobster dinners, urged me to marry before too long, and sent me on to my next appointment in Westfield, New York.

There a prominent woman said to me, "This evening my youngest boy and girl will be there to hear you. I want to tell you now you are NOT to try and persuade them to go as missionaries!" Other peoples' children, but not mine, thought I bitterly, but seized the chance to ask the lady if she knew Dr. Welch of Welch's grape juice fame and fortune.

"Oh, yes, I know him," replied the mother of the high-school children, "but would you have the nerve to go to him?"

"Why, certainly," I said. "All I want is an introduction."

Next day I ploughed through snowdrifts to Dr. Welch's office, to find a mild, delightful man. We were soon chatting like old friends, socially at ease, discussing common acquaintances. Within twenty minutes, Dr. Welch had written a check for Bao Lin. It was for two thousand dollars.

This was my token. On my knees that night, I talked to God. "Thank You, dear God, for showing me You can use me as I am. I don't have to masquerade in old-fashioned clothes or make myself sad and pitiful. Thank You!" I doubt whether Dr. Welch ever knew the peripheral result of his generous check, but it gave me the courage to stand firm when the committee in New York saw me next before I was to speak in the city and scolded me sharply about my modish appearance.

It turned out that the New York meeting was at the home of a rich woman and the gathered crowd were society women who knew little about missions. I made such a hit with them that the collection was not only high, but the fee my hostess gave me in an envelope was twenty dollars instead of two and a half. To cap my pleasure, the lady told me next day that she had ordered three hundred iron beds and shipped them to Nanchang. God was proving to me again that He could use me as I was, that clothes were superficial and that it was the spirit and dedication that mattered. I rejoiced. And the committee which had undertaken to remake me dropped the subject.

From then on I rode my own whirlwind. Making as many as fifteen talks a week, I opened most of my meetings with a song and closed them with a musical benediction. Money rolled in as the miles piled up.

A few who met me on my travels tried to stay me from my purpose. The good-looking president of a large bank in Chicago, a widower with two charming children, told me it was every bit as noble to be a "missionary to one" and suggested he be the One. If it was the school building I was worried about, he would build it himself and travel out there to see it with me—as his wife. When I wrote my mother of this temptation to give up and settle down, Mother said seriously, "Remember, these offers will not come forever." Later Mother mischievously clipped a page from a missionary report which had a list of those "Lost to us by death or marriage."

In another city, a bachelor brother of a missionary friend put his car and himself at my total disposal. I was staying at a deaconess' home and the women, looking out at the waiting car and chivalrous driver, teased me, "If that is what it means to go to China, let's all go."

Back in New York state, I did meet my fate in Ithaca, but was wholly unconscious of it at the time. I was invited to sing at a large gathering of Methodist laymen, conducted by Dr. Fred B. Fisher. Wearing my long red Manchu robe, with my hair in a coronet of braids around my head, I stood in the pulpit and sang, "Do you know the world is dying for a little bit o' love?"

Dr. Fisher, so he told me years later, nudged a Colonel Halford who sat beside him. "No young woman," said the stocky young man who was soon to be appointed a bishop in the Methodist church, "who looks like that has any business going around the world dying for a little bit o' love!"

I remember meeting him and looking into the brightest pair of blue eyes I ever saw. That was all that happened then.

The future bishop, my future husband, was married to his childhood sweetheart and it certainly never occurred to either of us that one day he would be a widower or that we would meet again in India.

Tom was still the man nearest to my heart. Resolutely I refused to look him up, even to let him know that I was back. It would not be fair to renew any relationship that romantic when I had no intention of marrying him—or anyone else, in spite of my mother's dear hopes.

An Ithaca banker, like the one in Chicago, made me an offer of more than "a little bit of love," and threw in a horse. He would go back to China with me for a year, he said, and help rebuild the school, if I would then come back with him. Furthermore, he would send out the horse, one of a pair in his stable, which I so loved to ride. "What would I do with a man in Nanchang," I asked facetiously in my diary, "where men and women are never seen together until they are man and wife, and seldom then? Not even the gift of a horse is a temptation. What would the little ponies of Nanchang think of that gorgeous, aristocratic horse?"

At the end of fifteen strenuous months, after six hundred meetings at which I sang and talked, in New York, Pennsylvania, Illinois, Indiana, Michigan and California, I had the money. An architect had made blueprints for me of three buildings, for nothing. And furthermore I had two recruits for my staff. A girl, Rosalie Mayer, whom I met, offered to go with me without compensation. Mabel, my dear sister, a musician and artist as well as a teacher, would also come, paying her own fare, and work for a year at a minimum salary.

It was with a sense of great relief and triumph that I set out again across the Pacific Ocean for Nanchang. In the agreeable company of my two new colleagues, I waved a blithe good-by to Rainier. I could hardly wait until Fujiyama hove into view. This was not a leave-taking from home, but a return home to my children in China.

11

I had left a troubled Empire and returned to the brand-new
and turbulent Republic of China. The revolution had been
accomplished while I rushed from city to city in the United
States pleading for funds to educate Chinese young women.
To my delight, schools for girls were springing up all over,
fostered by the new government.

One evening soon after my return Sun Yat-sen rode through
Nanchang on the back of a white pony. Crowds jammed the
streets, hailing him as their saviour. As he trotted past, all of
us—my American sister and friend, Ilien Tang and the Chinese
teachers, the student body and the orphans—collected to
cheer him. He resigned the Presidency soon after his appointment, yielding to pressure that replaced him with Yuan Shih-
jai, who was said to have a heart beating "for a monarchy while
his lips speak for the republic." But Dr. Sun never stopped
representing New China to the South.

Nanchang had been spared the invasion of troops and sub-
sequent looting, fire, and rape—but not merely by chance.
Local rich families had bribed revolutionary leaders and gen-
erals with large sums of gold to bypass the city. Although Ilien
Tang, the orphans, and girls who were staying in the hospital
compound spent many nights with bags of money under their
pillows, ready to escape, not even the ashes of Bao Lin were
disturbed.

Gone now the sable coats and peacock feathers, the pro-
cessions preceded by the red umbrella. Gorgeous insignia of
rank were on sale in the curio shops along Chop Stick Row.
Men had cut their braided queues and officials discarded their

long satin garments. Girl patriots, even those from ultra-conservative families, cropped their hair. My old friend and ally, the governor, survived in office, but he came to call wearing a Prince Albert, well-creased trousers, and a stovepipe hat, walking awkwardly in squeaking Western shoes.

Scarcely pausing to enjoy the tumultuous or ceremonious warmth of my welcome back, I plunged into the task of spending my funds, a job which proved much more ticklish than collecting them. I had determined to buy the twelve acres adjoining the walled compound of Bao Lin as part of the new school, and I ran into all the superstitions, tissue of etiquettes, and shibboleths of ancestor-worship which had by no means been swept away in a single leap into a democratic state.

The acres, contoured like a dragon and called Dragon Sand, were derelict for fear use of the land might disturb the beast it resembled. Two ponds, twelve huts, and the Temple of Last Prayer (where the criminals to be executed in an adjoining bit of field went to be shriven), and an old and neglected cemetery with five hundred graves dating from the nineteenth, eighteenth, and seventeenth centuries occupied the Dragon Sand.

Negotiations began. A bewhiskered elderly gentleman brought a deed which he swore antedated all the others. Tapping the tattered and browned parchment with his inches-long fingernails, he said, "You can see it is the original." To be sure it looked ancient, but my lawyer found that the parchment had been antiqued in hot opium.

To buy the Temple of Last Prayer, I dealt with the Buddhist priests. Money was scarcely mentioned, in air blue with proverbs, though it was uppermost in everybody's mind. By delicate indirection, a price was agreed upon at last, and the priests reminded me that with the Temple came eleven unburied coffins. "These await a propitious day of burial," the yellow-robed abbot told me. Necromancers, I suspected, would long since have named a propitious day if there had been any relatives to pay for the interments. "This black one has been here for fifteen years," added the priest.

The elaborate transfer of temple ownership and responsibility for the unburied coffins took weeks. While it was going on I was unwilling witness to a crucifixion. The man, brought from the city in the sedan chair with its top removed to indicate his disgrace, was not even allowed his moment for prayers. Strapped without ceremony to a rough cross in the place of execution beside the Temple, he was left hanging there, with keepers watching him casually until at long last he died. Christ's agony took on new vividness for me and it was several years before I could sing my old favorite: "There is a green hill far away/Beside a city wall/Where the dear Lord was crucified/Who died to save us all. . . ." Words which had only spiritual meaning before choked me thereafter and I wept not only for Jesus, but for the thieves, for all men condemned, and for the Chinese stranger whose silent suffering I had seen.

My plan was to turn the Temple into a kindergarten, its name changed from Last Prayer to the Temple of Happiness, and beheadings and crucifixions in the old spot beside the building must be stopped somehow. I went to a friendly official whose child was coming to kindergarten the following year. "It would not be the desire of your Excellency," said I, "to have public executions just there where your baby might be playing?"

"No, no, no," replied the father, predictably. "But no one can sell or give that bloody piece of land. When Little Sister Han builds her wall, perhaps she will be good enough to bulge it out a little to take in the spot?"

Little Sister Han would bulge her wall.

The Dragon Sand and the Temple and the plot for public execution were now mine, but it remained to deal with the dead. This was an exquisite problem. Any disrespect would create an impossible scandal, and respect for the departed was carried to elaborate lengths.

For the eleven coffins in the Temple, Ilien Tang and I found a daring solution. Taking council, we declared ourselves competent necromancers, announced that on August second the stars would be in just the proper relation to each other, and these unclaimed bodies would be transferred with all due ceremony to a new burial ground, purchased near the city wall.

Prior to the Republic, each new Chinese dynasty coming into power had sent out an edict to plow under all the graves in China. This restored millions of acres of land to feed the living. The Manchus had been on the throne since 1644, and no graves had been violated. Under the new republic, no man or committee felt powerful enough to give the ruthless if beneficial order to disturb that many ancestors of three hundred million citizens.

Fortunately for me, no great Mandarins lay in the Dragon Sand cemetery. The graves were humbler ones, with conical towers of cobblestones and earth or an occasional slab of red sandstone. Glad that I had spent minutes on my knees and hours pouring tea for the governor, I went to him for advice. He immediately issued an edict and had it posted all over Nanchang. Naming a price which Little Sister Han would pay to the rightful descendants of the buried corpses if the bodies were claimed within three months, he said I had his permission after that reverently to remove them all.

When the three-month period was up, it took three more months to rebury the lot. At first I hoped to carry out the gruesome business in private, forgetting that there was no privacy in China. No sooner had the ceremonial transfer begun than people appeared in droves to see how a foreigner would conduct such a matter. I doggedly supervised each move, making sure that proper rites were observed. Bones, when bones there were, were carefully placed in new coffins, in anatomically correct relation to each other. Dust, if dust was all that remained, was symbolically heaped into neat new boxes and reburied. Whenever a bit of jewelry turned up within a grave, somehow a relative appeared to claim kin and ownership, but I questioned no one as to his right.

At the same time I had to calm my students, from peasant girls to the nobly born, who feared the ghosts they claimed to see nightly. If I insisted on building the school here, they said, great calamity would befall us all.

Material for the new buildings piled up on the grounds: educational equipment; a pump and engine from the American Well Works, which meant that Bao Lin would have the first water system in the city; a gleaming new bathtub; the town's first phonograph; timber, cement, and the porous handmade bricks of the province.

I went over my American blueprints with a Chinese contractor, Cheo Lao-ban, whose name translated Old Board Complete. He maintained an attitude of blank disapproval and said they must be completely redrawn. At this point, I decided to do my own contracting and further that I would have temple roofs on the buildings, cornices, ridges, gargoyles and all. "It will look like a man in Western clothes and a Chinese hat," critics told me, but I was delighted with the idea.

Grave-moving over, no calamity other than the inevitable crushing heat of summer befell the school. I designed a bridge and had it built over the moat to Bao Lin's new entrance and awaited complaint from authorities, but instead the magistrate only asked who might use it. When I said that anyone who cared to could cross on the structure, he refunded the cost from public funds.

There was no way to "hustle the East," but in this land of plenty-of-time if you took it easy each problem seemed to settle itself before the next one arose.

Thanksgiving Day was celebrated in Nanchang, with the largest of local chickens as substitutes for turkeys for dinner that evening. Mabel and I walked to the city gate, closed at sundown as it had been for so many centuries, and I presented my pass, the half of a key which looked like a large wooden ladle. The guard at the gate matched it with the other half, then loosened the iron chain enough to permit us to pass. We lived in America for a few hours with the other Americans, talked and sang in English, and I even wondered where Tom was eating his Thanksgiving dinner.

Christmas came and the little girls waked us singing "Hark! the herald angels sing..." (only none of them could quite say *Hark*), dressed as angels in white robes with paper wings pinned to the shoulders.

New Year holidays brought all activities to a halt, as they always had, but winter ended soon after in a burst of blossoms. Spring ran by like a rushing brook, and I hired two hundred coolies to carry away baskets of sand to level the hills on my new acreage, using it to fill in the malarial ponds. Bamboos, magnolias, oleanders, and azaleas were planted where the stagnant water once bred mosquitoes.

Tragedy struck, when the second child I had adopted, Precious Pearl's first little sister, died of diphtheria. I comforted myself with the others and went on with my work.

In May there was a field day in the great court where the Manchu civil service examinations had been once held and where Confucian scholars had written over and over with conviction: "The aim of female education is perfect submission—not cultivation or development of the mind." Now young women, from all the nearby girls' schools opened under the Republic and from Bao Lin, competed in physical drills, and the School of the Protecting Spirit won first prize.

Though he had not closed the new schools, Sun Yat-sen's successor had imprisoned many young revolutionaries. One of his prisoners in Nanchang was Chang Tren.

This girl, to whom I handed her letters and who led the group of early patriots at Bao Lin, had gone on to Japan as a student, returned to China as a student-leader and, during the decisive days, had been the heroine who managed to open the gates of Nanking to the revolutionary soldiers. Her crime was great in the eyes of China's conservative dictator, and her father's property was confiscated before she was sent to serve her sentence.

Anguished at the news, I went to the jail to see Chang Tren. Making my way past the cells of the common women criminals to find her, I saw a murderess who had done away with three daughters-in-law, hugging an opium pipe, and female thieves and prostitutes sitting idly in filth and misery, surrounded by their children who, by law, were allowed into prison with them. Some of the women were in chains, although the modern-minded warden, who hung a picture of Thomas Mott Osborne in his office, did his best to alleviate conditions. Fortunately for Chang Tren, the warden had known her as a student in Japan and in his heart did not disapprove of what she had done. She had a cell alone where she received me with affectionate pride.

I found my former pupil far from despondent or unkempt. On the contrary, Chang Tren was radiant, spotlessly dressed, her short hair beautifully coifed. For the prison cot she had crocheted a white bedspread and on the scrubbed table she used as a desk were her papers and two open books, Carlyle's *French Revolution* in Chinese and the Gospel according to St. Matthew. She was writing an article on woman's duty to New China for newspaper syndication, and this she read to me during our visit. I left the jail uplifted. Here was an educated woman, undaunted by captivity, full of hope for the future.

The heat, when it came, was the worst I remember, and with an entourage of seventeen and sixty-one pieces of luggage, I moved up again into the mountains in a caravan. Will China never discover her beautiful hills, I asked myself again. Perhaps well-to-do people will some day start a fashion in summer resorts, and the poor will follow them. Perhaps my babies will remember this summer and be courageous enough to venture in the future. At present the rich people have no more comfort in the heat than their poor countrymen— except a punkah and a little more space.

On August 10, 1914, in Kuling in the mountains, I heard that Europe had gone to war. My Chinese friends could not understand what this might mean, in spite of recent revolution. The Kuling area had been untouched by fighting since the Taiping Rebellion. Among the foreigners, the British tried hard to maintain polite relations with the Germans, but even in so remote a spot the strain was impossible.

I went away for a few days' peace to camp near a Buddhist monastery, but when I tried to tell the priests of the war, they only replied, "Our Buddha says 'He who is strongest in patience, he is the great man.'" "No, no, Buddhist priest," I noted in my diary that night. "I love your temples and your trees and your calm, but I shall create if I can in the daughters of your people a divine discontent with 'things as they are.'"

Before I left Kuling, I agreed to rent my comfortable bungalow to a stranded German businessman and his family. He couldn't get out and he couldn't do any business and no Englishman would let him have a house, though he was known as a fine, high-minded man. Later the skipper on one of the Yangtze riverboats sent word to "tell that young lady she will stay in her interior city because we will not let her travel on any boat to Shanghai if she continues to rent her house to the enemy!" This was two years before my country was in the war.

When I got back to Nanchang, Chinese friends inquired with concern and politeness how the Christians' war was going. The war, it seemed to me, was the very opposite of Christian, although each nation involved invoked the Christian God to bless its own side.

My first job after returning from the cool hills to the heat of the plains was to count bricks. The brick-maker whose kilns I had kept running for nearly two years watched me with amusement. "Honorable Teacher Han is like unto our late Empress Dowager," he said with a low bow. From what I knew of that many-sided and formidable woman, I was not sure whether I was being complimented or insulted. "The Empress ordered one hundred boats to be delivered and the contractor, thinking she would not count them, sent only ninety-nine," went on the contractor. "She counted them and ordered him to be beheaded."

"Yes, I know," said I. "He saved his life by building her the marble boat in which I had tea in the Peking summer palace."

"Little Sister Han will find every brick there to the last brick," he declared.

"It is even so. I have counted them," said I.

The next fall brought rumors that a railroad would be constructed from the Yangtze to Nanchang, and that machine-made bricks were being manufactured in the province to build the stations. I set out to find the source of these bricks and to get a load for Bao Lin.

To track them down, I took a junk so squat that I could not stand up straight in its interior, though the owner and crew did not bump their heads. It was to carry me down to the city in the District of the Poles—so called because, to reach there, poles were used to guide the junks through the inland river rapids.

One morning the boat was gliding peacefully past a little walled town, when it was ordered loudly to halt. "I will examine your luggage!" called the voice.

"I have an Ocean Teacher on board," called back the boatman.

"Halt!" repeated the voice, this time angrily.

Sensing trouble, I came up to the deck waving the silk Stars and Stripes which I carried as a passport in the interior. I found the river police aboard my craft, with drawn swords in their hands. Seeing the flag, the chief dropped his weapon and grinned broadly. "Foreign Teacher," he said, "why did the boatman not say that you were of the country of the Starry Flag? Your honorable country is the friend of our unworthy country. I shall enter the city over there and tell the magistrate to make you the city's guest and grant you its key."

There was no way to avoid such a delay, and very soon the magistrate arrived with a wooden key as large as a suitcase, offering the freedom of the quaint, square village which no American woman had entered before.

"You are our first honored guest since the Republic and a feast is being prepared," announced the magistrate, and handed me on shore where sedan chairs were waiting.

Untouched by passing centuries, the town stood within wide fields. Four gates pierced the walls and a drum tower rose above the parapet to provide a lookout for approaching enemies.

To my utter astonishment, when I arrived I found that the Chinese town was a matriarchy. The women did all its business, owned all the property, and ran its financial affairs, permitting the men to work and to hold honorary offices, but that was all. There was everything in China if you looked long and far enough, even early suffragettes!

The story was that many, many years ago, the men of the city had gone to war and were away so long that the women had perforce taken over. A messenger arrived one day to tell them all the local men had been slaughtered or captured. When the war was over, this city of widows and spinsters sent out to get husbands for themselves and fathers for their children but married them only on condition that the women keep control of business and the purse strings. These women were delighted to hear that I was educating girls in Nanchang, and told me that I would find my bricks, or so they had heard, back in Kiukiang.

When I got to Kiukiang I not only found the bricks but also the new piano which had been sent from home. Through proper middlemen I bought 345,000 bricks and hired forty-nine junks to carry them across Poyang. Before I had finished filing the hand-painted bills of lading in a wicker basket, the three hundred iron beds showed up. Nine more small junks and nine more large bills of lading were added to the forty-nine—plus another one for myself, my piano, and my flag.

The wind was favorable. I provisioned myself for a five-day journey and the flotilla set sail. At the end of three days I was anchored in the Yangtze, imprisoned by a never-ending gale within sight of the lake. The days were as black as the nights. The boat tossed crazily on the wild, raging, rising river and tugged at its little iron anchor thrown into the mud of the shore. Rain poured in through a leak in the roof of my cabin. I put up my umbrella, spread an oiled sheet over my knees, kept a stick to hand with which to threaten the rats, and read the three books I had brought with me: Tennyson's *Collected Poems*, Meyer's *Medieval and Modern History*, and the Bible.

A brief let-up permitted us to enter the lake, but fresh storms blew up, driving us dangerously over the water, out toward the unfathomed middle. We sheltered in the lee of Great Shoe Island, in the center of Poyang, until another lull in the tempest allowed us to up sail for the safer lee of the shore.

My food ran out and the boatman's wife shared her coolie rice and bean curds. Every day, hearing the caged cock crow, I hoped that the time had come for a chicken dinner, but when we passed offshore the Official Buddhist Temple, the boatman's lady cut off the cock's head, let the blood drip into the tossing waves, and finally threw in the head *and* body so "his blood may mingle with the raging waters and calm them." Hungry, I remonstrated, but the woman, who could afford a chicken dinner no more than once yearly, said, "Wait, you will see. We have made the sacrifice, and the gods of the lake will be appeased."

The next morning was clearer and the boatman, who had concluded I was "bad joss," stopped glaring at me. On the tenth day at dusk, we reached the city of Wu Cheng, eighty miles from the mouth of the lake. Landing, the junk ran onto the sharp anchor of another boat and its shell was pierced. My cabin amidships began to flood and I crawled out on deck to find that we were in three or four feet of water, in no danger of drowning, but the junk was filling fast. There was my piano, its treble end under two feet of lake.

"Get coolies!" I commanded.

An hour later the maddeningly deliberate boatman returned with twenty or more local men, all talking at once and carrying ropes, pulleys, poles, and lamps.

"Will the Honorable Sister Han tell them what is in the box?" asked the boatman.

"It is a large *chin,* a musical instrument, very valuable, from America," I explained to the leader.

At this they all shook their heads and began to argue among themselves. It was dangerous to interrupt such exchanges and I listened with seeming patience while the coolies speculated as to whether the large wooden container was full of ammunition or of strange new devices for the foreigner's hospital.

In the end, as I knew it would, curiosity got the better of them. They attached a pulley to the mast, and hauled the piano, dripping muddy water in streams, from its case. It would drain during the night on top of the boat, I thought happily.

A self-appointed committee then informed me that one of the brick-loaded junks was also in harbor and that I would see it in the morning. "And now come with me," said an old man, "and I shall escort you to my humble, unworthy dwelling."

The little house was chilly, without a fire on the wet, raw, and windy night, but the welcome was as warm as the courtesy of the women and hot vermicelli could make it. Shaking with cold and fatigue, I tried to return their courtesy by answering a thousand questions about America before lying down in my coat and gloves to sleep.

"Please say just one word of American to let us hear the sound of it," the wife begged before I dozed off.

"For *fan* we say rice," I complied, and fell into exhausted slumber to a chorus of "lice ... lice ... lice ..." repeated by everyone from grandfather to the smallest child, kept up to see the foreign devil who spoke this exquisitely impossible language.

The harbor was a forest of sunken masts next day, among which was the protruding mast of the junk with one load of bricks. "You can always think of a way out," I said to the committee. "I want my bricks and shall stay here until you get them up somehow."

But the leader, calm and philosophical, spoke as if I were

a child. "Little Sister Han must wait just eleven months until the water is low again. Then we will get every brick for her."

The junk with the piano proved mendable and was soon afloat, so Little Sister Han sailed off, under fair skies and a brilliant sun. The lake was still too rough for landing when we arrived finally at Nanchang, but on the shore as we passed the school I could see dozens of children waving handkerchiefs frantically to welcome me home. I was finally put ashore two miles away and carried by squeaking wheelbarrow (all wheelbarrows squeaked) to the school gate, where a search party of men that had been out for two days and the whole faculty and student body greeted me with tears and rejoicing.

"While you were gone, Honorable Teacher Han," the children told me, "we thought you must be happy because you had a piano and watermelon seeds on your boat."

"My sufferings were nothing," I wrote, "when I looked over the papers and read of Europe and Gallipoli. Strange that one's concerns should dare to loom so large. Day after day Great Britain sees her splendid ships go down to the bottom of the sea. And yet how large, it seems to me, that one boat is at the bottom of Poyang Lake with 34,000 of my bricks."

12

Welthy Honsinger, headmistress of Baldwin, reported each school year to the Kiangsi Woman's Conference of the Methodist Episcopal Church. In the 1913–14 letter, I said:

For the past year, we have been one huge moving van, migrating hither and thither, from one house to another,—homeless. The foreign faculty, having walked five miles a day for half the year, and having camped out in no less than five different domiciles during the year, is glad to have shelter for the next ten months. . . .

But I am anxious that all our friends shall know, that in the thing that counts for most—her spirit—Baldwin is more beautiful than ever.

Miss Tang has opened a kindergarten where thirty-five are enrolled. A wheelbarrow goes from house to house gathering the children. . . .

The department of mathematics has been strengthened by the coming of Mr. Feng, a graduate of the famous Presbyterian College at Weshien, Shantung.

Our greatest blessing is the addition to our faculty of three of Baldwin's own graduates. Of the five who received diplomas last June, one is doing school and Bible Women's work in the needy city of Fu Cheo Fu; one is teaching in the Presbyterian School in Shanghai, while three are with us. . . .

Spiritually, we have been used and blessed of God. During Chinese New Year's vacation a number of the faculty made a preaching tour in the Kan River district where we preached to four thousand women and children. Every Sunday afternoon our girls and teachers scatter to three centers to tell to others what they have learned of the Master. Seven girls have been received into the church and two others are on probation. One hundred and twenty students have been taught in Baldwin this year.

119

An enlarged faculty; a higher standard of work; the first High School Commencement in its history; more Christian work and more students admitted into the church; these have been the milestones of the year at Baldwin.

Each succeeding report sounded more and more jubilant. The main buildings went up, in solid brick. Desks and chairs and blackboards, ordered from catalogues, were installed. Paths, shaded by camphor trees, pines, blossoming peach and persimmon, bamboo, and magnolia, wound through the enlarged compound.

The Chinese characters on the new arch stood for "The truth shall make you free," and under the arch the final dedication took place. Ceremonies were similar to American ones except that at the invocation the clergyman who led in prayer first slowly and devoutly removed his glasses, while everyone who wore them in the audience did likewise. The Chinese do not pray in glasses.

Spirits of criminals, supposed to linger over the grounds, were exorcized with tea parties and games. The Temple kindergarten was opened to all local moppets, including those from the squatters' huts. Now when I walked through the alleyways of the neighboring poor, tattered children ran to greet me, some crying "O Men Tsai Tien Shang Ti Fu (Our Father, who art in heaven)," while others lilted "Chu Ye Su Ai O (Yes, Jesus loves me)" and, most touching of all, one or another would try to say "good morning," which came out "Goo mawlin." I remembered the days when I heard in the alleys only "Watch out! The foreign devil is coming!" and parents used me as an ogre with whom to frighten their young. From big bad bogy to beneficent friend in so few years. . . .

Bao Lin had grown, then burned, then grown again in the same years until the small school of eight grades was a huge school, graduating its students to become teachers, preachers, welfare workers, and leaders in other areas.

My satisfaction was great, and only the war kept my ebullience in check.

A new teacher came out to me from California, a delightful girl whom Gertrude Howe soon nicknamed "our Bonnie Brownie." Miss Brown was to be there for five years, and what a pleasure she was immediately.

When news came of the death of my mother in the United States my sorrow was so profound I could share it with no one. Needing to get away by myself for a few days, I chose this time to take the long, lonely trip to Shanghai to make final purchases for Bao Lin, although Ilien Tang was away on her biennial pilgrimage to her ancestors. Miss Brown could take over for me for the time being.

No skipper denied me passage, in spite of the threat, because I had rented to a German, but when I got to Shanghai I found my British and Scottish friends inclined to be testy with all Americans. I understood that it was because they were so frantic over the course of the war, but their attacks were barbed.

How could America remain neutral when the world was on fire, threatened by the Kaiser's barbarian hordes? On the defensive, I wondered how the British and French could go on living their lives of extreme luxury in the Paris of the East while their countries endured the privations of war. In my diary, I commented that one of my friends had even bought a second car to run around at night and see what woman her husband was visiting. "Not my cup of tea," I noted, and kept my stay as short as possible.

Just before I left Shanghai a telegram came from Brownie. The yellow envelope contained a brief and dreadful message. "Wang Su-ling committed suicide yesterday hurry back tell us what to do."

My heart plummeted and I boarded the next river steamer up the Yangtze, praying that the north wind would blow when I reached the treacherous lake. Su-ling—the girl would have graduated in June. A charmer, inclined to mischief and insubordination, but beautiful and an outstanding student.

In Kiukiang I found a letter waiting from Brownie. For some misdemeanor, Miss Brown had sent Su-ling to spend the day in her room. When a student took up a tray with Su-ling's lunch, she found her hanging by the neck, dead, suspended by a silk scarf to the top of the door.

The whole school stopped, they told me later. Everything stopped. Even the clocks seemed to stop. Brownie kept saying over and over, "I know Welthy would do something, but I don't know what." She got in touch with the Chinese undertakers and had the body taken care of, but Su-ling's family in Nanchang refused to come for the coffin. It stayed in the Bao Lin gatehouse, while everyone said with the family, "The blood of Su-ling will be a curse upon the school."

As soon as I arrived and heard the whole story, I went straight into the city to Su-ling's house. It was not the loss of face in being sent to her room that had made her kill herself, but the fact that her father and mother were determined that she marry an uneducated boy, who had left school after the sixth grade.

Parents and I faced each other, Old China and the New World missionary teacher who had come to find and try to help New China. I believed as they did, but in a different way, that the spirit of Su-ling haunted the room.

Sad and angry, the parents attacked the Ocean Teacher. "Su-ling was an undutiful daughter. She refused to marry the boy we chose for her. She felt she was better—better than we are, than he is. It is because she saw your Chen Yi, your Precious Pearl, and she knew your child would never be told whom to marry. Little Sister Han, why do you set such a radical example? You are ruining our daughters!"

"More than one family belonging to the gentry," I said gently, "have asked for the hand of Chen Yi, but I have refused her hand."

"How can you do such a thing? You are destroying the life of your child, as you have destroyed the life of ours," accused the father.

"I think not only of my daughters and your daughter, but of all the daughters of New China. They must be educated for the New China. Your Su-ling was a beautiful young woman. She was a fine student, a girl to be proud of. Many a high family would have sought her in time, but she had to be given a chance to breathe freely, to study and learn longer, before marrying. She should have been allowed herself to choose an educated man."

The interview ended in tears. "Oh Sister Han," wailed the parents, "what have we done to our daughter?"

"Let us give her a beautiful burial," I said sadly. "That is all that is left to do. All her friends will come and sing songs before the last words are spoken by your Buddhist or Taoist priests. Allow us to bear all the expense and let us comply with your every wish. You have a younger daughter, too, and her we shall be glad to have as our student without payment. May we do this much in Su-ling's name because we loved her?"

Su-ling's parents came for her coffin. They asked that the songs be in English, because they believed this would please the spirit of one who had been learning this tongue, and they promised that her little sister would come to Bao Lin the next year. The agony was over and the curse was lifted.

In May 1917, I wrote in my diary: "America is too far away. The Pacific is too wide. Ten thousand miles stretch out to an endless distance now—letters, since we boast a railroad at last, come in a month—but a month is thirty days too long. For America is at war! My country at war! It is so hard to believe it, to imagine it. No matter how accustomed I have had to become to thinking of Belgium, France, England, Italy at war, to think of boys leaving American homes—to picture American camps and American last good-byes staggers me. Every thought of you, America, has so long been one of luxury, of peace, of sunlight. Here on this side of the world is such poverty as you could not imagine and unhappiness and misery. Here about me it has been continual dusk, with only now and then a ray of hope shining through. But now, America, the clouds of war are over you. I must come home. I want to breathe your atmosphere and share your fate. I cannot stay longer than to complete the School of the Protecting Spirit, and then I shall come."

Chinese officials were greatly disturbed over this turn in the war. "America, the country that loves peace, is at war—and China will follow her," they said. Then they questioned me on geography and politics, coming to call at the school for the purpose. I flew from these interviews to classrooms, to my little office where hair-bobbing went on, to the infirmary where I spent hours massaging and oiling the feet of the students who came to us crippled each year, to the nursery where the orphans were growing up, to the grounds where last-minute additions were being made on the buildings.

The thermometer climbed as summer advanced until I thought it would burst. Oregon pine, sent from the west coast of America, was attacked by an army of white ants, and the whole school turned out to help workmen pour pitch, kerosene, and boiling water on the precious lumber. The war news was grave, and the Chinese searched my face to find the answers I did not have, while the British recruited Chinese men by the thousands to work behind the lines in France, giving China her own participation.

Fall brought famine, the second since I had become part of the country. In spite of war, I knew that America would respond to faraway disaster and would send flour and money. The governor of the province appointed a committee to aid the starving and for the first time in history a woman was a member—Little Sister Han from Bao Lin. I rallied the Nanchang women to raise money, gave an entertainment at the school which netted a thousand dollars, asked the girls to go without meat for dinner until the famine was over, sending the amount their meat cost to the hungry in the North, where it was worse than in Nanchang, although even here the trees were stripped of leaves, the animals killed, hungry children moaned at night, and hollow-cheeked people crawling out to look for food dropped by the wayside.

By late December I felt that I had done all I could. The

time had come to turn my school over to a Chinese woman. It was a Chinese school and it should have as its headmistress a woman of New China. My beloved Ilien Tang was ready. Not only ready, but she was accepted. I had accomplished this much—and now the time had come to take my own part with my own country at war.

The governor wrote asking me to come back soon, for the sake of the province. Banners of red satin to cover all the walls of my office were presented with ceremony as farewell gifts from the officials of the city. The students gave me a gold bracelet engraved: "The pupils of the School of the Protecting Spirit will forever be as close to thee in spirit and love as is the gold bracelet to thine arm." And the faculty—this I can scarcely write of now without tears—presented me with the Temple Bell.

I would never again be far from the sound of the bell that had sustained me so long. When I came back, it would be with me. I had rebuilt the School of the Protecting Spirit and turned it over to the people to whom it belonged, leaving it in the care of my Chinese sister. Whatever happened to me, I was part of China, and for the rest of my life China was a part of me.

Indeed much sooner than I dreamed, China's Little Sister Han was acting again as a friend to the Chinese, but this time in France.

The YWCA accepted my services as soon as I landed in the U.S.A. As a member of the War Work Council I was in uniform by May 1918 and on my way through submarine-infested waters to Europe. When I landed in Le Havre, I found Chinese coolies unloading cargo at wharves. The men were from Shantung and understood me perfectly. Clustering around, they asked "Where are we, please? We don't know where we are!"

I stayed long enough to visit their huts, to talk to them all, to draw maps in the rich soil of France to explain to these homesick men where on the round earth they had arrived.

At the munitions factory in Central France where I was

to do welfare work, I found coolies again, trying to say a few French words. As soon as they heard me speak, they pled with me to help them. "Little Sister Han, did you cross two oceans to get here, too? Can you endure this French food with no rice and no well-cooked vegetables? Will you explain these people to us? They pay us much money to come from China, they pay us well to do their work so they can go and be killed. We cannot understand them at all!"

Then after I had tried to explain Europe to China as I had tried to explain China to the United States and America to the Chinese, they said to me, "Do you not have a pain in your heart for China?"

All the rest of my life, all over this wonderful world, I have always had a pain in my heart for China. No one will ever know how deep is the pain of Little Sister Han.

PART II

The Bishop's Wife

1

"Little Sister Han" had finished her job before joining up for war. Bao Lin, I knew, was where it belonged, in Chinese hands, and flourishing. In the gigantic redeployment from war back to peace, each citizen made the same decision I did in some form or another: to go back or to start over. It was a temptation to return to China, to embellish the never-completed edifice I had built, to preside over the work that could go on without me. I guess I am at heart more of a bricklayer than a caretaker. I loved China and longed to return—and did, several times, as a visitor—but I felt that the rich, building part of my life up the Yangtze was ended.

As I followed my own road to the crossroads from which we went on together, Fred Fisher and I, five years passed between World War I and the evening we kissed behind the pillar of a bridge in Springfield, Massachusetts, during the General Convention of the Methodist Church.

After the war I lectured for the Swarthmore Chautauqua (eighty-five times in ninety days) on "Women of the Allies" and you may be sure I brought in opportunities for mission educators, doctors, nurses, and technicians. Traveling over the country with the Robin Hood troupe, I spoke myself hoarse and exhausted.

In 1920 my Aunt Dorinda gave me a fat check for five thousand dollars, and off I went around the world. After Japan, Korea, a return to China and my adopted darlings, and on to Singapore, Malaya, and Burma, I went to India. There, again, I met Dr. Fisher, elected the youngest bishop in our church. I was not the "girl in the red robe" that was "dying for a little bit o' love" this time, but a properly introduced member of his church, my interests coinciding with his. I thought him the most dynamic and delightful human being I had ever known. It was a joy that we Methodists could command the services of so broad-visioned and great a Christian man. Without any designs on a married bishop, I reveled in his company and I knew he was pleased with mine. Then I set off for Palestine, Egypt, and France.

Back home, I took on the editing of a monthly magazine for young people, *World Neighbors*. An honorary degree from Syracuse gave me increased standing and authority and I was often called Dr. Honsinger. Working like a Trojan, I wrote and lectured and, in these lavish early twenties, was frivolous betimes, shortening my skirts, cutting my hair, and indulging in my first permanent wave—which cost me fifty hard-earned dollars.

I could never manage to feel as I was supposed to about my chronological age. Maybe I was too busy. The future always seemed limitless and I never stopped expecting something to happen, some invitation to another far adventure. I was forty-four years old when Fred Fisher promised me in the happy egotism of romance: "You're going to be loved as no woman ever was loved!"

When something so important and wonderful happens, one tends to consider how many hazards might have kept it from happening, how many sad, curious, and good things combined to let it happen. Before we went on together, Fred Fisher came a long way around to that bridge. He was a very lively fellow who led a lively life, and in 1904, two years before I sailed for China, he had gone off to India.

Fred's background was one kind of classic American: forebears who emigrated from Norfolk County, England, to the New World in the 1700s and settled in Pennsylvania. His own father pushed west as a railroad employee to Indiana in the nineteenth century. Mother and Father Fisher's second son,

Frederick Bohn, was born on Saint Valentine's Day, 1882, "back home" in Greencastle, Pennsylvania, where Mrs. Fisher had returned to her mother's house.

The baby was baptized in the town's austere German Reformed Church, nine miles from the Mason-Dixon line. Afraid that his wife's homesickness might be permanent, Father Fisher gave up his job and came back east. Fred's grandmother, Maria Bohn Shirey, was thus an influence in his childhood. She was a prototype of the gently bred Southern woman, raised in Maryland, with a soft, slurred magnolia-petal accent, a black velvet ribbon around her throat, and a lace cap on her white hair. But her ancestral home had been used in the Underground Railway for runaway slaves and at her knee Fred learned that "God is color-blind." An old Negro preacher had often been asked to lead prayers in his grandmother's house, "And, son, that old preacher must have had hold of the keys of heaven, because he could pray you right through to the city of God!"

When Father Fisher went back to Indiana because his career was there, they lived for a while in Elwood in a low white house with classic pillars called, for some unknown reason, the "shoo-fly house." They were neighbors of the Wendell Willkies and Mrs. Willkie was perennial president while Mrs. Fisher was vice-president of the Methodist Missionary Society until the gas boom lured the Fishers on to Muncie.

Little Fred was a bookworm. At twelve, when he first delved into his father's small but select library (Emerson, Carlyle, Dickens, Shakespeare), his dad suggested he tackle ten volumes on the Reformation and Martin Luther. Just before his boy finished this formidable assignment, Father Fisher handed him the life of Jean Jacques Rousseau. The contradictory influences lasted all his life. Fred defied conventions and did the unexpected with the gaiety of Rousseau, exponent of *laissez faire*, and, like the monk Luther, was an immovable rock when he knew a thing was right. Laughing at his boyish

confusion over these noble irreconcilables, Fred said, "When
I came to the page in Luther's life where he threw the ink-
well at the devil, I thought it was aimed at Rousseau!"

For "light entertainment" in those days before radio,
movies, and comic strips, family circles discussed with artless
seriousness Free Will, Good and Evil, Is Satan a Real Person?
Evenings with the Poets and Chautauqua Circles came in
season. Religion was all-year-round, all-absorbing.

When the Reverend Leslie F. Naftzger took over the Methodist pastorate in Muncie, the short, stocky, vital minister and
the short, stocky, vital boy immediately became friends. Fred
was a natural-born hero-worshiper, who already worshiped the
teacher-preacher Dr. Phillips Brooks from hearsay. Dr. Naftzger reminded him of Brooks, and the good parson, without condescension, made young Fred at home in his house and often
read him passages from forthcoming sermons or discussed
with him the nature of man's search for God.

Naftzger was his own evangelist. When he held his revival
meetings and called the faithful to declare themselves for
the Lord, the solitary Fred "rebelled against this parade of
one's most intimate life in public" and found it "repulsive
to watch my neighbors go forward and hear their shouts of
rejoicing and noisy public prayers." But he could not resist the
doctor's fervent appeals. The night he walked the center aisle
himself and knelt at the chancel rail, Dr. Naftzger came and
knelt beside him, put his arm around the boy and wept. From
then on Fred never doubted his own future in the ministry.

Under Naftzger's influence, he decided on Asbury College,
in Wilmore, Kentucky, instead of DePauw University, where
his father was a trustee and a scholarship was his for the asking. Asbury was a "holiness college," supported by Funda-
mentalists from the Methodist Church, South. It was an unlikely training ground for the boy who would later become so
broad in his views, range so far in his search for the deepest
spiritual values, offering as it did nothing except the most
strait-laced piety and puritanical restraint. Furthermore, to go
there Fred would need to borrow money.

Now in Muncie, the Middletown, U.S.A., chosen by the
Lynds for their sociological study, a righteous man did not
borrow. He paid cash or did without. Fortunately a far-seeing
patron, A. L. Johnson, for whom Fred had worked during his
high school years, insisted on lending. He gave the eager young
man a blank check to go and get his education and to pay
him back when he could, of course with interest. (When
Fred did pay him back, Mr. Johnson put the money into a
Missions-for-India fund for Fred to administer.)

Later Fred wondered why he, so rebellious by nature, never
balked at the narrow severity of his college. Rather he valued
it deeply, especially the spiritual unity that existed between
faculty and scholars in their simple asceticism.

In his second year at Asbury he was sent as a delegate to
the Student Volunteer Convention in Toronto. This was his
introduction to the world, to a picked, aggressive group of
students from all over, and to a number of famous religious
leaders. Among them was Bishop Thoburn of India. A short
man with a long beard, few gestures, and a voice like a soft
volcano, the bishop addressed the students. He ended his
talk, "Young gentlemen, I tell you the Man of Calvary is by
my side!"

The whole gathering of young men became his disciples
as he spoke, but Fred was the one who walked two miles in
the cold Canadian winter to see the good bishop alone. He
interrupted him at dinner.

"How do you do, young man," said Thoburn, napkin in
hand.

Fred beamed, forgetting frostbitten fingers and nose. "How
do you do, Bishop. I've decided to go to India."

"Oh? When?"

"Just as soon as I finish college."

"That's great," said Thoburn. He must have felt the difference between this one and the thousands of youngsters who
made the same resolution immediately after hearing him
speak. The two sat down to talk while dinner grew cold and
the bishop's hostess fretted and the bishop used his napkin

on which to draw a map of India. They were temperamentally kin, the distinguished old man and the provincial youth, impatient of red tape and wholly unself-conscious. When Fred left that night, Bishop Thoburn placed his hands on his head at the door. "Although no conference has elected you to ordination, I hereby set you apart for Christ and the world."

It took Fred, who never changed his mind, a little longer than graduation to get to India. First Dr. Naftzger presented him to the board of examiners to be licensed as an "exhorter" so that he could preach and prepare himself for becoming a deacon. The frock-coated elders immediately struck Fred's streak of stubborn honesty and independence.

"Do you smoke?"

"No, I do not smoke."

"Will you promise never to smoke?"

Fred looked straight at the elder who posed this question. "No, sir, I will not promise."

Fred had no intention of smoking himself, but his father and uncle, good men, smoked and he would not, by his promise, label smoking a sin.

In the end the examiners yielded to the candidate. He was a willful one, but he had good stuff. A typewritten certificate as exhorter was presented to Leslie F. Naftzger to sign on behalf of Frederick B. Fisher.

Sent as a circuit-riding exhorter to Kokomo, Indiana, Fred was paid $360 a year. His preaching soon packed the tiny Kokomo chapel and his pleased parishioners thought, perhaps on St. Paul's advice, he should marry and settle down fast. At their hearty urging, he returned to Muncie, where his childhood sweetheart had just come back from studying at the New England Conservatory of Music. He courted this lovely girl, a glamorous worldling in his eyes, and won her. Characteristically, the first article of furniture he bought on his thirty-dollar-a-month salary was a mahogany davenport so massive that the legs had to be cut off to get it into the single, all-purpose room he rented for himself and his Edith. (It followed them everywhere and is still in the only house he ever owned, in Hingham, Massachusetts.)

In his second year, his salary was raised to a thousand dollars. Kokomo hoped he would stay a while, but another unusual bishop took hold of Fred's destiny.

Charles G. McCabe was famous as Civil War chaplain of Libby Prison and as a rousing money-raiser. When the railroad tracks were being laid across the continent, McCabe was secretary of the Church Extension Society. Somehow he mesmerized the hardboiled railroad barons into holding a certain number of building lots in each raw new town for Methodist churches. Then he collected cash from well-to-do eastern churchmen to build frame chapels and persuaded young evangelists to fill these pioneer pulpits.

Once when he was blandishing a wealthy lumberman named Tom Collins into giving him funds, Collins said skeptically, "You're always talking about building new churches, McCabe, but how many have you built?"

McCabe sat down at the little folding organ he always carried with him and improvised a song that became a classic in the Methodist circles of the time: "We're building two a day, Tom," he sang lustily. "We're building two a day!"

Church empire-builder, now bishop, McCabe presided at the conference in Muncie in 1904 where Fred was to be ordained. As he was reading out the list of candidates he stopped at Fred's name and turned to Bishop Warne of India. "Say," he boomed, "is that the young man you said wanted to go to India? Well, how much will it cost to send him and his wife?"

"About six hundred dollars," answered Bishop Warne.

"And how much is the salary of a young married missionary out your way these days?"

"Nine hundred and fifty. . . ."

"Good! If we can get six hundred dollars plus nine hundred fifty right here this morning, I can appoint him to Agra, where you need a fellow. Right? Excellent! There's always a shrinkage in collections and things usually cost more than a bishop estimates. How about eighteen hundred?"

Fred sat stunned. Bishop McCabe was cheerfully interrupting the entire proceedings. Before he went on with the candidates' list, he got the white-haired ministers composing the Conference Cabinet to tear up sheets of paper and pass them out to the audience. Within fifteen minutes he had pledges to cover the eighteen hundred dollars. "I am ordaining this man Fisher a deacon," he announced happily, "and we are sending him to India."

2

The P. & O. ship left Tilbury docks in England for Bombay. Most of the passengers were British colonials, many of whom did not come aboard until the ship reached Marseilles, preferring a last fling in Paris and a comfortable train trip through France to the rough voyage across the Bay of Biscay and around the coasts of Spain and Portugal. Fred and Edith were the only Americans. With his artless friendliness and irrepressible good humor, Fred finally succeeded in breaking down the standoffishness of his shipmates, but when he did succeed in making friends with them he could scarcely believe his ears.

Conversation was right out of the pages of Kipling. Indians, whose history went at least as far back as the Egyptian era, were referred to as "niggers." "Mistake," they told him, "to educate the blighters, but one must have a supply of clerks to run the blasted country, mustn't one?"

Fred, proud to be a descendant of American abolitionists, thought at first they were pulling his leg. Finding them serious, he tried at least to look at the other side of the question and to give them full credit for their constructive achievements, for railroads, irrigation projects, and partial headway against famine and plague in the country they ruled with such condescension.

Agra, "City of Fire," was Fred and Edith's new home. Dust storms drove in to polish the marble of the Taj Mahal. Colorful bazaars and ornate temples were centers of Indian life, while in the compounds of the white sahibs, silent, barefooted servants moved about in turbans and long coats. Fred's pulpit was in the small Methodist Episcopal Church of

Agra and his missionary quarters were in the house of a Scotch widow.

He was charmed with the exotic city. At twilight he went as often as possible to the Taj Mahal, preferring the hour when the muezzin called all men to prayer even to the magic of it by moonlight. As ever, his primary interest was in people. No one was likely to discuss God in the corner grocery store in Kokomo, but in Agra they quoted the Koran or Gita in every bazaar. Many people in the city spoke English, but he wanted to talk also to villagers and illiterates. The first thing he did was to engage a Persian scholar to teach him Urdu, and the second was to begin inviting all sorts of Indians home.

"You are outraging the sense of decency which we British have built up through the years," his Scotch landlady told Fred. "If you must see your colored friends here, keep them on the veranda and never ask them for tea, young man, for I shan't allow them served from my kitchen!"

So, on the veranda, Edith brewed tea, using her own kettle and tea service. This was a Fred Fisher compromise. It involved no surrender and no battle and it worked.

Some Indian students delighted him by asking that he perform a wedding ceremony for one of their number. He spent long hours with the couple, discussing the sacrament and, in accordance with British custom, posted their banns in his church.

All Agra was thrown into a tizzy. Even American bishops were not allowed to perform marriage services for Christian Indians unless they met a series of fantastically complicated legal requirements. The British missionaries thought this brash twenty-two-year-old rebel from the United States might hinder their government-sponsored monopolies. They protested.

Fred, whose stipend was less than that currently offered members of the Peace Corps, took his Lord's tenth and telegraphed the Viceroy, Lord Curzon. Other U.S. missionaries then called him upstart for going over the heads of them all, even the bishops. To approach the Viceroy directly was un-heard of. A cordial reply came from Lord Curzon saying that he understood from his American wife that regulations in the U.S.A. were much broader than here. Mr. Fisher's mistake was a natural one. Then, setting tongues wagging much more wildly than before, an order came down rescinding the em-barrassing regulation and allowing much more latitude for ministers of other than the Anglican communion.

When the new statue of Queen Victoria was unveiled in the city park, the young upstart, Fred Fisher, delivered the in-vocation, by official request.

During the ceremony, an English prince pulled the ribbon to release the silk Union Jack and reveal the awesome pudding face of the Queen-Empress. Nothing happened. The prince gave the ribbon another firm yank, but this time the cord broke in his hand. Victoria's statue remained as veiled as some of her subjects, the Moslem women in their burkas, who watched from among the crowd. Nobody, including Lord Curzon, knew what to do.

On the outskirts of the crowd, the pariahs stood apart. An outcaste urchin in loin cloth and dirty cotton scarf broke away from them and wriggled through to the platform. Fred heard Lord Curzon say to his aides and equerries "Right-o," and the child began to climb the pedestal. Resting on the sovereign's knees, he boosted himself to her shoulders and finally stood upon her regal head. Then he loosened the Union Jack and climbed down again. As ringing cheers echoed through the park, the boy disappeared again in the gathered multitude.

Fred went home meditating. The unknown youngster came to symbolize for him the potential power of fifty million out-castes. They might one day achieve for India all that kings and queens and foreigners and potentates had failed to accom-plish. In later years he used the parable of the boy to help raise a million dollars pledged to interpret Christianity to the outcastes of India.

A visit to Akbar made another impression which lasted all his life. To the sixteenth-century town, Akbar, greatest

Mogul of them all, had brought chosen representatives of the major religions, Hindu pandits, Christian missionaries from Goa, Buddhists, Jains, and Parsees. What might have happened if, in this deserted ancient city of which only seven miles of wall remained, men of good will had succeeded in working out a reconciliation of faiths? What mountains might be moved now if men of different faiths only worked together?

In Agra, Fred invited Hindus and Moslems and anyone else interested in the search for religious truth to come to his house and talk. In these discussions, he garnered wisdom that cast new light on the Christian scriptures for him. "This is the pathway for mystics," he wrote. "It winds through the valleys of human reality and over the hills of vision. Except spiritual imagination accompany thee, enter not by this gate." The worst lack he felt in himself was having no grounding in philosophy, and when Professor Borden Parker Bowne of Boston University, founder of the personalistic school of philosophy, came to Agra, Fred listened in while Dr. Bowne talked with the Indian pandits. He was delighted at the doctor's invitation to travel around India for a while with him. "I would have carried his bags or run errands just to be near him!" he told me later.

Fred combined mystic and intellectual, organizer and administrator, the seeker of inspiration and the practical man in his person. While he studied the East and sought a meeting between East and West, he by no means neglected his mission. Thanks to his sermons, British Tommies began drifting to services in the little white Agra church. Their officers followed and then members of the British nonconformist community in such droves that the church could not hold them. Seated in carriages outside, an overflow audience listened to him through open windows.

"We couldn't find seats for them all," Fred said once, "but you may be sure the deacons passed the baskets around to every carriage during the collection."

The second year he was there, Fred witnessed the Mahg

Mela, a religious festival that epitomized all the power of primitive superstition and ignorant priestcraft in contrast to the beauty and poetry of Hindu life and philosophy.

Every twelfth year, the Kumbh Mela, a supreme festival, was held in the city of Allahabad, at the juncture of India's most sacred rivers, the Ganges and the Jumna. If true believers were there on a special day, once every twelve years, they were blessed with certain unspecified benefits.

Standing on the walls of an old fort, Fred watched the pilgrims packed together in their millions waiting for dawn. As light broke, water carriers standing in the river filled bullock skins and with a deft pressure of their arms squirted water over the crowd. Men and women in the front ranks had been standing for forty-eight hours or more. With cracked, dry lips and gaunt hands they reached for a few drops.

In the brutal undertow of the crowd surging toward the precious sprinkling of water, children, women, and men were hurt, some trampled to death. Their screams and groans, against the background shouts of camel and bullock drivers, were the very sound of human agony.

Fred came away intensely aware of the basic inadequacy of ethnic religions which assigned no importance to human life, failed to value the individual. Christians might not live up to the Golden Rule, but they believed in it. Salvation could only come through the ideal of the individual coupled with universal tolerance.

Although he was early troubled by arthritis, Fred paid no attention to the climate. With his boundless and indestructible energy, he found India a richly varied experience for himself, a challenging field for his endeavors. He would have stayed his five-year term and doubtless doubled it except for Edith's collapse. The difficult climate proved too much for her.

If he felt a sense of loss at leaving, Fred cut it off sharply. As soon as he had taken Edith home to Muncie for her convalescence, he went to see Professor Bowne in Boston to arrange for graduate study in philosophy. To support himself, Fred washed dishes, waited on table, sold gadgets from door to door, and served as supply minister in the district.

Soon he was offered a small mission church in North Cohasset, south of Boston, with seven hundred dollars a year salary and a parsonage. In order to take care of his parish and do his college work both, he followed the advice of John Wesley and rose at four every morning to study by lamplight. He also added to his income by supplying other pulpits now and then.

One Sunday he was flattered to be asked to First Church, Boston, a venerable and distinguished parish.

Later on the bishop of the New England Southern Conference heard that the deacons and elders considered calling Fisher as their next minister. He summoned the key men immediately and said indignantly, "I tell you gentlemen, I will *not* appoint this young man to your church!"

Fred went straight to the bishop. He had preached there once, and that was all, he said. He by no means considered himself eligible at twenty-five for a leap into an important city parish. His experience in foreign missions and country churches did not qualify him. "And, Bishop," he ended, "I'd like you to witness my note saying that I do not wish to go to First Church and prefer that it not come to a vote."

The bishop gulped, sighed, and rescinded his veto. The young man was called to First Church, Temple Street, Boston, with his blessing.

When Fred was a boy, his first summer job had been carrying water to the men working in gas wells. To "shoot a well" after it was drilled, the men dropped in a tin tube of nitroglycerine and then ran for shelter. The dangerous little object with a basket handle on top and a torpedo point was tagged "Don't touch me; I might go off" and called a go-devil. Fred asked the foreman if he could drop the next one.

"What?!!" bellowed the fat man, looking down at the little water-carrier.

"I can run faster than the men," argued Fred.

From then on he dropped all the go-devils.

"I confess," he said as a grown man, "it's been a revealing joy to me to drop go-devils—the song of freedom, the ideal of love, the glory of the Gospel of Christ—down into society. They go off!"

Blithely depositing go-devils from his new Boston pulpit, Fred stirred up many issues.

When he found the back slopes of Beacon Hill crowded with struggling, poverty-stricken immigrants, he set up committees of rich churchmen to provide help. Trust funds were established to continue that help.

Hearing that a Boston woman had just returned from Europe with a thirty-thousand-dollar collar for her dog, he contrasted this with a West End woman whose children were starving. His choler getting the better of him, he thundered against "the disgraceful demonstration of a thirty-thousand-dollar necklace on a thirty-dollar dog led around the streets by a thirty-cent woman!"

The papers carried the startling sermon and Mrs. J., the dog-and-collar owner, sent a demand that the brash young minister deliver a written apology. Fred refused, but offered to call on her. She received him—and later became a heavy contributor to his causes and a personal friend.

Promoting the ideal of church unity on the practical level, he was soon exchanging pulpits with the Unitarian minister, ignoring the protests of the ultraconservatives.

In the interests of the Christian Labor movement, he invited all members of the Boston labor unions to service on Sunday in October. To the astonishment of Back Bay, the response filled the church and the galleries and the vestibule with enthusiastic union men.

At the end of three years, he had finished his graduate work at the University, paid back the money borrowed from Mr. Johnson in Muncie, bought a small country place named Pilgrimthorpe in Hingham, Massachusetts, as permanent home base, and gained a local reputation as a mighty preaching man. Edith was entirely well again and he was ready to go back to foreign missions.

Bowne protested his leaving "Just when you are learning how to preach," but Fred's horizons were wide and he felt the need to stretch his wings. He preferred a return to India, but when his church offered him the job of field secretary to the Board of Foreign Missions he could not refuse. He knew he could do more for India in this work than by going there.

From 1910 on he crisscrossed his own country, covering enough mileage to circle the globe several times over. He helped to collect many millions for missions and he organized, among other things, the spectacularly successful Indianapolis convention for "Militant Methodism" abroad.

In 1917 Fred was chosen to head the campaign for support of the India Mass Movement. This time he felt he must see for himself what was happening in the vast subcontinent he had left a decade before. With Edith he set out for an extended study of the country.

The World War had diverted India's energies away from interior violence. A million Indians had served in the Allied armies and the whole country poured out money and supplies in aid of England and the Empire.

Traveling through the Punjab that spring, Fred went into a village a thousand miles north of Bombay. Usually the advent of a white man caused a stir. Was he here to collect taxes? To judge and punish? For what exercise of his power? This time Fred and his party found the villagers ranged on three sides of the central square, so absorbed that they paid no attention whatever to their visitors. Two local boys, veterans invalided home from France, were talking. One had a pointer and, drawing lines in the sand, explained where Europe was, where France lay in relation to Germany. Both of them spoke of streetcars, automobiles, high buildings, unveiled women, and different manners. As a dramatic climax, one of the soldiers told how during an emergency in the trenches all castes had eaten together.

The effect, thought Fred, of a million men returning from far places would be incalculable.

On this trip, Fred got to know that extraordinary Englishwoman, Annie Besant, leader of the Theosophists. In his opinion, the new Viceroy, Lord Chelmsford, made a sad mistake from his own point of view when he jailed her for seditious utterances from June through September. Fred was impressed with her genuine enthusiasm for Hindu culture, her political sense and gift of oratory, but it was undoubtedly the halo of martyrdom that convinced the members of the Indian Congress, some of whose wives stayed at home in strictest purdah, to elect Mrs. Besant President of the Congress for the ensuing year.

That year also Mr. Montagu, freshly appointed Secretary of State for India, declared that India would be granted many concessions in return for her war effort. Fred believed him when he said he wanted "the gradual development of self-governing institutions . . . progressive realization of responsible government," but how gradual? That was the big question.

India was not in the mood for gradualism. The most important man, the most important influence, in the country was Mohandas Karamchand Gandhi, who in 1914 had returned to India from practicing law in South Africa. Fred saw him first on a train journey from Madras to Calcutta. "No word of his presence had been allowed over government-owned wires," he wrote, "yet the curious grapevine telegraphy of India knows no censor. At every station human seas overflowed our train. Ladders of breathing, sobbing bodies were made so that some might climb to touch or merely see the man spontaneously called Mahatma (Great Soul). Rose petals covered our engine and peasants prayed in the fields as we passed. Every pole, fence and hillock had its worshipers. . . ."

Fred had found his foremost spiritual hero. Gandhi, he felt, was a true man of God, a saintly man. Later he wrote a book about him, *That Strange Little Brown Man, Gandhi* (a title dreamed up in the publisher's office), which was banned by

the British in India and smuggled through to Gandhi himself
in jail. Besides his admiration and respect, as he came to know
Gandhi Fred grew to have enormous personal affection for the
little man.

"How can you help liking a saint who always remembers
to ask about your wife and teases you for taking soda mints
when you eat too much?" Fred asked.

Gandhi was a great tease among his friends. He declared
that Fred was responsible for his silent Mondays. It was on a
Monday, he explained, that Fred Fisher came to see him
once so full of ideas and talking so much so fast that Gandhi
claimed he could not get a word in edgewise. "The rest did me
so much good that I have ever since kept Monday as a day of
silence."

During a discussion of Ahimsa, nonviolence, one time,
Gandhi took Fred's strong, determined chin in his hand.
Twinkling, he said, "Just imagine a man with a chin like yours
talking about peace!"

"And what will people think of a pacifist like you with two
front teeth missing? You look as if you've just been in a
brawl."

Gandhi laughed delightedly at this retort, but when Fred
went on to suggest that he come to Calcutta and permit
Fred's dentist to replace his teeth in the interests not only of
his appearance but his health, Gandhi refused gently. "You
know, Fred, some years ago I renounced personal property
and money. . . . I began to live on the scale that the poorest of
our people must live upon. I have kept my personal expendi-
tures within eleven cents a day. Now, you see, one of our
lowly brothers whom I call Sons of God and others call outcastes could never afford your dentist. I cannot accept, but I
thank you deeply."

Fred believed that Gandhi practiced what Jesus taught while
multitudes of professing Christians called Jesus "Lord, Lord,"
but did not follow Christ's way. This was one of the things he
preached about when he returned to his own country after
this visit to India. (In fact, one fellow complained that "Fisher

sometimes gave us Gandhi for breakfast, lunch, and dinner!")

The war was over when Fred completed his work in the U.S. for the Indian Mass Movement. He was then assigned to the Interchurch World Movement, which proposed to conscript for peace and construction the same vital energy that had been devoted during the war to heroism and self-sacrifice.

As head of the Industrial Relations Department of Interchurch, Fred met with the directors in Cleveland on May 1, 1919. After the morning session, the large group of business leaders, professional men, scholars, and clergymen broke up for lunch.

A Socialist-Labor parade turned into the Cleveland public square that noon. One veteran in uniform marched carrying a red flag. A lieutenant on the sidewalk snatched the flag and trampled it. To quell the rioting that followed, mounted police charged the crowd. The reserves were called out and army tanks and trucks thundered through the streets.

No one there could ever forget the sights and sounds of that prolonged lunchtime interval. Clubs descended on flesh, rearing horses plunged among the people, citizen battled citizen. Violence was loose in the public square and one man was killed and several hundred, including two Interchurch officials, were injured.

When the delayed afternoon session did take place, industrial relations was foremost on the agenda. Fred recommended a firsthand, impartial study of industrial disputes and, on September twenty-second when the steel strike began, he acted.

Appointing a commission of inquiry of the best and most fearless men he could find, he asked them to search only for truth. The resultant Steel Strike Report made history, contributing greatly in the end to the reduction of the twelve-hour working day. Seventeen years later, when all that it accomplished had long since been taken for granted, the man who wrote the report paid tribute to the courage displayed by Fred and its other sponsors.

"A commission of lawyers, of legislators, by my experience,

would have weaseled out, and scientists would have qualified.
These churchmen, faced by the simple 'This is the truth, shall
the word be spoken?'—although with some 'Lord-help-me's'
voted aye. Thus conscience does not make cowards of us all!"

As soon as Fred's commission was established, detectives
and spies started shadowing him. The Ohio Manufacturers'
Association came out with a statement that the Reverend
Mr. Fisher had only recently dropped the c from Fischer and
was secretly pro-German. Also, as if this were insufficiently
damning in those days, he was a Bolshevik. A more elaborate
and subtle attack financed by the Steel Corporation asserted
that Fisher was a radical and furthermore showed "a strong
trend toward mysticism," although what the two accusations
had to do with each other was never explained.

A special committee composed of John D. Rockefeller,
James W. Kinnear, and others of equally unassailable position investigated these charges and exonerated Fred. The Ohio
Manufacturers' Association was forced to print an abject
apology. Meantime his own church stood by him in the most
spectacular manner. At the age of thirty-eight, Fred was elected
to the Episcopacy of the Methodist Episcopal Church by the
highest vote on record. He was the youngest bishop in a century,
since the pioneer days of Coke, Janes, and Roberts.

Asked where he wanted to be sent, he said "to India."

The youngest bishop and his wife arrived in Bombay in late
October 1920. To the dismay of some and the delight of
others, he announced immediately, "When you agree on the
Indian whom you would like to have as bishop, I shall not only
do all I can to help you elect him, but I promise to resign and
turn over my office to him!"

As an American, he could take no part in the Nationalist
aspirations which had fired all of India, but he could work for
self-determination within the Indian Methodist Church. He
began at once by appointing as many Indians as possible to
head missionary schools and colleges.

The headquarters for his see was in Calcutta, but Fred was
taking no chances on Edith's health, good as it seemed after

her long stay in the U.S. The intense heat begins about the middle of March in India and increases until in May everything that grows on the plains withers and dies and human beings not born to its endurance wilt into a sad semblance of themselves. In March Fred arranged for the other Methodist bishops in India and for Indian church leaders to meet him there, and took Edith to Darjeeling, a hill station in the Himalayas with an inspiring view of Everest.

When the monsoons break, about the middle of June, the white man can safely return to sea level. A few days before Fred and Edith were to leave Darjeeling, she helped an outcaste mother carry her sick baby to the dispensary. A few hours later she came down with typhus and in three days she was dead. Fred mourned his wife deeply and had these words carved on her tombstone in Calcutta: "She died serving."

Plunging into his work, he preached and talked and met with churchmen the length and breadth of India, urging his countrymen especially to "keep up with India." His reputation as a great Christian liberal grew each month.

One day in his study in Calcutta a British visitor was announced by his houseboy. Fred could not place the young man whose face seemed familiar. "Haven't we met before?" he asked him.

"I don't think so, sir," said the Englishman, "but you may have seen me. I have heard every sermon you preached and every lecture you gave for the last six months."

"Now that's remarkably faithful of you and almost too flattering," said Fred, amazed, and sure the young man could not possibly have followed his peregrinations.

"Oh, it's been no hardship to hear your sermons," said the embarrassed man, "but last night you talked on motherhood and I felt such a beastly cad I decided to come this morning and make a clean breast of the whole thing. You see, Bishop, I work for the C.I.D. and this is on the books against you."

He laid a memorandum on Fred's desk: "In the confidential report of the C.I.D. dated January 1, 1921, it is considered that Bishop Fisher of Thoburn Methodist Episcopal Church in

Calcutta is a most dangerous Bolshevik and was sent to this country under an American passport under the guise of a Bishop to carry on his teaching. His movements are being watched."

"I'd be grateful if you would let me get back to England before you make this known," said the C.I.D. agent. "I have been so moved by your sermons that I want to get out of this damnable business of spying on men like you."

When the man had left the country, Fred took the matter up with the American consul-general, who took it up with Lord Reading, the Viceroy, who invited Fred to visit him in Simla and discuss the matter.

The charge was erased from the books of the C.I.D. and, as was usual with Fred, it was the beginning of a good friendship between himself and Lord Reading.

One primary difficulty developed as he worked in India, dropping go-devils of thought and spiritual challenge throughout the church he was trying to make strong and independent. The pledges made in the U.S. to carry on the mission were breaking down. Funds were exhausted. An "I Will Maintain" campaign was planned by the Mission Board and Fred was asked to come home and help. After a meeting in Singapore to discuss the work of the church in the Pacific Basin with all the bishops of eastern Asia, he went on to San Francisco.

I myself remember well the last of the "Bishop Fred B. Fisher dinners" in aid of the nationwide campaign. It was held at the Commodore Hotel in New York on October 30, 1922, and Fred's irresistible eloquence reduced my meager bank account by a hundred dollars, ten times what I could possibly afford.

3

By May 1924, when our courtship and the Methodist General Conference occurred simultaneously in Springfield, Massachusetts, Fred had long been a widower. It was perfectly proper for an unattached woman of virtue to set her cap for the bishop from India. That was just it. I had gone to hear him speak that spring every time I could and I knew I was falling in love with him. It did not bother me that I was over forty, a little older and a little taller than this man with the spirit of a giant and the sturdy, short body and impressive head. He was easy to idolize and I suspected that many women did. But I knew of myself that if I let myself I would love him so deeply I would never get over it.

Fred kept eyeing me, too. He told me later he had always known that I was a woman he could love. One day he came to the office of *World Neighbors* during working hours and asked for me. We sat there and talked of this and that and everything, formally enough, casually enough, and he asked me to go to the theatre with him that night. And I refused! Maybe I was trying to protect myself from my own heart.

My friends had hoped for years, volubly, that the day would come when Welthy Honsinger gave in to love. They found my spinsterhood absurd. But when those closest to me guessed that I was more than a little interested in Fred Fisher, they warned me. He was fine and splendid, but too maverick, too engrossed in India, too committed and absorbed. I would be asked to bury myself in another Oriental country, after I had given so much of myself to China.

In that spring, my dear sister Mabel died. She had returned not long before from China, where she had gone back to teach music and where one of her pupils had written the anthem used for China after Sun Yat-sen died. We understood each other better than any other two members of my family, she and I. I loved her wit and her artistic talents, and we enjoyed the same things and people. It was a blow to the heart when she died, and afterward Fred reproached me for not telling him. He would have conducted her funeral service himself, he said, and comforted me.

Instead I lay awake for many nights, my loneliness compounded by her loss. I was aware I might have cut myself off from the man I could love by refusing to go to the theatre that night and I might regret this as long as I lived.

So I wrote to Bishop Frederick Bohn Fisher. He kept the letter and quoted it to me often, teasing and loving. In it I told him I was coming to the General Conference and planned to stay at the Hotel Bridgeway. (I never dreamed he had taken a room there, too. It was not a very expensive hotel.) I added—forthright, or forward?— "Please look me up and give me a ring. I can't bear it if you don't!"

When I arrived he was in the lobby of the Bridgeway, waiting, and the third evening we had dinner together alone. The miracle is that he managed it at all. A bishop at a church conference is in demand, and Fred was not only one of the most popular among them, but his parents were with him.

The first day I saw Fred's father and mother in the two seats reserved in the gallery for his guests. The official members of the conference were on the floor and the elder Fishers leaned over from their aisle position in the front row upstairs to look for their dear son. On the second day they left for home before I had a chance to meet them, and Fred invited me to use his tickets.

I was grateful, because tickets were at a premium and accepted joyfully. Then I got skittish. How would it look? Miss Honsinger sitting up there, tall and looming in the bishop's front seats. I asked an old friend, a minister's wife, to come with me without explaining that I felt the need of cover and chaperonage at my age. To my distress, at intermission she said she must leave. Before I could say, "Oh, don't leave me alone," she was gone.

Ten seconds later the Bishop of India and Burma burst down the aisle, smiled like an angel and sat down beside me. You could almost hear the murmur that went up, feel the indrawing of breath all over the crowded auditorium.

I hope I did not look as flustered as I felt, but I said, "Do you realize, Fred Fisher, that there are one thousand pairs of eyes staring at us?"

"Wonderful," said Fred happily and clearly. "Wonderful. Just what I want. I want to be sure they all know it's my seats you're sitting in."

How could you resist a man like that?

When the afternoon session ended, Fred steered me firmly through the mass of Methodists from all over the world who wanted a word with him. He bundled me into a car and we left them behind, buzzing no doubt. And with reason. In the car, with the driver attentively listening to every word, my man proposed—and I accepted.

I tell each generation of girls I meet not to fear leading independent lives. I generalize, of course, from me. The gamble was whether I could eat and have my cake. I wanted to do the work I did, and I found in the end the man who loved me for this and also for me, for all of me. When I married him, I knew I could help him with the things that were important to us both. It was well worth waiting for.

Don't think ours wasn't a love story just because we were middle-aged and he was a bishop. Coming together because of mutual beliefs and work didn't make us sedate and sensible. No romance was ever more bedazzled and we were head over ears in love.

"I'm going to take you to India as fast as we can get there," said Fred with shining enthusiasm, "and we are going to have the greatest life two people ever had!"

In that town awash with Methodists and friends who knew

us both, we had to wait for dark to seal our engagement. Then
Fred took me out to the middle of the long bridge across the
Connecticut River. Behind a large pillar, he kissed me for the
first time.

The announcement of our engagement was a high spot
of the Methodist Conference. I had no sooner told a friend
than the bishops' wives descended. It was fitting and proper
that the formal announcement be made in their company, at a
tea they would give for me. Our romance was blessed by the
Episcopacy's kind ladies.

Even though we were smiled upon by those gathered together in the sight of God to do the work of the church, we
had precious little opportunity to see each other alone. We
dined together when we could, in inconspicuous restaurants,
and then walked out on the bridge to the same pillar, "ours"—
and kissed each other again, confirming the fact that we two
would soon be one.

When we both got back to New York, I was living at the
Allerton House for Women and he at the Commodore Hotel.
We still had no place to be alone, and began a pattern of
walking in Central Park at night. Bishop MacDowell of Wash-
ington was to marry us and he wired Fred suggesting a date
in July. Fred exploded. "I have no intention of waiting that
long and never seeing you alone except on bridges and in
parks!" he said crossly, and wired back asking for June. Bishop
MacDowell's reply was charmingly sympathetic: ALL RIGHT
WITH ME STOP MAKE IT JUNE STOP I SHOULD THINK ANYBODY
MARRYING WELTHY HONSINGER WOULD WANT TO DO IT SOON
STOP MACDOWELL

That night after walking a mile or two in the park, matching
strides as good walkers do, we sat down on a bench to make
our wedding plans. One question needed resolving. My cousin,
Dorinda, was having the announcements made. Tiffany said
firmly that since these announcements were going to many
lands, Fred should be engraved as the Right Reverend Frederick Bohn Fisher. Reverend Bishop was the common usage in
the Methodist provinces. But though some of his brethren

might be shocked, Fred said, "Old darling, this is your wedding. You and your cousin have it the way you want it." We did not care where the chips fell. We were in seventh heaven, and nothing seemed to matter much except us.

As we sat there on the bench, reverting happily to the sentimental foolishness proper to engagements, a policeman came up and said, "Move along there, people. It's time to go home!"

Since we were officially engaged, I could follow Fred about when he toured to make speeches in the weeks that remained. My admiration skyrocketed. Each talk was different, the fresh outpourings of a limitless mind. Each was inspiring. And then later we would be together a little while and I would learn that this powerful and brilliant man was as sensitive as a woman. We were two strong personalities joining our lives, but we knew that neither of us would bruise the other.

To him privately I became his Han and he was my Bohn, or —because we were very foolish and sentimental at times—my Bohnny boy.

Just before the wedding, one of my closest friends said to me, "But, my dear, aren't you afraid to marry a man who lives by such leaps? Do you think you can hold him down?"

"I don't want to hold him down," I said. "I'll leap with him!"

4

We were married on June 18, 1924 by Bishop MacDowell, the quiet wedding given for me by my cousin, Mrs. William H. Bliss. In our party were Fredericka Kiang, a Chinese girl with a Phi Beta Kappa key from Vassar, and Evangeline Thillayam, an Indian with a Ph.D. from Columbia.

A honeymoon in the U.S. would have turned hectic. There were too many churches to be dedicated, summer assemblies to be addressed, special missions urged on Fred. We spent a few days at Lake Mohonk, where we could be quiet and alone, away from everybody, even the clustering fellow passengers we would inevitably meet on shipboard when we sailed from Vancouver for India via China a little later.

This was a rare time of alone-together. There seemed no end of talking as we rode, swam, walked, or sat in our room or on the veranda catching up with all the years we'd spent apart. We thought of our future as an extended and infinite honeymoon. (And it was.)

From Lake Mohonk we went to the Cape to visit Fred's only property, the small farm in Hingham, and then, in a Model T Ford, drove all over the Cape. No day or night was long enough to encompass the understanding that grew and expanded and deepened every moment.

Several times Fred had to interrupt our days for a speech or a meeting. There were a few complaints that he had neglected his homework for one or another meeting, but he cheerfully explained, "I've been too busy loving Welthy!" They forgave him and I became "Welthy" to them all.

156

My Bohn insisted that he had married not only his Han but also the 450 million Chinese with whom I felt kin. He had been in China briefly twice during his peregrinations but only in the coastal cities and now he wanted to know my people, meet my adopted children, visit my inland city.

We boarded the Canadian Pacific steamer with fairly balanced luggage. Fred carried more books even than I did, being an omnivorous reader who snatched every odd moment to poke his inquisitive nose into printed pages. I certainly carried more of a wardrobe. As long as Fred had one excellent suit for state occasions, a few well-worn garments bought originally at the cheapest men's store in Boston sufficed. In his case, the clothes certainly did not make the man. The only reform I secretly planned as a wife was to dress the bishop better.

When we anchored in Shanghai Harbor, in August 1924, the Captain sent down word that passengers going ashore did so entirely at their own risk. Shanghai was on the verge of another revolution.

Sun Yat-sen was still alive, though keeping pretty much to his own southern province of Kwantung and its capital, Canton, where he was training young leaders to take over the revolution from his ailing hands. Among them was Chiang Kai-shek, who was appointed principal of the Whampoa Military Academy. Insiders claimed that he would surely be Sun Yat-sen's successor.

Perhaps the most important thing that was happening was the rising of Soviet Russia's red star to ascendency in China. In the treaty between the two countries, Russia was the first Western power to give up the extraterritorial rights seized by the West a century earlier, rights which rankled deep in every Chinese breast. As a result, the first national congress had reorganized the Kuomintang along Soviet lines, Chinese Communists were permitted to join, and Russia was asked to direct the establishment of the Whampoa Military Academy. I mourned with Fred that it was not England and France and the U.S. who had made so important and effective a gesture toward the Chinese nation, torn and divided as it was.

Chinese war lords were embattled over much of the country. In the North, the Chihli-Mukden war raged. Peking was in the hands of Wu Pei-fu, outspoken enemy of Sun Yat-sen. The Christian general, Feng Yu-hsiang, was planning a coup to rout Marshal Wu.

Nevertheless we landed. I was an old China hand and I knew that my Bohn could get along anywhere with anybody as an individual. As a matter of fact, he behaved like a boy on holiday. He talked to everybody and acted up, even when he spoke with philosophers. I had quite a time managing him at all or keeping up with him when he needed an interpreter. He wanted to see everything, know everybody, go everywhere.

Without any hesitation we took the Yangtze river steamer to pass through two revolutions into the calm interior.

The panoramic beauty of real China, away from the treaty ports and foreign devils, unfolded for Fred as we sat together on the boat's deck. Of course I talked of my early adventures and when we crossed Lake Poyang Fred insisted that the boat-man haul down sail and drop anchor each time we came to a commemorative spot: over the water where my bricks had sunk and my precious piano was inundated, in the isolated cove where I rode out the terrible storm. Ours was perfect weather, honeymoon weather of unclouded sunshine and moonlit nights.

At the Da Shen gate outside the walls of Nanchang we were met by the city's few Americans and by an immense crowd of Chinese. Thousands of firecrackers popped such a welcome that we could scarcely hear the speeches. Fred loved Bao Lin and admired the lovely structures built with the money I collected in the U.S. after the fire. I was eager to show him everything, but most important of all was the sight of my first adopted child. Precious Pearl had grown into a beautiful young girl and her immense lovely eyes were astonishing.

That night when we were alone in our bedroom, Fred

said, "Hmmmm. Those eyes are not very Chinese, my dear. I think you put one over on me!"

I could only laugh at him as a rascal. I knew nothing whatever of Precious Pearl's forebears.

"What a contrast to India," Fred went on, discussing our day as we always did. "There they hang jasmine garlands around your neck and recite their welcomes softly. Here— what a racket!"

"Firecrackers express happiness in China," I said. "The Chinese invented gunpowder, but not for killing people. It was to go bang in honor of birth and death and for welcoming friends home."

Nanchang was a real provincial capital, unconnected with the outside world, and it had not changed. There were still no telephones, no railroads; the sewage system was the army of men with night soil in buckets hung from bamboo poles, the water system a chain of wells without pumps. The city had never signed a treaty with any foreign power and was free. Fred was its first visitor from India and the gentry, officials, and scholars poured out from behind the walls or asked him in.

How far had scientific thought penetrated into Indian philosophical thinking, they wanted to know. Was the nationalist movement in India truly Oriental, or did it owe much to Western influence and backing? Fred was surprised by this last question. It came from Chinese who feared that the entrenchment of the war lords meant that China could attain unity only with the aid of foreign devils.

What about literacy, they asked. Did Bishop Fisher really think that people, ordinary people, were better for reading? Did India find this necessary? Were there telephones in India? In fact, wasn't India very much like the International Settlement in Shanghai? Did all the people of India look like Shanghai cops [the Sikh policemen]? What was Gandhi like? Wasn't he really a Buddhist?

Charmed with Nanchang, Fred wanted to go farther into the undisturbed interior back of the city, where during centuries nothing had changed. We planned a trip to the famous old town of King Tehchen, where for two thousand years the entire population had devoted itself to making fine porcelain.

My old cook, Tsung Tse-fu, who had crossed Poyang to meet us in Kiukiang although he was almost blind, arranged for a sailing junk. Even the smallest was too large and heavy for the upper river, so we had to transfer to a flat-bottomed boat which was poled, not rowed, and could ride the rapids. For the last two days of the trip we lived under a curved matting in the bow. When the men at the poles came to a sharp bend, they had to look through the matting tunnel and would shout in Chinese, "Down on your stomachs!" Fred and I, neither of us fat but both of us bulky, obediently flattened ourselves. Lying prone with our heads hanging over the edge of the boat, we looked down into the bed of the river. There we saw masses of broken porcelain in a thousand colors. We realized, with awe, that this was the accumulated breakage of all history. The Sung and Ming dynasty vases, all the precious Chien Lungs, examples of which are the pride of museums in New York, London, and Paris, had been brought along this river and over these rapids in just such fragile boats as ours.

For currency to use on land, we carried Mexican dollars worth their weight in silver anywhere. Three hundred U.S. dollars had magically become a thousand Mexican and gained ten thousandfold in weight. Tsung Tse-fu packed them in a wooden box in which we had brought two dozen cans of Carnation milk from America and hired Chao as extra man to carry the load. When Chao was tired, he deposited the box in the street wherever he was and sat on it. We created something of a sensation and people always rushed from homes, studios, and kilns to see the two "ocean men."

Invariably they asked Chao, "What thing you carrying in box?"

"A thousand dollars, no less," he replied laughing.

"Won't we be robbed, telling the entire countryside that he carried a fortune?" asked Fred.

But civilization in this teeming backwater was placid, dignified, and trusting.

"Oh, no," I told Fred. "The safest way is to let everybody know what you are doing in Old China. We're as safe as though we were in heaven."

Fred found the rural life heaven. He kept me busy translating his questions to the village pundits wherever we tied up for the night. All of them answered him with characteristic courtesy. Delightedly he planned to spend a sabbatical year with me among them. We would rent a junk, fix it up as a simple houseboat, and sail lazily along the rivers of the interior. Aboard the boat he could write his memoirs, ashore he could mingle to his heart's content with these people.

Easy victim to their charm, he understood the way their minds worked. In spite of his deep attachment to India, I think it would have been easy for him to stay in China.

We left King Tehchen with seventeen huge pieces of the glorious porcelain we had watched the artisans making. They were so well packed that they survived unbroken all our long way back to Calcutta.

To leave Nanchang again was not the wrench it had been before. I was going on to new adventures with the most adventurous man alive.

As we sailed across Poyang and through the rocky gorge where the Buddhists built their ranging monasteries up the steep slopes, Fred said, "Buddhism is the only power that has ever completely captured China. Her art and architecture, her culture and philosophy are saturated with it." Then he added wistfully, "How long will it take Christianity to become indigenous in this fascinating country?"

On the way across oceans to India, we stopped for four days in Manila. Fred and I both knew the islands. He had gone there in 1917 on a missionary tour, and I, oddly enough, was there in the same year studying their educational system.

Fred wanted to check up on the *Iglesia Filipina Independiente*, an Independent Catholic Church movement under

the leadership of Archbishop Aglipay. He had feared that the
movement might trigger rebellion against the American government and thus interfere with our Protestant missions to
the islands. Pleased with what actually happened, he recommended that this church be approached by us as a religious
opportunity and integrated into American plans for Philippine
autonomy. "It is a protesting and independent church," he
said.

Our next-to-last stop was in Singapore, which we took for
granted was impregnable, and our last was in Ceylon. From
the tip of India we traveled by rail to Calcutta.

It's not too hard to be a good traveler on shipboard and
Fred had proved that this applied to him even in rowboats.
(What a contrast between him and my Lady-Interested-in-
Missions as companion on a Poyang junk!) I thought I was a
pretty hardy, happy traveler myself, but on this first of the
many thousands of miles we were to cover on India's primitive
railroads, I found out how much I had to learn from him.

After long, exhausting hours over hot dusty landscape with
nothing to see, the screeching of the flat wheels began to drive
me crazy.

"Now, Han," Fred said, "just get into the rhythm of that
squeak, old darling. Make it a song."

He tried two or three old hymns until he found one that
matched that squawking, squeaking cadence. From then on
the rusty wheels sang "Faith of Our Fathers" for me, too.

Fred was an impatient, sometimes testy man (especially
when his arthritis bothered him), but he never would let petty
annoyances disturb his enjoyment of daily life.

I remember the first time I was subjected to a hot-weather
bird so exasperating it was called the "Brain Fever Bird." Its
endlessly reiterated refrain made white sahibs, already jumpy
with the relentless heat, go quite out of their heads. Fred told
me to listen carefully to its horrid shriek.

"Hear? The bird's shouting, 'Hallelujah, I love you!' "

What woman could resist a man like that?

5

In an optimistic misconception based on my Puritan name, the reporter said that the Right Reverend Frederick Fisher had married the "wealthy Miss Honsinger." Fred owned nothing more than his Hingham home, often as not mortgaged when he needed money for a mission survey or something, and I had only my elegant trousseau, the income from a small trust fund provided by my cousin, and the beautiful Chinese things I had collected in Nanchang bazaars (the best ones, lost in the fire, were never replaced). I hoped they would settle for me without that *a* in Welthy.

Rich or poor, my position as bishop's wife in India took a little getting used to. As former mistress of Bao Lin and as a lecturer on international affairs, I was accustomed to public life, but the difference now was as marked as my title. No longer Miss or Little Sister or even plain Mrs. Fisher, I was "My lady" as Fred was "My lord." Calcutta was a very British city, grown from a fishing village after the East India Company came there.

We were, of necessity, Personages, and our house was a public place. My first job was to furnish it appropriately. Fred had told me that two rooms were already fixed up in the six-room apartment we were to live in. It did not sound too formidable.

The apartment house had been bought by the church as regional headquarters. It was on Middleton Street, near the main thoroughfare, the Chowringhee, and the huge Maidan Park. Next door was the mansion of the Maharajah of Burdwan (he was a very nice neighbor) and nearby was the

Viceroy's palace. When I saw our apartment I was aghast. They were enormous, those rooms, twenty by thirty feet or eighteen by twenty-four, with dark red concrete floors and ceilings over twenty feet high. Enormous electric fans dropped from the ceilings on rods. As you entered a room, you switched them on. Except from mid-January to mid-February, our courtesy "winter," life would have been unendurable without those whirring fans stirring the thick, hot air.

I had survived the great heat of China, but such year-round discomfort was different. Calcutta lies a foot below sea level at a latitude of 21 degrees. Mark Twain said of the humid city that it has two seasons: when the door knobs are sticky and when they run.

Our lives were tempered to the heat—as whose there were not? Soon after dawn a barefoot bearer in his white turban and long white coat waked us with two trays of *chota hazri* (little breakfast of tea, toast, and bananas) which he thrust under the mosquito net beside each of us. We read and meditated or talked quietly as we ate. Sometimes we took our trays out on the small veranda where the crows joined us and tried to steal our bananas, but more often we stayed in bed. There no crows but my husband occasionally conspired to rob me of breakfast when I was not looking. I would reach for my tea and find the cup empty. Wondering how and when I had drunk it, I would catch him twinkling and find out that he had switched his empty cup for my full one. At seven, Sur Babu, Fred's Brahmin secretary, arrived, and the busy day began.

Anything that required physical effort had to be completed before the noon heat crushed the whole city into silence and people slept or lay still behind the closed doors and drawn blinds which even in the morning let in only enough shaded light to work by.

I found fascinating places to shop in Calcutta. There were streets like those in Nanchang named for the wares sold along them: Porcelain, Wood, Carpenters-making-furniture streets. The New Market, no longer new, was a hundred shops nestled under one great roof. You could buy anything there, from meat (which Indians did not eat) to pianos. Cheery little boys slept in the doorways at night and hopped about during the day offering to carry bundles for a pittance.

Officials returning to England often sold off their household goods, and auctions were frequent. From these I acquired our splendid Dutch bed, seven feet long and six feet wide, for which I had an enormous net made. During our siestas we could take our typewriters with us under the net. For the rest of the house I tried to be as Indian as possible, unlike most Americans and Britishers there, who had Indian cabinetmakers copy Grand Rapids or Manchester. I could not resist, though, such treasures as a Spanish *almirah* lined with blue satin and an old Stuart chest.

India has the largest unemployed population in the world and the climate made a long day's work impossible. Thus I had a household staff which seemed very numerous to me, all of whom were needed to perform their separate duties. A sweeper could do nothing but sweep, and so on. Laundry could not be done in the house at all, but must be washed by a certain caste in a particular part of the city. The launderers had a monopoly, a pond, and plenty of rocks. I think it was in Calcutta that Mark Twain quipped that it was the first time he had ever seen people trying to break a rock with a shirt. I soon gave up using my good linen.

Old Baroda, the cook, did the buying of groceries. I am sure he made his percentage from the merchants, but I think it was his right. The money was well earned. He sprinted two miles every day in his bare feet to bargain at market and only at my insistence, when his load was bulky, occasionally used a ricksha to come home in. There was no refrigeration and no kitchen. Kitchens were cook-houses, little mud huts separate from the main building. The stoves made of mud had no chimneys. Our oven was a tin box improvised from two Standard Oil tins and I don't know how Baroda fed us so deliciously. Also he was, luckily for us, a Christian and had no prejudice against meat. It was nice to have beef now and then, though we lived chiefly on chicken and fish and never served meat when Hindu guests were present.

Baroda fixed tiffin at noon and then the whole city lay down. Workmen slept where they happened to be. The bazaars were still as deserts and the streets empty. Even the sacred cows wandering along the main thoroughfares lay down in what shade they could find.

Our "living doorbell" curled up on his veranda to be ready for four or five o'clock when life began again. He was an out-caste boy about fifteen, schooled enough to read names on cards, and was a necessary part of a household where no bells were installed and no doors locked and where chits carried about by hand served instead of telephones. I dressed him up in a red velvet embroidered cap, a little red coat, and white trousers with stripes down the sides. He was a charming Buttons and everyone loved him.

We cut down as much as we could on the life in our British quarter where tea, tennis, golf, rugby on the Maidan, dinner parties, and bridge took up the time from five o'clock on, but a bishop must entertain and be entertained. At least we did not have to serve liquor—the bachelor bishop of the Anglican Church (the Metropolitan) ran up a whiskey bill of some nine hundred rupees a month.

I remember getting into an argument once at a formal British banquet. Each of us had three or four wine glasses and when I turned mine over so they would not be filled, the official on my right remarked, "Of course you people have the Statue of Liberty but no liberty." This was when Prohibition was the law of our land, and I replied with some asperity, "Quite the contrary, Sir George. We have so much liberty we are free to refuse alcoholic drinks, not like your poor little clerks who pile up drink bills in order to be like the others. No, no, we're free!"

My friends in China had commented on a change in me. "What has happened to Welthy? All through dinner she never said a word!" The change didn't hold good when I was sitting out of earshot of Fred. I had not become subdued or taken any conversational veil, it was just that he was the most interesting talker I had ever listened to in my life. Silent to hear every word he said, mine was a lively silence, tribute from a chatterbox to a fascinating man. When I was separated from him, I was apt, as ever, to take part in any discussion going—even when the other women kept quiet during religious or political arguments. I was not much of a theologian or politician, but Fred loved it because I could hold up my end.

We lived in concentric rings of Calcutta's society. There were the faculty professors—many from Calcutta University, then the largest in the country, with thirty thousand students and a very modern curriculum. Of the Christian colleges, some were run by Scotch missionaries, highly intellectual men, spiritual descendants of such giants as William Carey, who learned the languages of India and the ways of the people, and Alexander Duff, who actually started Calcutta University in the old days. British university colleges abounded.

There were many churches, Christian churches and cathedrals, mosques, Hindu temples, Jain temples, and hundreds of religious groups. Fred liked nothing better than to spend evenings with non-Christian thinkers and spoke whenever he could in their crowded town halls.

In fact, though we were separated somewhat from the life of the city's mass of people by the demands of Fred's position, most of our congenial friends were Indian.

We knew a great many of the Calcutta Brahmo Samajists, a society that went back to the days of those first intellectual Christian missionaries. These men had converted so many Indians to Western thought, the Brahmins felt that too many were becoming Christians. Ram Mohan Roy founded a church to be all-Indian and called it the Brahmo Samaj. Christ was adored, and one of the greatest tributes to our Lord was written by its Keshab Chandra Sen, but it was not a Christian church. Some of India's early reformers came from among the members. Their wives and daughters gave up purdah and caste and both men and women were broadly educated.

My own closest friends were among the followers of Gandhi.

The two ladies Devi (no relation to each other) were as dear as sisters.

Sarala Devi was a niece of the poet Tagore, whom my husband loved so and whom I too was to know and love. She was a proud woman and did not want her sons to be colonials, barred from all the top places in the life of the country. Deciding that the only answer to the force of imperial government was force, she had raised them as expert fencers and shots. Then, under the influence of Tagore, she went to see Gandhi and told him she was anxious to serve her country.

"I sat with him," she told me, "and he looked at me with sad eyes. At the pearls in my ears and the jewelry around my neck. Then he touched my garments woven of fine linen and gold thread. 'What have you in common with the villager, the untouchable?' he asked me.

"I knew that my uncle was no ascetic and continued to wear his own kind of clothes and live a semi-Western life though he was at one with Gandhi. 'I am an Indian and I want to serve, but must I change?' I asked Gandhi. He said, 'It is for you to decide. If you wish to serve the people you must feel more at one with them.' "

Sarala was still for a moment as if going through the struggle again. She referred to the Bible parable of the rich young man, and went on, "Like him, I turned unhappily away. But one day I went home and took off my gold-threaded gown and high-heeled French shoes and prepared to sell my expensive wardrobe. I began to spin cotton and when I could dress in homespun woven with my own hands, I went back to Gandhi, barefoot in sandals and asked, 'Now may I serve our people?' Since then I have been at one within."

Urmila Devi, whose brother, C. R. Das, would be first Indian Viceroy of India when the day came, had seen the light long before Sarala. She was more flexible in her ways and lived closer to the highest-placed Indians. But at the first congress I attended, in 1925, it was she who cooked the Mahatma's meals when his wife could not come.

When Miss Ting, the first Chinese National Secretary of the YWCA, came through India and stayed with me, I used her as an excuse to mix all sorts of people. Lady Bose, who ran a girls' school in Calcutta, came, and several Scotswomen on the Indian YWCA National Board (which had no Indian members), and the two Devis. How we rattled teacups and enjoyed each other. I was grateful that English was the true lingua franca of India and we needed no interpreters.

During my first weeks, I had on principle begun to study Hindi and Bengali. Unlike China, where the native language is all tones and idioms and utterly alien, the Indian background is in Sanskrit with genders, declensions, tenses and all, readily translatable. I soon found that even the lesser workmen in Calcutta spoke English. It was not in the form of pidgin, that degrading verbal shorthand, either. It might be limited gutter—or, more accurately, sparrow—English or it might be used as if the speaker had swallowed Webster whole, but it served for real communication. Education in English was mandatory in the schools and the Indians added to it local honey. In their soft, mellifluous voices the language sounded as it does nowhere else except below the Mason-Dixon line.

Everybody came to our door sooner or later, but the man we cherished most was, or at least was born, an Englishman. He was a saint, with a saint's face and beard, and his name was Charles F. Andrews. Charlie had come to India an Anglican priest as a young man. His faith in England and her democratic institutions, justice, and freedom, went deep and he could not believe that his country would or could do anything to bar independence to other people. At Delhi and later in Agra, he met the Indian teachers, professors, and social workers, many trained at Oxford or Cambridge, who believed that no foreign government was right for India. The country must be ruled by its own.

After prayer and thought, he resigned his priesthood. "I am still a Christian," he told his distressed bishop. "More so than ever before, but I want to teach the Gospel in India as a servant of India and the Indians." Like My twenty-years-in-China Saint, he gave up his life to them and wherever and whenever Indians were in trouble he packed his battered suitcase and went to them—all over India or South Africa, the Fiji Islands or England. Of course he became a Gandhi man, and later served as go-between for Gandhi and the British Prime Minister.

The first day I met him, in the fall of 1924, he had just come back from Gandhi's famous forty-day fast in Poona.

Fred asked a hundred intent and eager questions and Charlie, his face lighted with glory, told us of those days in the house of Mohammed Ali, one of the Moslems who worked with Gandhi for the independence and freedom of India.

"The things that so many people in the world were doing at the moment seemed petty while this great man of love, this man of God, was letting his life go for unity, for harmony, for love among the brothers who separated themselves into Hindus and Moslems. He seemed near death. Even his powerful will and intensity of purpose could not be enough, we feared, to raise that frail, feeble body from the little rope bed to be the great leader he will have to be. We all came close to weeping and then hung our heads for shame at the little we were doing."

"What was your part, during the fast?" asked Fred.

"I was Gandhi's nurse because his wife could not be there, and I was also the doorkeeper." Charlie laughed a little, thinking of the time when he had been made Gandhi's treasurer, but could not refrain from giving anything he had to anyone who asked for it. Gandhi had gently taken this job away from him. "They seemed to think I could keep out his adorers and disciples better than an Indian could. I don't know about that, but I did my best. At the end, all of us tried our hardest to persuade the Mahatma to put just a little salt in his water, to take just a little orange juice."

We waited, breathless, as if wondering whether the Great Soul had died.

"When the fast ended," said Charlie, "and we knew he would live, the Mahatma looked over at me and said, 'Charlie, I want you to sing my favorite Christian hymn.' He had been near death and sacrifice had been his passion. There was no one with whom I could compare him except Christ himself. I sang 'When I survey the wondrous cross/On which the Prince of Glory died/My richest gain I count but loss/And pour contempt on all my pride. . . .' "

As Charlie ceased speaking, there was silence in the room. All three of us were praying and meditating on the fast. Charlie said only, very softly, "Gandhi once answered a question by saying 'I consider myself a Hindu, Christian, Moslem, Jew, Buddhist, and Confucian.' He has certainly made me more of a Christian than ever in my life before."

At the end of our meditation, my practical husband asked, "How is he now? All right?"

"Of course," said Charlie. "He can live through these things."

Charlie was a visitor whom Buttons never bothered to announce. He came when he wished and left when he was ready. Our home was his.

Fred and I tried to work out a program for home life that would give us as much time to ourselves as we could thieve from a bishop's schedule. We always kept our morning quiet hour. How I wish I had a tape of only a few of those deep, intimate conversations, but when we were silent we spoke even more closely together. Every day my Bohn was full of ideas. Some were possible to carry out at once, but no matter what he proposed, I was inclined to begin the first step before he finished talking about it. "You don't have to do it now, honey," he would say. "Let's wait and talk some more."

On afternoons when he came in weary from financial committee meetings or other onerous chores, he often said, "Han, old darling, be a British wife!" And I took off his shoes and loosened or changed his socks for him, brought his slippers, made him tea, and kept everyone away from him for a little while.

Whenever we could we dined alone, at nine, and afterward walked for miles in the Maidan, long happy walks in the cool of late nights.

Fred suffered even more than I did from the heat with which the Indians lived in an at-homeness inherited from their forebears. In May, before the steaming monsoons of June broke the worst of it, the only sound in houses, banks, shops, and offices was the occasional flutter of papers under brass paperweights and the whish and murmur of fans. Even a raised voice took too much energy. The Indian slowed to a special tempo, slept long hours, and moved languidly in his comfortable, scant clothing.

It was hard for me to temper my habitual energy to the heat, to buy clothes big and baggy enough to go on over my sweating body as I stood under a fan. It was even harder for Fred, who could not divest himself of his jackets and whose stocky body rejoiced naturally in the freezing winters of Indiana. His greatest longing was for a cool bath. Plumbing in Calcutta was casual and pipes attached to outside walls caught the full force of the sun. Before he went to bed, Fred filled the bathtub and as the water cooled off through the hours of night, I heard him up and splashing two or three times between midnight and dawn.

At least the heat made Calcutta more beautiful than ever, did not wilt and brown it, and this was compensation. On our Sunday-vesper pilgrimage to Edith's grave, we drove down Gol Mohur Avenue, named for the peacock whose colors it outshone. May was a perpetual fete of blossoms, cassias in rose, purple, and gold, jacaranda trees loaded with blue-purple blossoms the color of prestorm tropic skies, acacias in misty yellow. When we got there, we smothered her grave in fragrant blossoms.

A bishop could not stay home for very long, though. His was a far-flung domain. We were forever asking our man Friday, Kamal, to pack the paraphernalia needed to travel in India—bedrolls, pillows, and tiffin basket, to go along with a few clothes, our typewriters, and the all-important tin book trunk that accompanied us everywhere. Then we left Calcutta, at daybreak for an early start or at night for a cool one, and set out for somewhere: Lucknow, Kanpur, Jabalpur, Darjeeling, or by ferry across the Bay of Bengal to the bishop's other province of Burma.

6

No matter where we were going, for how long, or how often we left one place for another, Fred was ready an hour or at the least half an hour ahead of time. I learned to check our accommodations and tickets and to leave Kamal with the luggage in order to join him. Then we sat together and meditated.

What were we going for? What did we hope for, expect to contribute? What did we want to bring home with us in our notebooks, our hearts and lives? Departure was as calm as a prayer.

But not our arrivals! Deputations invariably met us at the station and rushed us without pause into a receiving line. Public Personages are never expected to need privacy, even that of the bathroom. Fortunately Kamal was usually along to take care of our mountain of baggage ("What would Gandhi think?" Fred asked once, chuckling. "Why can't we do with less?"), and I soon got in the habit of making my toilet before we left the train. In those little rooms at the end of the cars, scarcely large enough for my bulk, I came to be an expert on what is inelegantly known as the spit-bath before changing into fresh clothes.

While Fred held conferences with the men, my duties included presiding over the women's meetings. Women missionaries, wives of missionaries, women teachers and nurses, or the wives of teachers and doctors from the church's hospitals and schools all came. It was the custom for the Indian women to be quiet and let the white ladies do all the talking and voting, but custom was not my mistress. "We had a great lift, almost a shock," Mrs. J. R. Chitambar, whose husband

174

became the first Indian bishop, told a group later. "Mrs. Fisher asked the opinion of the Indian women. And she insisted that we stand up and give it. It was the first time."

Fred did all the things he was supposed to, handled conferences, finances, internecine struggles, tended the temporal and spiritual well-being of his flock and preached in the box buildings our church put up all over the place in complete disregard of indigenous architecture and local traditions. But he had a much broader conception of his function in India. He wanted to cooperate with *all* Indians who were groping for a better life. His influence in promoting the Christ-way began to be felt in wholly new ways.

One January we went to the Bengal village of Bolpur, two hours by train from Calcutta, where mango trees shade the baked earth and bamboo screens the jungle from sight. Met by the usual deputation, we were garlanded with marigolds as we stood bareheaded on the station platform. Indian heads popped from every carriage window in curiosity to see who these Sahibs might be.

In the bare, nondescript building which was our church, Indians and missionaries of the Bolpur Conference were buzzing, for even in India a church acquires an accelerated tempo if it is administered by Americans. Fred added glow and color to energy and faith as he led the people in meditation and worship.

The morning that his theme was "Character Marks of the Modern Christian" he first noticed a young Hindu Brahmin watching him and listening with peculiar intensity. A day or so later the young man accosted him as Fred was leaving the chancel.

"I am Sudha Kanta," he said in a soft voice. "May I speak with you for a moment, Bishop? I have heard every word you have spoken here this week and I wish to be ordained with your other minister-candidates tomorrow."

"Ordained!" exclaimed Fred. "Are you a Christian?"

"No," said Sudha Kanta. "I am a Hindu, but I want to follow your Christ and interpret Him to my people."

Fred looked into the eyes of this Indian who wore a white khaddar dhoti, a piece of cloth draped at the hips and hanging to the knees, a collarless shirt with tails hanging loose, and a homespun shawl thrown gracefully over his shoulders. Most Indians turning to Christianity adopt European clothes, but Fred was looking into his soul. Using the words of John Wesley, he said to the Indian, "If thy heart be as my heart—give me thy hand."

Sudha Kanta Roy Chaudhuri, former librarian at Tagore's University at Shantiniketan, did not wish to be baptized or to disenfranchise himself from his Hindu community. He had accepted the Christian message as his ideal. How could he serve?

Fred Fisher considered it his privilege and responsibility to help non-Christians realize common ideals rather than trying only to convert them to outward orthodoxy. On that Sunday, he consecrated Sudha Kanta to a new form of service. Laying his hands on the head of the Hindu Brahmin kneeling before him at the altar of our church, he said: "Sudha Kanta Babu, I set thee apart as a social servant of Jesus Christ and may His living presence guide you."

A typical Bengali town, Suri, eighty miles from Calcutta, was selected for Sudha Kanta's experiment in this form of service. He took his family and household goods there and rented a small house. In a short while he had shattered local complacency and tradition by making friends of Brahmins and outcastes alike.

One sultry day in June an outcaste dropped dead on the main street of Suri and the police came to Sudha Kanta. The outcaste was penniless and they did not know what to do. Sudha Kanta went to three of his Brahmin friends. "This outcaste lying dead on the street offers us a chance to show that every Indian is truly our brother."

As a crowd, far enough away to remain uncontaminated, watched them, the four high-caste men picked up the gaunt, ragged Untouchable. Laying him on a stretcher, they carried him to the river bank, built and lit his funeral pyre, and sat like sons mourning for a dead father until the corpse was ashes. Then, with due ritual, they cast the ashes into the river to be borne away into the sacred Ganges.

Such an extraordinary happening was discussed everywhere. Sudha Kanta's reputation spread. When he translated the Sermon on the Mount into Bengali, it was distributed and taught throughout the schools in the district. His articles on temperance, illiteracy, and the decadence of Hindu festivals were reprinted all over India and his influence helped the Hindu Committee to abolish gambling and nautch girls at their Melas.

My unorthodox Bohn had a way of starting things that gathered momentum like dunes piling in the desert winds. He believed that the white people in India were there on sufferance and that the country belonged to the Indians. Christian principles should be spread the Indian way.

Chakravarty Babu was an ordained Christian preacher. One day this emaciated Bengali came to see his bishop and pled, "Bishop Sahib, I want to teach in the way established by my forefathers. You know when you visit the temples in Puri, the priest is always there. He doesn't run around entering people's houses unless he is sent for in an emergency. Such visits are intrusions on Indian privacy. I would like to sit in a Christian ashram by the side of the road where the stream of pilgrims pass and wait for them to come to me. *And,* Bishop Sahib, I want my ashram under the eaves of the temple of Kalighat!"

Kalighat was a gory place, as untypical of Hinduism as the Ku Klux Klan of Christianity. Every noon goats were killed in sacrifice and to many Indians and almost all Americans, the rituals were revolting.

As usual there was no money in the mission budget for such a daring experiment. On faith alone, Fred rented a house and installed Chakravarty and his wife. It grew quickly to be a real ashram. Fred and I went there to sit, Indian fashion, on the bare floor, and listen to the pilgrims speak of their lifelong quest for the eternal. Many had walked the dusty miles to

Benares, to Allahabad for the Mela, and came now to Kalighat. Where was peace to be found? Of the thousand who stopped at this ashram door, many carried away the message of Christ.

Fred said, "Victory is not won by destroying other religions but by respecting and honoring them." In India he was tuned in to the Hindus and Moslems but when he went to the other land which was under his episcopal jurisdiction, he tuned away from them and in on Buddhism. Born and bred in India, Buddhism was all but extinct there, but in Burma it flourished —as it did in Ceylon, Siam, and farther east.

Missionaries in Burma complained that the Burmese was the true forgotten man. Nobody remembered that the country existed, they said, except when some baritone sang the song written to Kipling's verses. Certainly dawn thundered 'crost the bay and Burma girls waited by the old Moulmein Pagoda. In fact, turning away from the Great Gawd Budd many a girl had kissed her Tommy Atkins all right, and been left flat, often enough with a buttermilk-eyed Mongolian baby to support unless a Chinese, Indian, or Burmese husband (in order of preference) adopted it. If husbands proved in short supply, the babies wound up where? In Christian orphanages.

Fred was dissatisfied with his hurried visits there and wanted to know more about the country as well as to pay more attention to the neglected American missionaries. We managed somehow to go down for a monsoon season, the only time Fred could fit into his heavy schedule.

Our fellow passengers on the British-India ferry disappeared the moment we set sail from Outram Ghat on our way down the Hoogly River into the Bay of Bengal. The rain poured down, foghorns bellowed, tarpaulins were up, portholes closed, and the air had the weight of lead. Fred took out his typewriter and ensconced himself in a corner of the dining saloon, working happily away at his area bulletin, the "Calcutterean" and his book *Building the Indian Church*. I studied books on Burma so that before we landed I could summarize my reading for him.

Rangoon was a real melting pot. Races and nationalities mingled with abandon. Aryan, Mongolian, Chinese, and Indian characteristics blended and it was a guessing game to figure out any man's ancestry, although Fred insisted that all Burma's cheekbones came from China. It was a better place for most women than India, with no caste, no purdah, no child marriage and gaunt child-widowhood. Women laughed in Burma.

Buddha was God and his likeness was everywhere. Buddhas with Grecian noses or Negroid lips, in a state of placid Nirvana or with wide-open eyes; reclining, standing, seated cross-legged; from huge to miniature, in rich gold leaf or crudely carved teak, they topped every hill, guarded every street or bend in every river. In the town of Pegu we saw a Buddha 181 feet long, and no village was so worthless it lacked a pagoda and an image.

Back in the hill country, the Burmese had not yielded to Buddhism but remained Shans, Kachins, and Karens. It was among these last, about a million people, that Christianity was first accepted. The Karens formed the nucleus of the Burma Christian Church.

Fred, being Fred, made no bones of his opinion that the Baptists did the best work in Burma. They got there first with the most and so my Methodist bishop, a true and practical believer in Christian unity, advocated turning over to the Baptists all the Methodist schools, hospitals, churches, and parishes. Nothing so simple and idealistic was done, naturally. Only Fred could have suggested it.

To learn the secrets of Burma from its past, we went as soon as we could away from the polyglot towns to the ancient one of Pagan, from which our word *pagan* is probably derived rather than from the Latin *paganus*. Fred wanted to meet U Wilatha, ranking prelate and head abbot of the Buddhist monastery nearby. This was the man responsible for the extraordinary restoration of the Ananda Pagoda, an ancient and beautiful structure Fred loved next only to the Taj

Mahal. The tall, spare, shaven-headed abbot in his saffron gown and the bishop in his business suit took to each other as friends and brothers. For one thing they both had considerable talent for raising money, in which pursuit Fred Fisher was hats off to U Wilatha!

U Wilatha took us to see the oldest Buddhist landmark in Burma, a pagoda built about 150 B.C. To our surprise, it was as simple and chaste as a mosque.

"And you will see, my lord," said the abbot gravely, his eyes twinkling behind his glasses, "that there is no semblance of any graven image or likeness of anything that is in heaven above or in the earth beneath or in the waters under the earth."

Fred acknowledged the complimentary quoting of our Old Testament with a smile and asked him what kind of religion the original Buddhist missionaries had found when they came.

"Animists—idolaters," answered U Wilatha. "The Buddhists preached to them the gospel of committing the least possible harm, of practicing love, pity, truth, and purity. Ahimsa—nonviolence."

"Ahimsa is being used by our Gandhi in India," commented Fred.

"Yes, that wise Hindu borrowed it," said the abbot, and went on, "There were no idols in any early Buddhist temples. They've gradually crept in."

As we talked with him in his monastery, where life had changed very little since Marco Polo paused to write his journal there, other monks drifted in. Fred was something new to them, a Christian bishop from one of the youngest countries on earth. And a seeker of truth like themselves.

When we left, the old prelate brought from his cell a small Buddha, heavy with gold leaf. It had been brought to Pagan when the Ananda was built, in A.D. 1091, and was made from the Bo tree from Bodh-Gaya, India. He handled it with great reverence and then, with his blessing, gave it into our keeping.

Fred's arthritis began to trouble him badly in the monsoon

rains, but he refused to give up any part of this trip. Doctors had already warned me that he would never be free of it in the humid climates of India or Burma, but Fred only said, "I shan't leave on account of health!" So on we went, determined to miss nothing.

There were the modern oil towns, such as Kyauk and Yenan Kyaung, which resembled the rest of Burma not at all and were like American frontier settlements at the moment of oil strikes. In one of them, Fred baptized the sons of an American driller, brought up a Methodist in just such an Oklahoma town, and I added three sturdy Burmese half-castes to my godchildren. Near another oil town we saw a glorious estate among the trees and asked our guide who lived there. "A retired English forest commissioner," he said, "and his wife, but he can't take her home—or, well, you know sir, she's Burmese and he *doesn't* take her home. But he gets up at two every morning to listen for four hours to London on the radio."

In the tiny poor villages along the banks of the Irrawaddy, the pagodas were lit with electric lights every night even though a saucer of oil with a wick served the people at home, and in one interior village we found a Sikh temple, a Hindu temple, a Baptist church, and an Anglican church as well as the Buddhist pagoda. Fred said it reminded him of places in our own Middle West where a "Church of God" and a "Church of Christ" competed on opposite corners for the souls of fewer than a hundred inhabitants.

One day along our way we saw a spiritual miracle. On Mandalay Hill an old Buddhist woman was climbing the hundred steps to an altar, supported by her daughters. We followed at a distance and saw her reach the altar and try to lift a sizable stone from it. She gritted her teeth and grimaced, but it would not budge. Closing her eyes, she rested her head against the shrine and began to pray loud and long. We knelt in prayer, too. Our God was everywhere, why not at a Buddhist altar? After fifteen minutes, the old lady straightened up and lifted the stone as though it were a baseball. Then, her sins forgiven, her burden gone, she trotted down the steps, spry and happy-looking.

Fred said, "That's the altar in Muncie and I've just risen from it. It's the same experience, Han."

Our welcome everywhere was warm and we were shown everything—ruby mines, oil wells, schools, factories, hospitals. In the bigger towns there were invariably three receptions: by the Burmese community, which we always accepted first; by the Indians; and by the sturdy Chinese, who were never to be outdone by anybody.

At one of these in the interior, an Indian Christian carefully read out a greeting that charmed me so I copied it verbatim:

"Welcome, generous expert gentleman," he said, bowing to Fred. "In my eyes there is a seat of beautiful tigers' skins spread for you [in reality a plain teakwood chair]. There is an adorned coronation seat in my heart for you. I will wash your feet with my eyelids and give you a bath with my tears.

"With my lips will I drink the water washed by your feet and will never be satisfied. The ocean of my heart is agitated and there arises the willows of pleasure in which there came out precious and attractive pearl lines."

Before we could try to figure *that* one out, he ended dramatically, "Oh, my lord, I wish I should present it at your feet. Well, dear, speak, speak. What else I should bring your worship?"

In Thongwa we were staying with Burmese friends, in spite of some raised eyebrows among the white sahibs, when a delegation of Buddhist elders called on Fred *and* (this was the surprising part to begin with) me. They asked my lord Fisher to honor them by visiting their shrine. He should speak as he was moved to speak and a skilled interpreter would translate his words.

"It will be the first time a Christian enters and the first time English is spoken in the sacred place," the leader told him. "And we would like to use this great occasion to open our temples also for the first time to women. The appearance of your wife who travels with you and is also interested in our people will gratify us and the Memsahiba may bring her Burmese friends who follow the Christ-truth. Some of our Buddhist-faith women will join them."

In the courtyard a colossal brass Buddha outlined in lights looked benignly down as the saffron-robed priests used the Western form of shaking hands to greet Fred and he entered the temple, followed by the other women and me.

"In this place is One greater than the temple," said Fred Fisher in his mellow, beautiful voice, opening the first Christian sermon ever preached there.

The next morning when we went to the station a C.I.D. man picked up Fred and questioned him long and closely about his entering the shrine. We almost missed the train. When we arrived at the next station, the senior Methodist missionary sent word that he could not come and sent his gardener to show us around. Fred commented that the mission was an ugly barn of a place where Christians looking through dirty windows could see pagodas glowing with gold leaf. Called to worship by the clang of a school bell, they could hear outside the deep-toned gongs and tinkling bells of Buddha sound nocturnes in the wind.

"Why are we so static?" grieved Fred. "We could reach these music-loving, beauty-loving people with our magnetic message if we only would."

One of the finest philosophers in Burma was U Ba Sein, who earned his living by compiling government statistics and in his own time delved into old Buddhist scriptures. Before we left Rangoon, he presented Fred with his book, *The Mathematics of Buddhism,* and asked for a debate.

"No," said Fred decisively to U Ba Sein, who had become his very good friend. "I never debate my religion. But if you want to present Buddhism, I shall be delighted to present Christianity in a discussion between us of faiths."

To a sultry Burmese hall came a thoughtful audience of some eighty scholars, men who refused to copy the West and wore long skirts, short silk coats, and delicate kerchiefs tied around their heads. The head trustee of the Shwe Dagon Pagoda (the Westminster Abbey of Burma) presided. Only three Christians were present—Fred, me, and one Burmese clergyman. I was the lone woman, but my husband wanted me there and I had plowed through *The Mathematics of Buddhism* as a sort of intellectual ticket of admission.

The meeting was conducted in quiet, mellow English. U Ba Sein covered the walls with his charts and posited, within the Buddhist circle, the evolution of the race, the present scientific era, and the future of the universe. He came back and back again to Planck's Constant Pi, as if he relied on it to prove his spiritual circle. I must say he got beyond my depth, but Fred took Constant Pi as his own opening.

Using the quantum theory as the most significant element in Planck's discovery, my husband cited the law of the radiation of energy and the law of coordination and response in nature, showing how these physical laws illustrated and supported our belief in divine energy emanating from God. In the heart of that circle, Fred Fisher, student of Bowne, posited the Divine Living Christ and challenged Buddha's claim not to have found any God.

A gentle breeze from the river refreshed the sultry night and the little electric bulb lighted the faces of the two men until long after midnight.

At the end, one of the greatest scholars rose, profoundly moved. "The ethics presented here tonight by this Christian Bishop," he declared, "have almost persuaded me that a good Christian is better than a good Buddhist."

Fred said to me later as we spoke of this shared and splendid experience, "If there were more of both, it would be a different world."

7

If I do say so myself, I am a fair organizer and a bit of a hustler. I like to get things done, see the results, and then try something else. I am also as distractable as a child and wander afield in search of many butterflies.

Fred drove toward aims of such magnitude that he rarely failed to relate everything he did to his purposes. Because of his prodigies of work and concentration, his one hobby, his one frivolity, and his occasional breaks away from the mainstream of his life were all the more important to him.

His hobby was collecting walking sticks. To symbolize his arrival at man's estate on his way to Asbury College, he bought his first one. Classmates and family teased him for carrying it, calling him a "dude." A man's cane, he proclaimed, becoming its champion, commemorated the first time man broke a branch from a tree and used it to defend himself. "It's the staff of life, symbol of prestige, sign of civilization, a support, protection, and companion," he argued stoutly.

As his collection grew, Fred insisted that each one come from a place or person he knew and loved, represent an important experience or tell a story. The 350 canes that ended up in Pilgrimthorpe included the one Andrew Jackson carried when he stamped across a Washington lawn to end an argument as to where the U.S. Treasury should be built. "We'll put 'er there," boomed Old Hickory and thrust the twisted, heavy stick into the ground. And there the Treasury still stands. Fred was given the small ivory-headed Malacca that Daniel Webster had carried and a stout Hoosier hickory that belonged to James Whitcomb Riley. Rudyard Kipling pre-

185

sented him with a bit of ash and he had another Kipling stick, the one described in *The Overland Mail*. From the head of this bamboo staff, metal catalpa beans jangled in a rhythm that helped the dispatch-carrier run, mile after mile, along India's dusty roads. Some of his sticks were curios, some beauties, many gifts from friends, like the Maharajah of Mysore or an African chieftain on the Zambesi River, and they came from all over the world.

When Fred broke away from one environment into another during his life, he used his one frivolous pastime to "wash his mind." Setting out on a long trip with our tin trunk of books, most of them on philosophy, theology, or history, we always included two or three detective novels. I was soon as much a fan as he, delighting in unlikely murders among the teacups and never-never detectives with infallible deductive powers. For the first day or two away, on shipboard or train headed for a far place, we had an orgy of pure escape.

Once, during our years in India, we took more than a day or two of artificial escape from the absorptions and activities of Fred's work for the Indians and the church, a trip to the "top of the world." It was a strenuous undertaking for two middle-aged Americans, but it was wholly glorious, utterly soul-satisfying. The whole thing came about through one of our varied Indian friendships.

Sadhus were wandering priests who gave their lives to poverty. Indian Christians sometimes joined the Sadhus. "Foxes have holes and birds have nests, but Sadhus have no place to lay their heads," was the saying, and our house served many of them as temporary shelter and mailbox. One of our best friends among the Sadhus came down from Himalayan fastnesses that summer and told us that we must make a pilgrimage into the peaks to the border of Tibet.

This man made the Jesus-way of life so attractive that the generalissimo of the Dalai Lama's armies became his friend. "You must meet him," our Sadhu told us, "and he is now in Calcutta."

Warned that the generalissimo was not accustomed to the

"knife and the prong" and found our Western food tasteless and disagreeable, I wrote asking him for tea, penning the invitation in my best Oriental English and importuning him in a fashion usually successful in the Orient. His Excellency accepted.

What a picture he made when he arrived! He wore a rich satin gown of deep yellow and high Tibetan boots in spite of the climate. Over his well-kept hair with its long queue, he wore a soft felt hat, which he kept on in accordance with time-honored custom. Why change your etiquette just because you modernize your hat? With him was a smiling Tibetan girl who interpreted for him. It took me a moment to catch on that she was no less than Princess Mary of Tibet, who had spent three years at Queen's Hill School in Darjeeling.

My household was ready, instructed in ceremony. The best Chinese teacups with silver saucers were set for the Dragon Well and jasmine tea I had wangled from a Chinese merchant. We ushered His Excellency to a high seat, especially prepared for him, and our mutual friendliness grew as the moments passed. I pulled only one boner, I asked where Princess Mary would continue her education in English. The generalissimo flashed her a look of stern, fierce anger and said she would return with him to Tibet for the rest of her life. My heart ached for the charming girl who had associated so long with the free children of Europe and America at Queen's Hill School but, like all cultured Orientals, Mary controlled her face.

"We would like some day to come and know you, your country and your countrymen," ventured Fred.

"My country is closed, Sir," answered the Tibetan.

"Will it always be closed?" asked Fred with a warm, friendly smile.

"Always. Even to those brave men who would climb Mount Everest."

Skating diplomatically over thin ice, Fred asked him to explain this attitude.

"We have considered letting you missionaries of Jesus

come," said the generalissimo, bluntly but kindly. "Your message is one of love and friendship and our people like you. But you would teach our people to desire things which you have and they do not have, things which I admit are attractive and useful. Your Western traders would learn of the desires in my country and come along. Trade grows then and traders get into trouble and need protection. Then soldiers come. There is war. People are killed. By and by we look at our flag-pole. It is not our flag we see, but your flag, and our country is no more. No, Sahib, we will not let your people in even with a message of love. It is too dangerous."

Of course the Sahib took pardonable pride in his truthful assurance that our own American government never spread its power through selfish conquest, but when we decided indeed to go into the mountains, we understood why we must sign a document promising not to set foot on the soil of Tibet, though we hoped to reach her wild borders.

This dramatic adventure, taking us far away from our normal daily concerns, began with a trip through the plains and jungles of India. For fifteen hours, while hot winds howled outside like a blizzard, we struggled to exist in our dusty, fan-less compartment until the sun went down and we dared open windows and blinds. When we reached the twisting upward course we must take for Darjeeling, we scrambled, transferring mattresses, pillows, mosquito nets, cooking utensils, and personal belongings, all needed to travel in India, from train to smaller-gauge train and then to one with a still smaller gauge. I felt better able to endure the comforts of modern travel in India when an old gentleman told me about the good old days when there was no train after Sahebganj and you crossed the river by ferry and then waded a mile through sand in the blazing Bengal heat to be loaded onto a jolting oxcart.

It was a pleasure to be among mountain people after the plainsmen, even though they spoke less English. They were friendlier and easier and had no caste distinctions.

The bishop had built a haven near Darjeeling for missionaries and their families to escape the deadly heat of the plains.

Our own small eyrie was a one-room shack set like an eagle's nest near to heaven, where every look took the eyes upward toward the eternal snows above.

When Bohn's fire blazed high on the hearth we shed the layers of coats we had gradually put on as we ascended to Darjeeling. Then we walked out of the eyrie to take one look at the crescent moon over the white glaciers and prayed, deeply aware of our own small stature and the expansion of our souls.

It took many days to prepare for the Himalayan trip and the essentials were too many for the eyrie to hold. With the help of a skillful Indian, Fred made a canopy for protection against rain and sun and we ate out there where we could watch the thousand-hued, ever-changing view.

First, my Bohn said, we must find Naspati, a Tibetan guide of extraordinary qualities. The people in Darjeeling said he had "gone." There was nothing to do but let the Oriental grapevine operate to find him. Naspati turned up one morning, and what a ceremony the reunion between him and the Sahib was. As I looked at him, with his placid Buddha face, his red Tibetan cheeks, and the nonpacific knife he wore in an embossed silver case, I trusted him instantly.

To carry the mountain of supplies Naspati insisted on, we hired ten coolie women, those extraordinary creatures who wear their black hair smoothly parted and brushed, are proud of their heavy jewelry and trot up perpendicular paths with loads that Fred could not even lift off the ground. Then there was the cook, who was also a climber, and one little boy as sweeper. Buddu ("Blessing") was a thin little fellow from the plains. I worried about him from the beginning.

The weather did not break for us and finally Naspati decreed that we leave in the rain. We were an odd-looking group, and got used to being laughed at by cheery bystanders. Fred and I wore riding breeches, boots and jackets, with high-collared starched shirts and four-in-hand ties. We added raincoats against the downpour and I was persuaded to put up an eighty-cent umbrella. With Naspati in his long silk gown and sash, we were mounted on three horses, white, black, and brown. The girls were dressed as if for a party, with turquoise dog collars and strings of red beads, and Buddu wore his only warm garment, a discarded morning coat of the bishop's that came to his heels.

For fourteen miles we battled the rain and wind. As we went through the tiny villages hugging the mountain paths, everyone turned out to see us and to laugh. "For *pleasure* they go—to *play*," commented one old wise chief of a hill tribe. "The Sahib and the Memsahib go to see the snows in the rain. Queer people. How hard they work to play!"

Naspati had sent word ahead to the landlords of the Dak bungalows. These had been built by the British in the same places where the Buddhists had established rest houses for travelers in these remote regions before the Moguls came down the path made by Alexander the Great through Afghanistan. After hours of walking and riding through gales and cloud, fording streams, descending steeply into hot valleys and then climbing even higher in the mountains, it was bliss to arrive at the Dak shelters, to sleep, to wake and eat breakfasts of Quaker oats, bacon, eggs, bread, celery, jam, and coffee, which barely lasted us until lunch.

The descents were more terrifying than the climbs. Fred's pony shied at the slightest rustle and I was afraid he would trip over a precipice. My old brown kept his hind legs together and slid straight down wet, slippery narrow paths. At night I shivered with fear as I thought of it and resolved to walk all the next day.

Every day we ended up two or three thousand feet higher than before and the altitude began to bother us. The paths grew ever narrower and the precipices deeper. Clouds enfolded us and we could see scarcely a few feet ahead and had to feel our way on foot. Avalanches filled the paths with treacherous ice and at any sudden turning an abyss was likely to drop beneath our feet.

But every rift in the clouds brought more glorious glimpses of the mountain ranges, topped with snow and covered below the snow line in the green and browns of virgin forests, the colors of a thousand flowers. Each day the cook prayed *"Om Mani Padmi Hung"* (Hail to the Jewel in the Lotus, Hail) to the Pure One for good weather. We were all awed into worship as we moved more and more slowly upward. Sometimes this was expressed in deep silence, sometimes in an outburst of adoration. Seated on his pony or walking on soft leaves, my Bohn would suddenly shout a prayer of praise. It was wonderful simply to be honest with God—to pray when we felt like it, which we often did.

I wrote a book about this trip, *The Top of the World*, and told of many things since become familiar to everyone through the conquest of Everest, when so much was written and said of the prayer wheels revolving endlessly by mountain streams in the wildest places, of the lamasaries lost in craggy isolation, of the character of the country and its hardy inhabitants. Now, I myself remember best the mountain women, smiling in beauty as they carried unbelievable burdens held by head straps, often knitting as they climbed. And little Buddu.

I had watched the outcastes of India crouch low so that their shadows would not pollute a high-caste man on the street and I had felt vicariously with them. It took this delicate, undernourished little boy to bring tears and real understanding to my heart.

One of the coolie women noticed Buddu, sitting as always far away from everyone, with his back to them, and carried over a cup of hot tea. He refused it. This child of ten had walked the miles with us and he needed food, but he only shook his head when Naspati and the cook also begged him to eat. Tradition was stronger than love, stronger than hunger, stronger than the words of wise Naspati. For three thousand years his ancestors had not eaten in the presence of men of caste. When we were finished, and went away, he took our plates and ate the scraps as a dog would. I realized what the words scavenger—sweeper—outcaste—meant.

The final days of our trip were ones of blinding, cutting wind and dense cloud, deeper abysses, more dangerous paths.

Our pith helmets acted as water sheds and when we stumbled, after the last march of fourteen miles, into the last Dak bungalow over two miles in the sky, we were soaked, and dead tired. Here we must wait and pray for a break in the weather.

We had only a few books with us, but found one—*An Affair of State*—left behind by another climber. Sitting in the mountain dugout, reading by candlelight, we felt a million miles away from governments and the intrigues of political men. Smoke made much reading impossible, the altitude made cooking laborious and lengthy, and the minimum exercise we must take for ourselves and our ponies if we were ever to get home again exhausting. Now and again we would see a patch of sunlight on the floor and run out. Sometimes, if the sunlight lasted a minute, we ran up the slope with hearts beating too fast. One day came Naspati's shout: *"Blue sky!"*

We swiveled to look in all directions at once, to see the bit of sky, the first in days. The wind drove mercilessly and our ears were frostbitten, but we screamed at each other, "The blue grows larger!" When the sun did not break through we were heartsick. To see the wonder view of the whole world, we had studied, prepared ourselves, come this far while the women carried those packs and little Buddu kept up with us and Naspati guided us.

That evening Naspati took out the smaller incenser and prayed to the east, west, south, and north, planting bamboo poles from which he hung prayers to flap so that the horses of the wind would gallop with his prayers to heaven. We were deeply honored that this Buddhist friend should pray so exceptionally for us, and added our prayers to his.

We broke camp next morning in a blizzard. On that final march we passed no human being, no hut, not a domestic animal. The rest of them taught even little Hindu Buddu to mumble the proper prayers and everyone prayed the whole day long. That night when we camped, all of us were electric with expectation. At four-twenty in the morning, Naspati waked us. It was bitter, bitter cold.

"Heaven has granted our petition and the sky is aglow," said Naspati. "Arise. Come to the hilltop."

As he aided us up the last difficult step, reaching for our hands, Naspati said, "Sahib, Memsahib, close your eyes! The glory of heaven and earth is before you!"

When we opened our eyes, we beheld infinity.

8

In the winter of 1925 we set sail for South Africa at the suggestion of the Indians and on their behalf. If this sounds unlikely it is because from a distance one rarely associates the two countries, but South Africa has a sizable Indian minority. In the old days, British sugar planters, finding the nomadic African Bantus unreliable, sent to India for indentured laborers. Recruiting agents dazzled villagers with tales of rich land and persuaded them to sign with thumbprints contracts they could not read. They were told that after one or two terms of service, they would be allowed to purchase land and become citizens. These hard-working people saved, bought, and prospered, but were never granted citizenship.

A new bill was pending to curtail their meager rights. Fred was urged by friends, including Gandhi and Tagore, to go there and study the effects of the proposed anti-Asiatic legislation on these settlers. Coming from him, an independent American of established integrity with no axe of his own to sharpen, a report might have some effect.

Nothing loath, we left the 120-degree heat in Calcutta for the South. We routed ourselves by way of Australia to enjoy its nippy winter and to see this continent. For one thing, Fred had an eager interest in the Australian aborigines who had delighted Darwin when he was twenty-three.

As we went through the frontier railroad stations, Fred was like a boy over the strange primitives. "Look, Han, there's one! And another. A whole bunch of them!" All they seemed to do was throw boomerangs to charm the tourist trade, but Fred never tired of watching the uncanny flights of the dark wooden arcs and cheered when they doubled back and unerringly dropped at the throwers' feet. He would have liked to stay among them and pick up their dialect, but we had little time and the Australians deserve their reputation as the world's most hospitable people.

We had arrived in the country at the same time the American fleet had. The newspapers ran columns on "What the American blue-jackets like to eat" and lists of "gobs' slang," and the whole dominion canceled its other engagements in order to entertain Americans. Caught in the round as if we were part of the fleet, we found every place, including churches and colleges, *en fête*.

An American had only to express a wish to any Australian. Some of the boys from the flagship *Seattle* happened to mention that a kangaroo would make a nice ship's mascot. Next morning a motor truck and a small car arrived at the pier. In the truck was a full-grown kangaroo, in the car two wallabies, small marsupials like kangaroos, and from his pocket one driver pulled out a baby kangaroo no larger than a kitten.

Fortunately Fred did not fancy live souvenirs, but when our host in Melbourne found out that Fred collected walking sticks, he presented him with seven, each one made from a different Australian wood.

The press was as friendly as the people. Of Fred the *Christian Advocate*'s editor wrote: ". . . Bishop Fisher came unheralded among us and entered without ostentation our life, so we took him to our hearts at once. A Methodist bishop is somewhat of a curiosity, and at first we scarcely knew how to treat him. To an ordinary bishop we give due respect after the casual manner of our race, secretly smile at his gaiters and apron, and with democratic reluctance address him as 'my lord'; but Fisher dresses like the rest of us, so we pounced upon 'Doctor' as the most suitable form of address. We find the doctor a strong, lovable, human sort of man, with a piquancy of speech, a touch of humor and a widely roaming mind. He talks to us in his frank, easy, almost laconic way about the big things of the world and little by little there is revealed a man of broad culture and of daring mind, disciplined by much experience to practical use. Yet with it all there is a gentle humility which softens even the most challenging and critical things he says and makes us feel that he came to learn. . . ."

And of me: "We liked Mrs. Fisher just as much and see in her the best type of 'college woman,' a type America alone produces. Being also a wise woman, she allows the spotlight to rest mainly on her husband, though now and then there are flashes of independent thought that make us feel that even a bishop is molded by his wife. . . ."

Melbourne for business, Sydney for gaiety, Adelaide for culture, and the island of Tasmania for beauty! We went out back-of-beyond, too, and found that the Indian and British passions for tea were but tepid emotions. The ranchers served you tea in bed at dawn, tea for little breakfast, tea for big breakfast, midmorning tea, tea with lunch, afternoon tea, tea with dinner—and at night before you went to sleep a servant wheeled in the tea cart.

We carried away with us, besides warmth and lavish friendship and a new respect for tea-drinking, two disturbing impressions.

Fred was so worried by increasing Japanese unfriendliness to Americans that he prophesied that this antagonism might lead to open aggression (a prescient opinion to hold in the mid-twenties).

And the Australian angle on the race question perplexed and upset us both. Everyone we met stoutly maintained the White-Australia policy was the best one. Here they were on a South-Pacific continent, completely surrounded by yellow, brown, and black races, with 96 per cent of the inhabitants northern whites. They intended to maintain this ratio. Why, we asked each other, should there be only six million people in an area the size of the U.S.? What was to become of the vast unpopulated wastes? Only the patient Oriental could make these arid deserts bloom! The Australians admitted this, yet maintained their bar against Asiatics, insisting that the faces of Australia must remain pure Anglo-Saxon.

We took the nineteen-day trip due west across the South Seas from Adelaide to Durban, South Africa, as private time in which to be alone. Though we'd have missed it if we had not been welcomed so lavishly everywhere, it was marvelous to diet unobserved at a table for two, to take our constitutionals in stride around the deck while we decided on a topic to discuss at dinner that evening, to have hours for uninterrupted work, Fred on six months of Sunday School lessons, me on a series of articles on Australia for a young people's journal, *The Class-mate*. Diet, sea air, and tranquility relaxed my stoic Bohn and for the first time in many months his arthritis, sometimes so crippling he could scarcely walk, troubled him not at all.

On the dock at Durban, a delegation of Indians waited for us. We were garlanded with flowers and escorted to the hotel driveway with ceremony. Then they bade us a dignified fare-well. Indians were not allowed in the hotel except as servants.

"How can the Christian Church tolerate such things?" Fred asked me rhetorically. "We do exactly the same at home! Will Anglo-Saxons never learn that men should be free to be with their friends, no matter what color their skin?"

After several days at the luxurious hotel, Fred went to settle his bill. The hotel cashier told him it was paid "by your Mohammedan friends."

In South Africa the blacks were called "natives" and the white men "South Africans." Indians, whether Christian, Parsee, Hindu, or Mohammedan were not exactly anything. The new bill up before the legislature contained the state-ment: "Indian is an alien element in the population and no solution will be acceptable unless it results in considerable reduction of the Indian population."

The mayor of Durban talked to Fred without mincing matters. "This bill has not a leg to stand on ethically, but ninety-nine per cent of the white people are in favor of it and we shall adopt it. It's a matter of self-preservation. Give them equality, and my children could not compete with these Indian traders—and what we whites cannot do through fair competition, we must do through restrictive legislation."

"So the Indian, cultured, sensitive, and successful, becomes the Jew of South Africa," Fred said bitterly to me.

When he was to preach in the Wesleyan Church in Durban, all our Indian friends met us early outside the building. After Fred went into the sacristy with the clergyman to prepare for the service, I told the usher I would sit with these friends instead of joining Sir Liege Hewitt, with whom we were dining later.

"But, Lady Fisher," protested the usher, "we only let the coolies come at all because of the Bishop and they will have to sit in the last pew."

So I did, too.

In Pretoria, we met an Indian couple whose eight handsome, well-dressed, intelligent children ranged in age from twenty to ten. Fred knew they had been devout Christians when they left India and asked what church they attended.

"Bishop Sahib," said the man of the family, "we know only English and no African languages so we cannot attend the African missions. When we were—not welcome—where they speak English, we——well, we go to the Moslem mosque where all races are the same!"

As we visited mission churches over the country the subtle influence of the Indians was apparent everywhere. The white sahib had put African women into blue calico Mother Hubbards, the Moslem Arab swathed them in black, but the Indians brought back the color in which they reveled. Where the Indians outnumbered the whites, all women wore gay India prints.

Sightseers that we were, we went to Victoria Falls whose proper, translated African name, "The Smoke that Sounds," describes its quality so vividly. In one of the kraals along the river, we heard the familiar theme of "Swing low, sweet chariot, comin' for to carry me home. . . ." Here, obviously, was its source and through an interpreter Fred asked the local chieftain, a huge man in a loincloth, with skin like black satin, about the African lyrics.

They told of a legend. In ancient times when the kings of the region were near to death, they went out in a bark alone and slipped over the falls and drowned. The eldest son of the wisest and best king of all decided to hasten the moment of his succession and forcibly placed his father in his bark and shoved it out into the current. It was not the moment for his death, and the old man sang, "Come down, angels, and take me!" When the bark went over the falls it was empty.

"His spirit still paddles down these waters," said the chief to us. "That's his song we sing. 'Come down, angels, and take me. Come down, angels, and take me....' "

So much that we found in Africa was moving and stirring. Fred was especially delighted with the elemental humor and music of the indigenous people, and though we were deeply impressed with the work missionaries were doing, he said, "If we only took from these people all they have to give, what a contribution they could make to our drab Anglo-Saxon Christianity!"

When he was to preach before six hundred black Christians in Salisbury, Rhodesia, he asked me almost pathetically, "Have I truly a message for these people?"

Of course he did, and they understood it. He never talked down to them, and if they missed some of the words they did not miss his message. After the service, he baptized the local pastor's baby; when he kissed the shiny black child and the child smiled up at him—for he had a way with all babies—the audience sighed as one man with pleasure. Then eight young men stood up and went forward to lead the huge congregation of men and women in singing. To our amazement and delight, they sang the Hallelujah Chorus as I have never, in all my musical days, heard it sung. It made me cry.

"Handel wrote that chorus on his knees," said Fred, "and that's the first time I ever heard it sung as it was written, Han."

All the long trip home, Fred discussed with me or meditated alone on his report, as a neutral American and an unofficial observer. When we got back, he conferred with the Anglican archbishop, Dr. Westcott, and with Charlie Andrews on the responsibility of the Christian community. These two Christian gentlemen told Fred to write it as he saw it.

"The newly proposed anti-Asiatic bill intends to take away

the well-earned land which the Indians have acquired," Fred
stated at one point. "A strip thirty miles back from the sea is
to be confiscated. Let him who has a conscience answer
whether this is justice or perfidy! 'Scraps of paper' has become
a favorite expression of the Anglo-Saxon race of late . . . but let
it not be forgotten that when nominal Christians break contracts . . . they will have to answer to the consciences of Hindus
and Mohammedans for their actions and will stand condemned at the bar of enlightened public opinion."

By Christmas week the report was on the desk of Lord
Reading, the Viceroy, and he sent for Fred and talked to him
for hours. Later it was published in India and mailed out to
all Christian bodies and to the secular press. It caused quite
a furor.

One of the speeches Fred made on this report was before
a large mixed group of Western businessmen and Indian in-
tellectuals. He pulled no punches and some of the white
sahibs were bitter. "As a bishop," said one, "you have a right
to present the ethical implications of this bill and to expose
the sins of the white man. But I strongly object to your talking about it in front of Indians. It works havoc with our
prestige."

It was a man from Africa who best expressed for me the
way Fred was, the way brave, strong men of conscience should
be. For years I have carried with me this paragraph from Alan
Paton's *Cry the Beloved Country:*

I shall no longer ask if this or that is expedient, but only if it is
right. I shall do this, not because I am noble or unselfish, but because life slips away, and because I need for the rest of my journey
a star that will not play false to me, a compass that will not lie. I
shall do this because I cannot find it in me to do anything else.
I am lost when I balance this against that. I am lost when I ask if
this is safe. I am lost when I ask if men will approve. Therefore
I shall try to do what is right and to speak what is true.

(Left) Welthy Blakesley Honsinger, Secretary of the YWCA, in France during World War I. (Right) Youngest bishop in the Methodist Church, Frederick Bohn Fisher, appointed to India.

(Left) The only home we ever owned was Pilgrimthorpe, in Hingham, Massachusetts. (Right) My adopted child, Precious Pearl.

(Left) Fred Fisher watching a football game with the Reverend Dan Poling; an unidentified friend; and Coach Yost of Michigan. (Right) When China was overrun by the Japanese, I took student refugees into the house at Pilgrimthorpe.

At Literacy Village, Lucknow, India, they welcome me back from fund-raising tours in the States with song, ritual gestures and an art form created in colored chalk on the ground. In the background is our House of Prayer for All Peoples.

Literacy Village trainees stop for four o'clock tea after a strenuous day of classes.

Indians come from all around to watch our educational puppets.

It's faces like these that keep me young in my eighth decade, that are my reward. (Below) On my eightieth birthday the children of the United Nations honored me with a special cake symbolizing literacy.

9

It was our privilege in India to know three men for whom no other adjective except *great* will serve.

The first was Charlie Andrews, our close personal friend, frequent member of our household, man of our faith, of Anglo-Saxon origins and thus tribally kin, born to our language, Indian by adoption and a saint through dedication to saintly ideals. He was a handsome man, with humorous eyes and a splendid beard.

Rabindranath Tagore, Nobel prize-winning poet of India, aristocrat, educator, innovator, intellectual and spiritual influence, was the most beautiful male I have ever seen in the flesh. When he rose from a low chair to greet me the first time I met him, unfolding to a towering six foot four and pressing the palms of his hands together to touch his massive forehead, I felt that I was looking at a portrait of a Bodhisattva. Silver hair framed his elegant features and deep-set eyes. His skin was ivory and simple robes fell gracefully the length of his superb body. He was a seer, but not a visionary seer, reaching up for spiritual things from the platform of the real world. Cecil Rhodes was obsessed with the idea of building an Anglo-Saxon Empire to dominate the world. Tagore—or, as he was called, Gurudev—wanted, above all, a university where everyone should learn cosmopolitan tolerance of all cultures and religions in preparation for world cooperation.

Sarojini Naidu's nickname for Mahatma Gandhi was "Mickey Mouse." Yet the other two men were the first to do him homage, acknowledging that within this skinny frame dwelt the most glorious soul of all. He was the spiritual giant of the twentieth century, exerting the most profound influence over three hundred ninety million people and affecting the history of the world.

It seemed to me natural that all three of these men should choose my Bohn for friend, knowing that he who was a doer had also a strong streak of poetry and mysticism in his nature and the courage to battle for his beliefs.

One morning a letter arrived from Tagore inviting Fred to spend the week end with Andrews and Gandhi at his home "Shymali," near his university at Shantiniketan. I could hardly wait for Fred's return to share the experience with him. The first thing he said was "I've been sitting cross-legged so many hours these days I'm beginning to like it!"

Then he tossed me a cushion and we lounged Indian fashion with the tea tray on the floor between us while he talked of the two days alone with these three great men.

"You know how Brahmins treat their guests. Royally by treating them casually. And Hindus make no fetish of eating. We ate together less than half the time. If I wanted tea when tea wasn't served I had only to speak to a servant. Our relationship was not pursued at meals. Afterwards we drifted into Gurudev's open room, I in my socks and the three others barefooted, and sat on cushions talking for hours.

"I'm all for Indian clothes in this weather, Han," he remarked in passing. "Charlie wore a thin silk Bengali shirt with tails flying in the breeze. Gurudev was in his flowing gown and Gandhi in his homespun. I went vestless, but somehow I just couldn't take off my coat, only my shoes. How convention-bound we are, we Western men!"

Saturday, Fred said, they had discussed India vis-à-vis the Empire and the problems of the Indians domiciled overseas.

"Then at sunset we took our walking sticks and walked cross-country. Gandhi's staff was almost twice his height and was nothing but a rough branch of a tree. The poet carried a product from his own handicraft shop, the handle carved like the head of a pheasant. Charlie's was a black ebony cane inlaid with ivory that an Indian friend had given him. 'Too

good for me,' he said. I had the stick Lord Reading gave me
in Simla. We made an odd assortment, legs and sticks, strid-
ing off toward the sunset. I believe Gandhi could beat us all
if we were in a walking race. That little giant's ninety pounds
has every muscle counted and at work. He likes to talk while
he walks, in the rhythm of it, but the poet likes to stride on
alone, so I walked with Gandhi. He sent his love to you and
'hopes your ankle [which I had recently sprained] will soon
be strong enough so you can keep up with me!' "

There was so much to say, Fred paused and digressed. "Do
you know, Han, what the Mahatma uses to sleep on? Thor-
eau's *Civil Disobedience!* 'Makes an excellent pillow,' he says.

"We passed one of Tagore's cows from his new agricultural
station for the villages. Somehow she winked at us and Gandhi
pulled up some grass and fed her.

" 'Isn't she the best friend of man on earth?' he asked. 'Of
course I believe in reverence for the cow. To me she symbolizes
the basic teaching of our Hinduism—that all life is part of
God.' "

Then they went back to talking of *Ahimsa,* nonviolence.

"Sunday was the great day of our week end," Fred said.
"In the morning after our solitary meditations we casually
wandered over to the poet's doorway."

"And which of you," I broke in, "got up to pray with Gandhi
at 4:20 in the morning?"

Fred grinned. Gandhi had prayed alone.

"We all felt like Sunday," he said. "The sky was a clear, hot
blue. The locusts shrilled to announce more heat. A reverent
spirit pervaded us. Gandhi talked of God. Tagore talked of the
Formless lifting us always to the Infinite. Charlie talked of
the mystical Presence and I talked of the Living Christ in this
modern world."

The buildings were covered with murals (and one of them
had a royal palm growing through the roof). On the gateposts
were bas-reliefs of Indian villagers. "These dark, silent figures,"
said Fred, "brought us round without premeditation to discussing the outcaste. We asked Gandhi whether they liked the

new name with which he had christened them, *Harijan,* son of God. Charlie and Gandhi said yes. Tagore made the point that to give them another name was to put them into another caste, a higher one, to be sure, but still a caste."

Fred smiled at me. "You know it was grand to remember, Han, when I was talking with these great liberators of the outcaste, that Christian missionaries were the first to look into his eyes and call him Brother!

" 'The outcastes' little red painted stone altar under a tree,' Gandhi maintained, 'is important. It's the only tangible symbol of God our half-starved brother ever had. They are doomed and their children are doomed to a hopeless future unless we four men seated here can arouse our worlds to white heat.'

"Tagore picked up the Mahatma on that. 'You, Gandhiji,' he said, 'and your Jain ancestors long ago left your chanting and singing and telling of beads! We all know that God is not only in his temple; he is where the tiller works the hard ground, in sun and shower, bound with us forever.' I'm proud," digressed my American husband again, "that in all the world Tagore chose to send his own son, Rotindranath, to the University of Illinois for his English education. He said it was because he 'expected democracy to be the vital environment and the labor of one's hand to be honored.' " Then he went on, quoting Tagore's argument with Gandhi concerning the outcastes. " 'No, if idols and idolatry, if beads and painted stones are not needed by us in this room, then they are not righteous for any of our people. I'd like to sweep up every idol of every kind and make one great heap, then sweep them into the sea, and so cleanse our stables.' "

The men were then silent for a moment, Fred told me, contemplating the poet cleansing the temple, before Gandhi said gently, "You dare not take the crutch from the lame man's arm until you have taught him how to walk. That is the Bishop's task, it is Charlie's, it is yours, Gurudev, and it is mine."

I asked Fred how Gandhi and Tagore differed basically.

"Tagore is like—Everest," he said slowly. "He towers majestic and, I think, alone. He seems to be in touch with the Infinite, a seeker for abstract truth. Wherever he finds it he makes it his own and it adds to his stature the way snows add to the glacial heights of Everest. Gandhiji is like the leaping cataract on the mountainside trying to reach the stream so that he may add his life to the parched plains below where the people thirst."

I came to know both the mountain and the cataract during my years in India. No literate alive but has read much about these major prophets among men. I will only add the personal memories that belong to me because they are very much part of my life, of Fred's, part of our growth and part of our religion and love.

We visited Tagore's university at Shantiniketan frequently. In the early days, Tagore lived there in a one-room mud hut of exquisite design, among his students, teaching, tutoring, laboring, carpentering, and cleaning, washing his own clothes. Life was Spartan in the assemblage of thatch-roofed huts, in the mango and sal groves where banyans and the sacred neem tree grew, and all members shared in learning and labor. The original aim was to teach boys to live with restraint, free from evil passions and greed and to gain knowledge of their cultural heritage.

In Tagore's own home in Calcutta, a house of many mansions where his princely family had lived for a thousand years and where I first met him in 1925, I saw no single lavish object, but was enfolded in an aura of warmth. Later he sold many of his own valuable properties and helped build replacements for the huts at Shantiniketan, proper buildings but as low and indigenous as the huts and the classes were still held outdoors, where slates were hung.

After Tagore won the Nobel prize in 1913, his concept of his school broadened, perhaps as a result of his having crossed the "black water" to Europe. He made his institution co-educational and opened courses in all religions and cultures.

To Fred and me, Tagore said, "The Gaekwar of Baroda

has endowed a chair of Hinduism and His Excellency, the
Nizam, a chair of Moslem philosophy. What of Christianity?"

Fred took pleasure in adding to Tagore's faculty an American, the Reverend Boyd Tucker, missionary from the Bengal
conference. It was the first time any Christian body had cooperated with the poet who wanted men to learn all wisdom
and all religions. When he could not raise money to endow
a chair in the U.S., Fred was afraid that the cooperation would
not continue after he left the country.

My meeting with Gandhi took place after we got back to
India from South Africa. We had stayed with Monilal Gandhi,
the Mahatma's son, at Phoenix, and I was eager to tell his
father about him. I went to Kanpur, where he was attending
the All-India Congress. Though I arrived on Monday, he sent
word that he would see me.

When I came in he took my hands and, without speaking,
smiled me to a chair, which I refused, preferring a white mat
on the floor where I sat cross-legged as he did.

His spinning wheel was beside him and now and then he
coaxed fine cotton thread from it, then read a little, then wrote
or closed his eyes to meditate. I spoke to him about Monilal
and South Africa for a minute and then stopped talking,
afraid to interrupt his meditations. After a while, he wrote me
a note and handed it to me with twinkling eyes. It said: "You
may speak though I may not." But I remained silent and
from time to time he turned to me and smiled and so we
became friends silently. While he meditated, I suppose, on
God, I meditated on Gandhi.

We talked together many times in the years that ensued—
in Bombay, at Birla House in Delhi, in Calcutta, in Sevagram.
I came to feel that I was a part of his circle, and I think this
was the secret of his power, that he could draw millions of
people into that circle with him.

Once when I visited him it was 128 degrees in the room.
I was dressed in the equivalent of what a woman wears for
strenuous tennis on a summer's day, while he sat, head shaved,
in nothing but a loin cloth. I realized that for all his English

schooling, eight trips to Europe, and his African life as a lawyer, one should not think of him except as a man of his own race and his climate. Otherwise one cannot understand him. He reacted against wealth and power and was reborn to his own roots. A man of two natures, one renunciatory, the other driving along practical lines to conquer vast political problems, he was, in both aspects, the very essence of modern India.

On a railroad trip with him, on the narrow-gauge line through the heart of Bengal, I was awed as Fred had been by the thousands of people who waited outside the great brick government-built stations surrounded by iron palings, by the peasants lifting their heads in the fields as he passed, crying "Gandhiji! Victory to Gandhiji!" like a national anthem. India walks in beauty and all the waiting people had bushel baskets full of flowers to throw over engine, engineer, passengers, conductor, and Gandhi.

I said, "This is beautiful! Do you deserve it?"

"Oh, no," said Gandhi. "I don't. It is not for me. They are offering the flowers to themselves." And he picked up a handful and sucked the honey.

I sat once with Agatha Harrison, a British Quaker, and Charlie Andrews, on the steps at Birla House. After Gandhi had made his Hindu prayer and the Sita Ram, he asked his "three Christian friends" to sing his favorite hymn. Charlie raised the cracked voice with which he had sung the same hymn at the end of Gandhi's long fast, Agatha lifted her soft, typically Quaker voice, and I sang in the voice I once thought would be heard in the opera houses of the world: "When I survey the wondrous cross/On which the Prince of Glory died. . . ." All religions belonged to Gandhi. "I consider myself a Hindu, Christian, Moslem, Jew, Buddhist, and Confucian," he had said.

10

It was appropriate that Fred Fisher should preside at the General Conference of the Methodist Church on May 16, 1928. The order of the day was the report of a Commission on Central Conferences recommending changes to obtain self-determination for the church throughout the world. The Negroes, South Americans, and Chinese, as well as the delegates from India, were passionately interested. When the report was adopted Fred envisioned for all churches in the mission field a heightened sense of responsibility, mounting self-respect, and a trend toward his dream of indigenous organizations.

This was a triumphant moment, worth waiting for, but by this time he felt that he had made his full contribution to the episcopate. He wanted to resign.

Fred's doubts about himself in the role of bishop were not new ones. After he was elected and before he accepted he wrote an article on "To Be or not To Be a Bishop." In it he frankly confessed his own failings, irritability, dislike of living in the limelight and being so much away from home. He also spoke of the inflation of the ego that could come from the unmerited adulation accorded men with this title and from the security such a position afforded. His greatest qualms were over the kind of decisions a bishop must make and the dangerousness of power.

"Welthy, if you ever see me using power for its own end, let me know," he said more than once. "I'll give it up then and there."

In 1927 Fred wrote a forthright criticism of the Methodist

Episcopacy, concluding with direct simplicity, "the fundamental difficulty is that it has too much power." Among the various remedies he suggested was one that would require every bishop to lay his resignation on the table at each General Conference. In a personal note, he added: "I think I should like the experience of being an ex-bishop, taking a local church and attempting to see whether, by personal merit of one's life, one could again achieve helpful influence uncoupled with this unprecedented power."

Other denominations have plans whereby their bishops may retain the title as nonjuring bishops and still do the work for which they feel they are better fitted. The Anglican bishop of Calcutta, a close friend of Fred's, caused no stir when he left his diocese of Assam and became dean of a theological college. The Methodist church had no such arrangement. None of our bishops was on record as resigning for reasons other than health.

Fred hated to leave India. He considered resigning to stay on as a missionary, building an ashram on Indian lines for the discussion and teaching of Christianity to all Indians. There were practical considerations that stood in the way of this— it would be hard on him to serve in an area where he had exercised a bishop's power and hard on his successor to have him.

Although he had sometimes been called "iconoclastic" or "restless" and some of his peers objected to his probing criticisms of the office, Fred had the warmest affection and respect for his colleagues on the Board of Bishops.

"I only wish, sometimes, my darling," he said to me, "that my chin would allow me once in a while to follow some easygoing line of judgment and action."

The Committee on the Episcopacy listened to Fred's arguments that he leave his office in 1928, but disagreed with him. Instead they reappointed him for a third quadrennium to Calcutta. We accepted this as God's will, and for the next two years Fred gave himself completely to the Indianization of the Church.

"I've just one string to my harp," he said to me, "but no outside nation ever has or ever will have the wisdom to solve another nation's problems."

In May 1930, he came to the conclusion that he hadn't the patience to plod along in this groove any longer. He had done what he could. As the youngest member of the Board of Bishops, he addressed his fellows with Puckish humor as "Dear Fathers and Brethren" and wrote a firm and final resignation.

India is no different from another country in respect to gossip and the suspicious natures of small, bourgeois minds. The rumor flew about that my husband and I were requested to leave India. In a fairly recent book, Krishnalal Shridharani picked up this canard, saying "Even American missionaries had to mortgage their right to free judgment and free conscience to the British before they were allowed to enter India. . . . Now and then there are noble examples of defiance like Bishop Frederick B. Fisher, who sympathized with the nationalist cause and befriended Gandhi and Nehru. He was thrown out of India."

There were equally unfounded rumors that we had ceased to believe in missions. Fred believed more than ever in missions. He thought the roles of those coming over from the U.S. were changing and that they must come not as superiors and guides but as trainers and teachers to help citizens of the country carry on the work.

On our way home with Fred's written resignation locked in his briefcase, we stopped over in Paris and picked up a cablegram from Dean Edward Kraus of the University of Michigan. He asked to see Fred as soon after he landed as possible and offered to meet us anywhere. Fred did not know him, but Dean Kraus had taught me German at Syracuse University.

"I expect he'd like to lecture in Calcutta," I said, guessing cheerfully, quite wrong.

What he wanted was for Fred to take the pulpit in Ann Arbor.

Fred's resignation went through this time, although it seemed to the Board inconceivable that a man on the sunny side of middle life (he was forty-eight) with apparent health and in good standing should of his own accord give up a life position that carried such privileges, emoluments, pensions, and opportunities for service.

The Board wished him a resounding Godspeed and the Indians mourned his refusal to return. For Fred his ten-year bishopric was crowned with joy when his dearest wish was fulfilled and an Indian, the Reverend J. R. Chitambar, was elected to replace him.

We went off with light hearts to reverse the usual sequence by passing from world service to a parish. Though I'd have liked to be near Boston and our own home, Pilgrimthorpe, Fred said, "No house can decide anything." Ann Arbor was an exciting assignment, a liberal parish in an intellectual university community.

Fred and I agreed with Gertrude Stein, who once told me: "There is no such thing as middle age, old age and youth. We are all contemporaries. We all have to adjust or we're already dead." We took a house large enough to try the joint-family system, so successful in the Orient, and four generations of us settled down there happily together.

There were Mother and Father Fisher, Fred and me, my niece Helen and her husband, Gordon Halstead, and their three-year-old boy, Scott, born in Lucknow, India. The second baby was born in Ann Arbor and named Welthy. John and Minnie Kopsi, Polish-Americans, completed the family.

Now we had to adapt to America instead of away from it. "The telephone is both messenger and chit," said Fred, and began to use it like a teen-ager. We tried to stir up our blood, thinned by winterless years in India, by walking miles in the late evenings when the snow made the avenues as quiet as siesta time in the East. In spring and summer we remembered the days when Fred would say to me as we crawled under our mosquito net in the stifling heat, "Tell me, Han, what would you give for a foaming ice-cream soda?" and visited the local drugstore with childish regularity. Fall was a joy. There are no falls like those in the U.S.

Town and gown in Ann Arbor responded to Fred's freedom of speech and personal magic by overflowing the church. Amplifiers had to be installed in the vestry. "How they keep pouring in," I wrote in my diary. "Today students sat on the steps leading to the pulpit and choir. Three hundred were packed in the vestry and five hundred turned away. The ushers say every Sunday is like Easter."

At a faculty banquet, the professorial toastmaster said, "One of our faculty who hadn't been to church in years heard so much about Fisher here that he thought he'd better go. Afterwards he said, 'That man asks God for more things than most preachers ever knew God had.' " Then the professor added, "As for myself, I feel as though I should apologize for eavesdropping when Dr. Fisher prays, he seems to be on such intimate terms with God."

Children adored Fred. Not only did the Sunday School grow, but more and more of them attended church. One precocious boy, brought up permissively to do anything he liked, was taken to service by his parents. Fearing his uninhibited impulses, they impressed on the boy that he must behave in the presence of God. To their surprise, he was angelic. On the way home they asked him how he liked the service.

"Well," said Junior, "God hollered just as loud as I thought he would, but he looked so young."

In the parsonage, I had my hands full. I am an impatient housekeeper and of course had my busy fingers in a dozen church and college pies. We were a huge household and Fred was apt to say, a few minutes before dinner, "By the way ...," and I knew he had invited some extra people. If it was only his secretary or one of our foreign students, he forgot to mention it at all.

If there wasn't anyone coming, he tended to bury his nose in a book and I had trouble prying him out. Once when just he and Gordon Halstead were at home, both men refused to hear the summons. Helen and I decided to teach them a lesson. We went ahead and finished the soup. The table had been cleared for another course when the men finally arrived.

"Let us pray," said Fred, and we all bowed our heads. "Oh, Lord, we thank Thee for what our wives have already eaten."

Sunday noon was a gala meal. After the morning service, Fred showered and dressed up in one of the red velvet coats I had made for him. The sermon always came in for close analysis during dinner.

Father Fisher, a staunch Lutheran G.O.P. seventy-eight-year-old, usually had a reprimand for his son. "You went a little *too* far this morning, Fred!"

"Not one inch too far," Mother Fisher invariably sputtered in reply. "I believe every word you said, Fred."

We were so occupied we had little time to miss India. Besides, we found plenty of the East in the Middle West. Among the students were boys and girls from Siam and South Africa and Ceylon, and there were one hundred and thirty Chinese to make me feel at home. Some of their smiling faces were always around our hearth. I took pleasure in introducing everyone to everyone in Ann Arbor, American Negroes to young Canadians and Arabians, Young India to Young Brazil. On Thursdays Fred held an at home to which came Hindus, Parsees and Buddhists, Roman Catholics, Shintoists, and a Moslem or two to mingle with young Protestants and take spiritual sustenance from the former bishop. They needed it in the land of plenty.

What discussions went on! One echo came back when a student, as many of them did, brought the discussion with him into the classroom. "When I criticize religion as I do," said one professor with asperity, "I am *not* referring to Dr. Fisher's religion."

There was always time in our house for visiting Indians. Fred would as soon have dropped his subscription to the Methodist *Christian Advocate* as to the *Indian Social Reformer*, on whose front page for fifty-two years were printed the flaming words of our own William Lloyd Garrison, the abolitionist: "I will be harsh as truth and as uncompromising as justice; I am in earnest; I will not equivocate—I will not excuse, I will not retreat a single inch, AND I WILL BE HEARD."

When K. Natarajan, editor of the *Reformer*, came to the U.S., Fred arranged for him to speak at the University of Michigan. We gave a dinner for him and his daughter, Kama Khoti, who was deaf from exposure in prison for nationalist activities. It was a rare and exciting evening. "Why don't you ask him something?" I prodded one of the younger professors who had not opened his mouth.

"How can I?" he asked in a whisper. "He knows our Bible, our Shakespeare, and our classics better than we do. And in addition he knows his own."

Next day we thought of a friend of ours who made a hobby of blooded cows. He had entertained us often, though he made Fred promise not to put him in a sermon. "I'm on to the fact that you put everybody you meet into your sermons as illustrations of something or other, but I hear every time you preach, in my pew or over the radio. So don't you break your promise!"

He cordially invited Natarajan to see the famous "three hundred and forty cows with college educations," and as our host stroked the back of a thirty-thousand-dollar bull after showing the trophies and prizes garnered by the animals, Fred said, "See, Natarajan, I told you India isn't the only place where the cow is worshiped."

Fred talked often about India and about Gandhi in Ann Arbor, interesting many people in the true evaluation of this huge country and her strange latter-day saint. If Gandhi should come to America, he felt that the danger of unfortunate publicity based on general misconceptions must be avoided. An advance program should acquaint groups in this country with his philosophy and platform.

When we heard that Gandhi was to attend the London Round Table conference of 1931–32, leaving India for the first time since 1914, we spent hours discussing the matter, consulting with friends, writing letters, sending telegrams. If by any chance he did come to the U.S., we planned to turn over our home to him so that he would have it as a private place.

One day the representative of a newspaper syndicate asked Fred if he would talk to Gandhi in London.

"Hello, Bapu [Little Father]," said Fred, and they talked fast. Neither was a man to waste words on transatlantic calls. Fred asked if he would come.

Clear as crystal, Gandhi's voice came back. "It is more important to return to Bombay and a new struggle for liberty. . . . God has not cleared my way to go to America. I will go in God's appointed time. My inner voice tells me it has not arrived."

"A miracle," Gandhi exclaimed in London as he hung up the receiver. When he was told the conversation had cost a hundred twenty dollars, he said, "Well, the Bishop should not have dropped so much money in the middle of the Atlantic ocean!"

Several years later Gandhi referred to the conversation in a message published in the monthly bulletin of the Indian League of America. "In America," he wrote, "I suffer from the well-known malady called hero worship. Good Dr. Holmes, until recently of the Community Church of New York, without knowing me personally became my advertising agent. Some of the nice things he said about me I never knew myself. . . . Dr. Holmes was followed by Bishop Fisher, who knew me personally in India. He very nearly dragged me to America but fate ordained otherwise and I could not visit your vast and great country with its wonderful people."

As our crowded, swiftly moving days fled by, I think I was the only one who knew what a quiet, heroic fight my husband put up against his increasing physical handicaps. Now and then he would take a few days in the University Hospital or drive to Mount Clemens for the baths or stop at Martinsville Sanitarium in his own state of Indiana for a brief respite.

Fred learned of the possible mental and nervous results of arthritis. "I think my spirit has often been broken and marred by a suffering body," he confessed. "I can see myself now and am determined to react as Paul did to the thorn in his flesh instead of the way Byron did to his club foot. The doctor thinks my ideals and my career in the ministry have saved me. My trouble is organic and had I chosen a worldly career, he says, by now the wheel chair or grave would have me. . . ."

He controlled his malady, which could never be cured, and still set himself an unmerciful schedule. To get the quiet periods he so deeply craved, he rose at four in the morning; his working day lasted until late at night. For refreshment we read together constantly and our book bill was frequently bigger than our food bill for the month.

I tried to get him to take the full three-month vacation his church offered him, but summer school brought to Ann Arbor a mature group of three to five thousand students. He loved the summer audiences and they crowned his year.

There were five or six weeks at the end of summer school before the fall session, and this time we packed with play, study, and work. We began our vacations with our ritual of transition, an orgy of detective-story reading, and then were ready for life on the farm in Hingham or to live close to nature in some shack where tides lapped our doorway and we could spend half our time in the water.

When we were in Hingham, Fred turned into a real dirt farmer. It was most impressive. "Wherever did you learn so much?" I asked of this man who was as much a product of cities as I was myself. "On Uncle Henry's farm," was my Bohn's reply, and he would make me reread *How to Get a Living from the Land.* As with children, he had a way with animals and even the birds and squirrels gathered around to eat from his hand.

Twice we went to Europe, and were in Germany the tragic year Hitler came to power. The Passion Play was produced that year in Oberammergau in celebration of the three hundredth anniversary of its first performance, though it was not the regular schedule. We lived there with the Unrepentant Thief who had to hang on the cross for fifty minutes. "My great uncle on my mother's side was once the Christus," he told us. Fred was so impressed with the fact that Judas and his confession held the stage for forty minutes that he selected this scene for enactment in his own church.

In June 1934, he was away just before our tenth wedding anniversary and he wrote me a letter which I quote in spite of its intimate nature because it reveals, I think, what ten years of marriage meant to us. It was scribbled on rough notepaper in pencil on a train in Canada.

Dear Old Sweetheart:

Rest in calm joy and peace. We shall need your beautiful strength and vision as we plan the new days together. I do not know what is just beyond our horizon—but it is glorious. You married a mystic—a leaper—an ultimist—but one who loves you with the deepest and highest artistry. A week from tomorrow will be our *glorious tenth*. We have at least 20 more at high level and then maybe ten more at quiet, reposeful reminiscent water level. And He shall lead us beside the still waters. Meantime there is work in the world for us to do. I feel a stirring within me—what it forbodes I do not quite grasp.

The unknown God! The unknown Lord! . . . Our Resource is within us—we draw it from the everlasting energy of life. Those were lovely but costly words you said ten years ago—"for better for worse—for richer for poorer"! And Riches untold in spiritual values have been ours. People have fooled us—and I have not always been wise—but there is no scar on my soul. Silver cups of ours have dissolved in the acid of experience—but God's grace is even now precipitating the silver for another richer, rarer one. I hold it to your lips as a sort of communion chalice. Then when your lips have kissed it in consecration I shall hold it to mine.

I gaze at the far-off and stumble over the near. And you too are like that—really! We belong together. The open road is our home. Tomorrow beckons—and casts her shadow on today. What does she offer us?

Glorious joy—salted with a little pain; beauty—wrinkled with a little disappointment; eternity—limited with a little time; love —pricked with just enough thorns to require kisses of comfort and healing. And, forsaking all others, I keep me only unto thee so long as we both shall live—and that means always. . . .

The following summer was the only one in which we took separate vacations. Wives were not invited to the meeting of the Continuation Committee of the World Faith and Order Conference in Hindsgaul, Denmark, and the trip was expensive. Fred refused to go unless I went somewhere and did something I wanted to do, so I took off for Mexico and a six-week course in Spanish at the old university and then went on to visit Yucatan.

Fred came back by way of Norway, Sweden, Finland, and Russia. From Finland, he wrote, "Really, if anyone who's always sighing for the old-fashioned Sunday talks to me again, I shall rise up and smite him. Death is stalking the streets today. No color, no joy, no pleasure such as you see in French families wandering the Tuileries in Paris on Sundays. It is Reformation Lutheran to the core. I've been to church three times and feel sacrosanct and have sent forty postcards. . . ."

In Moscow he took time to buy me a present. Most husbands would have selected a bit of sable, an ikon or samovar, but not Fred Fisher. My Bohnny spotted a curious painting on wood. "That is Catherine, Madame La Ressource (Madame Quick-wit)," explained the owner. "The painting marks the secret entrance to the apartment of her French lover." And this is what he brought me, lugging it across a dozen borders and displaying it to the authorities. When I met him at the rendezvous in New York, he had to display it before all the passengers, eager to see what the former bishop had brought his wife.

How could you resist a man like that?

11

When Fred came back from Europe, he was always filled with a sense of terrible urgency. Once as we drove across a peaceful landscape in Ohio, a vista of village and farmland, he groaned as if in pain, "You know, Han, I feel we must arouse them. Stop and ring their doorbells to warn them. Danger is so much closer than they realize."

He did what he could, but it was a cry in the wilderness. Then, when Bishop Blake pleaded with him eloquently to leave Ann Arbor and take Central Church in Detroit, it was as if Fred himself realized that he had very little time left in the world he loved and worried over. The church was in the heart of the fourth largest city in the U.S., center of our industrial complex. It had been through a series of calamities and was dying. "It will take a giant to swing it. . . ." Blake had said.

"I tell you, Han," said Fred, "the biggest problem is how to keep our scientific civilization from bursting. Either we've got to run the machines or they'll run us. That old church in Detroit must keep its spire pointing to God—and you and I must learn a new language. Detroit speaks a different one from any we've learned. It's the language of tomorrow."

As soon as we moved there, we set aside Friday evenings for the study of Detroit as if it were a foreign city. One Friday we met with labor-union leaders, another with a group of Negroes, who represented one tenth of the population, another with some of the Poles, whose newspaper had the largest Polish-language circulation in the world. One Friday Henry Ford was our host and said to Fred, "I should like to meet your friend Gandhi. I think maybe you'd find we are more alike than we look."

We discovered China in Detroit and after meeting with some of the twelve hundred Chinese residents there, carried on a mission for them from Central Church.

Those Fridays, as Fred had predicted, were necessary to an understanding we might have thought we already possessed if it had not been for Fred's sure humility about his own knowledge.

When the inexorable growth of the city reached a certain point, it was necessary to widen the main traffic artery. Our old church, a landmark since 1825, must be cut in two and moved.

Taking off twenty-four feet of the structure was no particular feat for Detroit's master engineers though a huge crowd came to see the gap when the auditorium was sliced away. "Did you hear about the split in Central Church?" became a current wisecrack.

To move the church tower, which weighed four million pounds and reached to a height of one hundred and eighty-three feet, required not mechanical genius but a modern miracle. Men had machines to shove large, heavy buildings wherever they chose as a matter of routine, but no machine was equal to the task of moving the slender, beautiful spire. Michigan insurance companies refused the gamble, but the intrepid Lloyd's of London ventured to accept a fifty-thousand-dollar policy.

Seven strong men were selected to man the jacks and perform the exquisitely exacting work for which no machine was suitable of turning them in unison. Five of the men were of Swedish ancestry and three of the seven were brothers.

A new cement foundation was laid, the seven jacks were placed, and at dawn the men came to rehearse the rhythm with which they must turn the jacks. Engineers were nervous, city fathers frightened, churchmen prayed.

When the day came, people watched from every hotel

window and from behind the ropes that kept them back. All day long people came, watched, and then went reluctantly away when they had to, a changing crowd of everyone: reporters, dentists, patients, shopping women, bootblacks, clergy, salesmen, laborers. Would there be miracle or catastrophe?

The head engineer had slept in the park, too nervous to go home. Now as the seven huskies manned the jacks and the foreman blew his whistle, the engineer watched only the doves in the bell tower. If they stayed, it was all right. The men turned and turned their jacks in harmony. No doves flew. The tower was moved four inches to the east, and now it was only a question of time. The miracle had happened.

In three weeks, the tower rested twenty-four feet east and six feet south of its historic foundations. Seven men had triumphed in the machine age. The doves cooed undisturbed in the steeple.

This church in an industrial community was transformed by the act of faith from meeting house into sanctuary. Fred determined that it should be suitably beautiful. The interior was redesigned with carved oak stalls that held a choir of one hundred fifty voices. To the left was a pulpit with statues of the four evangelists, sculpted by Alois Lang of Oberammergau. The deep red dossal cloth was woven with gold thread and the reredos marvelously carved.

Fred and I had walked many a steamer deck discussing clerical dress. He did not feel that it was right to perform the sacred offices of the ministry in street clothes. The first Methodist in Ann Arbor to wear an academic gown when he preached and held service, he now wanted something more symbolic of the moment when a man mounted God's pulpit. "Surely it is appropriate to set apart garments for worship," he said and decided to wear cassock, surplice and stole and to vest the choir.

After years of bewailing the lack of beauty and color in our churches, at last he had achieved a dream: a free pulpit, a beautiful sanctuary, and a group of dedicated laymen who,

like him, were convinced that the church must enter the
everyday life of the man in the street.

We rented a house in the suburbs, away from the traffic
and confusion of Grand Circus Park. Fred wanted this particular one because of a barroom which his imagination transformed into a private chapel.

Here we were influenced by India. As guests in a Brahmin
home, we had watched the mother of the household rise at
dawn and enter her chapel after her ritual bath, light incense,
kneel, and pray. Then she rouged the soles of her bare feet to
symbolize the hope that as she pattered about her daily duties
she would leave the imprint of holy matin prayers. In India,
we had built a private chapel in the apartment house which
was church headquarters where all men could go to pray and
meditate. Now we wanted one of our own.

"To what corner of our home, Han, could we take a guest,
as Brahmins have taken us, and say 'Enter my room of
worship!'?" Fred asked when he saw that bar. It became indeed a place of worship, partaking of all religions. The dossal
cloth was Moslem, the candlesticks Hindu, the vases from a
Confucian temple in Nanking, the brass tabernacle came from
Buddhist Tibet, and over it all towered the Cross of Christ.

Fred, fresh from Russia, held a symposium downtown on
religion in relation to communism, fascism, the totalitarian
state, and secular state socialism to which came Jews, Catholics, and members of all the Protestant denominations. Our
way of life was doomed, he felt, unless it had God in it.

"Russia made me more religious than ever," he told his audience. "Beheaded bishops, exiled priests, despoiled churches
mark the path of victorious materialism."

Yet one newspaper accused him of fellow-traveling, called
him a "Red" because he said prophetically, "At this moment
in the world, we shall have to fight first against fascism rather
than communism."

He stirred up another hornet's nest as well as generated
a surge of enthusiasm when, in the interests of church unity,

always dear to both our hearts, he exchanged pulpits with
Dean O'Farrell of St. Paul's Protestant Episcopal Cathedral.
On a Maundy Thursday evening, Fred invited Dean O'Farrell
to read the communion service in Central Church and to administer communion with him jointly to the combined con-
gregations. In spite of vigorous protests from the ultras in both
churches, a thousand people came.

Fred's energy seemed inexhaustible, although I privately
tried to spare him all I could, aware that he was using himself
up. Besides his duties in Detroit, he lectured, headed Theta
Pi, an honorary society for the clergy, and was president of the
Free Church Fellowship. We were very much occupied at
home but, as usual, we did a good deal of moving about.

One trip, in March 1938, was to Southern College in Lakeland, Florida, for a week of sermons and lectures. I drove him
down. In our fourteen years we figured out that we had
traveled together four hundred thousand miles, sometimes
moving so rapidly that I would wake up on a morning not
sure what country I was in until I heard a newsboy shouting
outside the window or some other sound proclaiming language
and place.

In Lakeland, we fell in love with the campus. Orange
trees, mangos, and jasmine reminded us so much of India that
we decided to give to the college the Hindu temple we had
brought home with us from Benares. The temple was meant
for our Hingham garden, to enjoy in our old age, but the New
England climate was proving too severe for the red Indian
sandstone. Besides, it scarcely seemed as if we'd ever get old
enough really to settle down, however much we talked about
it. I don't think either of us was by temperament a retiring
person.

On the way back, we had an automobile accident. We
were badly shaken up, but both of us were used to rough going.
At the time we had no suspicion that Fred had sustained a
serious injury to his heart.

Perhaps I should have suspected that he had been hurt,

though he did not modify his strenuous life. Once in a while he'd say, "Han, I'm so tired!" And more often than usual he would ask at night, "Darling, be a British wife!" and I would scramble for his slippers, take his shoes off and change his socks, and bring him a cup of tea. He spoke then of our life together often, wistfully, as if it were something we must keep firm hold of, repeating to me, "and forsaking all others, I keep me only unto thee, as long as we both shall live. . . ."

While he was preparing his Easter sermon that year, he said to me, "I get awfully curious, Han, to know what life beyond is like." I knew that he was preoccupied with the Easter message of resurrection and did not recognize his premonition.

Maundy Thursday morning he went to the front door on his way to make a parish visit. "Han, darling," he asked me, "did I kiss you?"

"Yes, dear," I said, "but why not again?"

On the way downtown in his small Ford, he felt a vital stab of pain. Friends took him in to an office and sent for the doctor, who carried him by ambulance to the Henry Ford Hospital.

When I reached him, he told me the pain was like bolts of lightning, striking his heart and crushing it. Gandhi was to say of him, "He seemed to me to be one of the few Christians who walked in the fear of the Lord, and therefore feared no man." He had no fear of death, either, only curiosity, and I think he knew he was dying. Dozing under opiate that evening, he said he had dreamed that he went to church to administer the first communion to the children he was to have confirmed that night. In his dream he laid his hands on their heads.

During the night he rested under the oxygen tent, but at 4:57 on Good Friday morning, the nurse called the doctor and me in haste. Before we could cross the corridor, Fred's spirit was gone.

Some of his dear ashes were placed in the Muncie church where he found God, some near the altar in Central Church. Some I kept to take back with me to the high Himalayas in his beloved India to scatter to the winds.

When I looked for an inscription to put on the bronze plaque in the Central Church Sanctuary, I found one in a poem by his friend, Tagore. So it is inscribed:

FREDERICK BOHN FISHER

Bishop   Missionary   Preacher

And when you had taken your leave,
I found God's footprints on my floor.

PART III

Literacy Lady

1

"Sometimes I feel we live together more when we are far apart. . . ." This was a line from a poem I had written before Bohn died, while he was away from me on a trip. But then he was returning on Friday. The line failed to comfort me when I knew that he would never return, never as long as I lived.

My loneliness was intense, however kind my friends were. We had shared our lives even more completely than most happy couples, I think, Fred and I, and after you have truly shared your life it is hard to go on alone.

I tried to tackle the projects we had planned together. Could I establish an Indian ashram, in Hingham in the summer, in Lakeland, Florida, in the winter? ("If we had been spending our last years together," I wrote in my diary, "this is exactly what Bohn and I would have done.") I went back to live in our Hingham home and spent a good deal of time in Lakeland supervising the installation of the Hindu temple from Benares, his gift and now a memorial to Frederick B. Fisher. Then the Methodist church licensed me as a lay preacher and I was confirmed a week later as a deacon. Parish work was not my main interest, though, and I continued to search for a way to use the undiminished energy that needed focussing. I did all sorts of things for many purposes in that first year of my widowhood, and found that whatever I did only deepened my sense of being alone. Sometimes I longed to join my husband in the hereafter.

As panacea for all my ills, I decided to go around the world in 1939. That was the only trip I have ever taken with no basic reason other than to find nothing but myself. I was not going for the sake of some piece of work or to study some facet of education and religion. I did want to build a memorial chapel to Bohn at Tagore's university in India and I wanted to scatter the last of my beloved's ashes in the Himalayas, but these were objectives related to the past, confirmation of what had been, not contribution to what would be. Perhaps I would find my way back to living by returning to the sources of my grown-up self, India, where Welthy Honsinger had been reborn as Welthy Fisher, China, where I had been reborn as Little Sister Han. Perhaps I would be helped by seeing new countries of which I knew nothing.

Practical enough, even in grief and distraction, I arranged to do travel articles on my way and to lecture when I returned. Then I set out. There was a cold drizzle the day I sailed. Faithful friends and relatives stood on the pier, among them my adopted Chinese daughter, now married and living in America. The last thing I saw was my tiny Chinese grandchild and namesake held high by a tall friend and then the tugs nudged the *Excambion* into the current.

On that ship I met two people as different from me as they were from each other.

One was a small, ancient shriveled Jewish woman, born on Hester Street on New York's lower East Side nearly eighty years before. She had made a long and difficult journey in her life, not in space but in immeasurable distance. Now she had a room of her own on Central Park West with a view of real trees and to crown her life she was crossing the Atlantic for the Mediterranean and Palestine.

What did she look for there? To find her roots in the arid land that had so grudgingly nourished, centuries ago, the twelve stern tribes whose precepts and desperate measures of survival had rigidly framed her own life? Was Jerusalem her Golden City?

Not a bit of it. "Jerusalem is old and dirty," she said. "I'm going to Tel Aviv. It's all new and modern, with apartments and central heat and movies, like Central Park West. Jerusalem? We tear down old rubbish like that in New York and build skyscrapers!"

The other was a Texan, who had set out on two hours' notice for the Red Sea area where he was needed to keep oil flowing in the pipelines. The laconic young man did not know or care in the least where he would be for the next period of his life. "I'll get my orders in Alex," he said casually. "I go where I'm sent." Like the Jewish woman, he carried his environment with him.

I, too, carried my past with me—and the heaviest thing in my luggage was sorrow. It was the first time I had gone forth laden with the past rather than leaving it behind while I went on to new adventures. In the harbor of Naples, I saw again that impressive symbol of enduring life, of noble purpose and belief in the future, a glorious mountain. Vesuvius sent blood-colored flames into the sky from its snowy crater. My heart made an effort to lift, to respond as it had to Fujiyama, to Everest. I could only remember the terrible battle the men below Vesuvius were waging and losing in 1939 against fascism.

India was home again, almost heartbreakingly so. For distraction, I rushed about, met people, saw old friends, spoke to girls' schools, began to work on plans for my chapel. (I'd have thrown plans and the temple, block by block, into the nearest pit for another day with my beloved!)

Then I went on my pilgrimage to the mountains. In Darjeeling I rose at three-thirty in the morning and was taken in an old Ford to the spot on Tiger Hill where one can see the sun rise on Everest. I left the car and climbed alone, along the winding paths, until I found myself at a height of 8400 feet. There I waited in silence until the sun came up, hours later. The Indians had wanted the last of Bishop Fisher's ashes for a large Hindu institution, and the Christians wanted me to put them in the Christian chapel I was building to his memory. But I was sure it was right to take them to the Himalayan heights, where together we had found God so near. These great piles of mountains, covered with tender orchids and rich green trees, and topped with snow, represented to me his strong intellect, his tender soul, and the universality of his spirit. So just as the sun was coming up over Everest and Kanchenjunga, I stood and cast his ashes out. With them I left part of me.

"Oh God," I wrote in my diary, "help me to keep my sanity and not to live in the past, for I am sure Bohn is still living in the future, as he always did here."

Revisiting the places and people we had known together was too painful, too much a clinging to the sights and sounds of the past. The Taj Mahal was as beautiful as ever, white as when it was built about 1630, scoured through centuries by sand blown from the desert. But I could not bear to enter it as we had done so often together. To see that beautiful poet and man, Tagore, was almost more than I could stand, and the spiritual presence of Gandhi was too strong for me. I knew I talked too much about Fred in the presence of these great men who were our friends; I was unable to keep myself quiet. If anyone did not speak of Bohn, I was hurt and when they did, I could not let them change the subject. Jestingly, because I was taller than he was, Bohn had sometimes introduced me as his "better two thirds." It used to make me laugh. After his death it was a long time before I could laugh again, and I still felt more as if I had been his lesser one fourth.

At one point, I seemed to try to revert wholly to the girlhood I had known, before I had been to China or married my Fred. I got a young American companion, Frances Sheppard, to join me and we set out to be gay and foolish tourists. In my diary I scolded myself for crazy shopping: 15 rupees for a silly hat! I told myself sternly I should stop somewhere remote and work seriously on my biography of Fred Fisher, and so Frances and I set off for, of all places, romantic Kashmir, "garden of the gods."

Determined to have a good time, I looked at everything with wide, appreciative eyes. At first I ardently admired the fine,

free stride of the men in Kashmir, until I found out that the
women carried all the burdens and did all the work. The
women were gay enough, though, and each one wore her
dowry in the form of as much junk jewelry as she could carry
on her person. Most of them dressed in silver and red but
even those who wore the hideous burkas, like Ku Klux Klan
shrouds, to hide their faces, were hung with jewelry from their
ears, necks, arms, and ankles as they washed clothes, rowed
boats, or collected cattle dung for fuel.

I rejoiced in the watery land, the canals, lakes, rivers, creeks,
streams—such a contrast with the dry plains of India, but I
soon discovered that the water-happy Kashmiris were the
dirtiest people in the country.

Tiring of muddy land, Frances and I went houseboat-
hunting and found one large enough for three ($4.35 a day,
including meals). The living room had a lovely red Bokhara
rug, a red sofa, and red curtains. I love red. Two large and
colorful bedrooms with a bathroom between, a dining room
with elegant china and cutlery laid out for our inspection, and
a cooking boat (called a *doonga*, meaning "side dish") tied
on the stern completed the floating home. With it came its
owner, Mohamdoo, as major-domo, his son as bearer, and a
cook, all Mohammedans.

We changed her name from *Astora* to *Miss Kashmir*, persistently refused a "good address" along the Nagin Bagh, gold
coast for houseboats, and finally anchored her on the Dahl
Lake, five miles from the resort of Srinagar and the tempta-
tions of tourist shops.

My plan was to settle down and write, to find again purpose
and work. Alas for my choice of spots. Loads of people were
there, many of them charming, and social life among the
houseboats was very lively. As for peace and quiet, there
wasn't any. Ducks and pilgrims went by in a water traffic
busier and noisier than a highway intersection's. Living on
water had a destructive informality of its own. One wore
slacks (also to ride the local ponies on land) and one's hair

grew wispy. Yet teas and lunches and dinners aboard were very formal and chic. I began to feel like a combination of an old Erie canaler (they had seemed the scum of the earth to me as a girl) and a resort socialite!

Also I had reckoned without the ingenuity of Srinagar merchants, who had only the brief tourist season in which to make their year's income. One day when I had firmly ensconced myself in my cabin with pen and paper before me to write, I looked out my window to ponder a phrase and to my amazement saw a delightful silver teapot suspended between water and sky at my eye level. A soft insinuating disembodied voice began describing the delicate outline, the graceful spout. By the time a speculative eye appeared above the level of the window sill, I was captivated. A head emerged, undulating slightly as a passing water-taxi rocked the boat which the salesman had brought alongside mine.

Ah, well, of course the teapot was "not for sale" and was "ordered by a distant maharajah." It was just for the "lovely lady" with the "artist's eye" to admire. The same story with a bit of embroidery and a candlestick. . . . I would never be the sort of mean "black beast" who would refuse merely to look at such treasures by an artist, would I? And of course, I succumbed. I bought the maharajah's teapot and the candlestick. When my first "artist" had gone and I saw an amethyst necklace appear at the window, I fled ashore, resorting to the oldest of female refuges: I had my hair done.

It was all exceedingly jolly, this attempt to be a carefree young woman again, but I wrote in my diary: "I seem to accomplish nothing, for all the time we are wondering what we are going to do next and where we are going to do it. . . . I am very restless."

It was no use, my being purposeless and frivolous. I just had to work or study. But I was still on the run.

That year and for the next fourteen, I combined one purpose or another with visits to strange and familiar countries or to strange and unfamiliar ones. I thought back on it all as the car bumped and jolted its way to New Delhi and I—trying to settle my future—let memories flood in as they would in a tide, in a jumble.

The twelve hours it took to pass along the hundred miles of the Suez Canal, the casuarina trees along the silting banks and glimpses of Mt. Sinai from the deck of my ship. . . .

How the Red Sea was hot but not red and how the Arabs in any boat, large or small, poured a pail of fresh water into the salt sea when they neared Port Sudan, where a saint, returning from Mecca, died of thirst in his rowboat within sight of home. . . .

Egypt, where the veils of women that used to be impenetrable black became coarse fishnets through which they could peek and be peeked at and where the whole town of Alexandria brooded in prayer for two days before Farouk's first child was born. When the guns began to boom all traffic stopped, radios were turned off, everyone appeared in the streets and counted silently: forty-one for a girl, one hundred and one for a boy. The silence after the forty-first burst was instinct with disappointment. . . .

A new China where over the doorways in sixteen provinces hung a blood-red triangle in which two characters were painted: *Gung Ho* (Work Together). Chungking, bombed past recognition. We flew above eighteen thousand feet to avoid Japanese bullets. My afternoon in Hong Kong with Madame Sun Yat-sen, and her belief in the cooperative movement. Born of a war emergency, it would lead, she believed, to salvation for China. . . .

I visited Madame Chiang Kai-shek in a little house, passing the rack in the hall where her large "coolie" hat hung. Before this, ladies in China wore no hats—they did not walk in the streets. Madame Chiang had made work fashionable and with it the coolie hat, with a little flower topping the center of the crown. Hers had a wide, rust-colored tie brought down through slits in the braided straw to tie under the chin. On the slim shoulders that brim shaded was the financial, educational, and physical responsibility for thirty thousand children orphaned by the war.

There was the week I spent at Gandhi's Congress meeting. A week is a long time for a Western woman to sit on her haunches and there were no chairs. My rope cot in my shared tent sank to the floor with my weight in the tent city that housed tens of thousands of people where several hundred usually lived.

The women in the purdah section applauded and voted— but kept on their veils. And there were the elephants, fifty-two of them, grazing on the opposite bank of the river. No one could figure out what to do with them when the triumphal procession was called off because Gandhi was again fasting unto death. Speeches were in English and Hindi, and no translations were made. When I left there, I was desperately ill for four days in Calcutta, and then rose like a jack-in-the-box and began to study Hindi.

Thinking of elephants, I remembered that a male elephant, disappointed in his life ambition to be leader of his herd, turns morose and solitary. When I was in Ceylon, two women were chased and trampled to death by a ninety-year-old misogynist from among the wild herd nearby. . . .

In Peshawar, I met the prime minister of the province, the nonviolent Dr. Khan with the face of a saint. A Moslem married to an English girl, he also had a Pathan wife and ran two establishments very happily. "Militarism has failed," he told me when I spoke of barbed wire and soldiers in the Khyber Pass. "Nonviolence will win here on the frontier if all tribal matters are entrusted to our care."

Japan's peeresses took hours of lessons in how to present a fan to a superior in rank. Very prettily done, I thought, and after all they have learned not only etiquette but the art of forgetting themselves. . . .

In what I called my "school-years"—1942–43, 1945–46, 1949–50—I spent my "semesters" studying educational systems in Mexico, Peru, Bolivia, Brazil, and over the whole Middle East. (It was the last year that I broke my knee, but I jaunted on crutches, limiting myself to Greece, Lebanon, Syria, Iran, Iraq, Jordan, and Israel.)

Each time I returned to the U.S. I found more people speaking of how the world had "shrunk." The time it took to cover the great distances between the world's capitals was foreshortened, but did the bullock carts in India move faster or the canoes of Ecuadorean Indians cover more miles of river? One world? Was it any closer to true than in the days of sailing ships?

2

On the fifteenth of December 1947, on my way back from a trip to China and through India, I sat again with Gandhi. We spoke tenderly of the beloved wife he had lost and of Fred Fisher, whom he had loved. As we parted he took my hands and said, "When you come back to live in India, go to the villages and help them. India *is* the village." On January thirtieth he was dead.

Time gathers speed as you grow older. Months peel from the calendar as they did in old movies, add up to years and are gone. It was fourteen years after my Bohn died and four years after Gandhi died that I went back to India to start a new life. I had no plan, but I had to go. Was Bohn's voice calling me? I was seventy-two years old, but I felt young and vigorous. In the two-year-old Republic of India, a free India neither Fred nor Gandhi had lived to see, perhaps I should find fresh inspiration.

In New Delhi I registered at a hotel, which made me feel an outsider. I told myself I would soon find an apartment. During those wandering between-years I had learned to speak and read Hindi, now the national language of the country which at last ruled itself. I was excited and interested—and I would stay a while.

One evening during that first week the desk clerk handed me a telegram. Dr. Mosher, an old friend working on a research program for the Agricultural Institute, wanted me to come to Allahabad. Leaders were being sent by the government to learn how to train teachers in villages to instruct illiterates. Would I serve as a consultant on this training?

238

Illiteracy is a real tragedy for a modern man, I thought. As a nation becomes democratic and industrial, there's no time for the wise men, for the cultured illiteracy of simpler civilizations, where remembered words were handed down in the village square. Now a man who can't read is cut off from participation in his own government, in choosing his leaders. He can't progress or improve himself because he can't read directions or handle the workings of machines. In this new India, men and women needed to read as never before.

The next evening I was on the train for Allahabad, laden like a camel with the bedding I needed for an overnight trip. No faithful Kamal Dutt carried it, or made me coffee and tea whenever I needed it. This was the new India, and strenuous. I felt lucky to be a part of it.

The Agricultural Institute in Allahabad was primarily dedicated to the simplest aims: sanitation, crop improvement, child care—goals first set by Presbyterian missionaries. More or less under its able wing was a pilot project to modernize five hundred villages. The administrator was an Indian, Dr. T. A. Koshy, who held a Ph.D. from Ohio State University and who knew his own land and people as one of them. The experiment was, I believe, underwritten by the Ford Foundation. I never did find out just who paid for what but, of course, there was never to be enough money.

The first morning I was given what could scarcely be dignified by the name of a "briefing." The Institute's practical work, they told me, was hampered because the Indians could not read. Indians are seldom stupid and embrace change. They wanted to learn and that was why I was there. Until they could read, the moneylender, ancient destroyer of village happiness and security, could always get them in his power. One bad crop and they were caught by him in a net of words and documents in exchange for the little money they needed to buy seed and begin again.

It was an answer to prayer to be asked to help educate the villagers of India. My old Bao Lin days came back to me, and Gandhi's words. I had not taught for a long time, but if teaching was needed, I was raring to go. Immediately I prepared to settle in.

Where would I live? A man who had been expected to join the staff had not come and his half-bungalow was empty. Was it furnished? It was not. Where would I sleep tonight? They sent me off to Dr. Hayes, an American medical missionary, and she made me very welcome. Her agronomist husband was equally cordial and I could stay with them as long as I pleased.

That night I slept without dreaming. At dawn I woke with a sense of great joy and bounded from my bed saying to myself: *I have a half-bungalow of my own.*

At breakfast Dr. Hayes, despaired of listing all the places where I could find the best matting, the best ironmonger, the best sheets. Laughing at my urgency and determination to sleep in my own bed that night, she sent a bearer off to see if a friend could shepherd me through the day's shopping.

From the moment I walked up the steps of my half-bungalow and stood looking from the wide veranda across the sward that sloped to the Jumna River, I loved it and knew I was suited. The river had its own peace and its own sanctity. Allahabad is a sacred city because it stands on a sacred river. Two or three miles farther down, where the Jumna joins the Ganges, is the spot where five million people try to bathe in the same spot on the same morning once every twelve years.

There was shade around the bungalow—bushes, trees, palms, and mangos, those blessed shade-givers which never drop a leaf without putting out another.

Inside was a living room, ample for students to gather in, and a funny little fireplace for the brief but very chilly cold spell that came in December and January. For the long hot months, the ceilings were high and equipped with overhead fans, the floor cement. The dining room was an open space, big enough to feed my guests there, and upstairs were two bedrooms and the unbelievable luxury of two baths. Only cold water, cold as only well water can be, ran into the home-made cement tubs, but there was a stove in the kitchen to heat pans of water for the pitchers that were brought upstairs. That kitchen stove was another bit of unexpected luxury. It was of the native variety, a gnomish thing of baked mud, meant to sit on the floor with the cook on the floor beside it. The former tenants had propped it on legs, bringing it to waist-high level, closed in the top with a metal plate and punched holes so pots sat over and not in the fire. A pipe had been installed to carry smoke out of the house. My improved, "advanced" stove was to prove a powerful aid in teaching the Indians that even a little knowledge could bring comfort and a better life.

Then, to my delight, I discovered that I had more of a house than I thought. A staircase ascended from the middle of my bedroom to rooms on the roof, more like twin water tanks than the "penthouse" I called them, but they were airy and bright and I immediately planned to take in boarders from among my group.

I must admit I drained my slender resources to furnish my new home. Big aluminum pots and pans, to feed however large a family I acquired, matting and fabrics, sheets and towels, brooms, mops, and mats. Dr. Mosher, who was away, had left a note saying I could have the loan of his dining-room furniture, which I accepted, and as soon as my beds were made, my house was ready.

By *made*, I mean built. It was done quickly, before my eyes. Indian beds are simple objects, four legs, four side bars, webbing woven from side to side. They may not be very comfortable, but I was pleased with mine, made to my large measure and equipped with a tent of mosquito netting in time for me to spend my second night in Allahabad on my own premises.

My first employee was a cook. In the "new" India, other services might be disrupted as individuals sought to lift themselves from old stratified positions into better ones, but there were many advantages to being employed in a kitchen in a hungry country. There is always an extra cook rapping on doors and wanting to show his "chits," or recommendations, some of them old and yellow and ready to fall apart. The cook has kept them lovingly as proof of his skill. All my guide had to do that first day was to let it be known in the bazaar that the lady wanted a cook.

I looked at Baroda's chits politely and hired him. By the time I got home, he was waiting on the veranda. When he saw the stove he was radiant. To cook standing up and to have the smoke wafted out of his kitchen! Baroda was in heaven.

Determined to please me and to stay with me, Baroda was prepared even to give up his precious privilege of commissions from the merchants, but through the long years I had learned better than that. Your Indian cook does your marketing and there are those who weigh everything with which he is laden to make sure they are not "cheated." I said to Baroda, "Use the merchant who gives you the best commission," and we understood each other. I knew he would make something on the side, an infinitesimal percentage by our standards, and he knew that I knew. It was his prerogative, and had been for centuries, and now he, in his turn, would make sure that no merchant cheated him on the price of anything and therefore me.

Baroda had been trained in English military establishments, which had not improved his cooking, but had its points. He was scrupulously clean, did not mind cooking bacon or meat, though he never ate it, and at night made me puddings, all too often steamed, but I love them.

When I gave my first big tea for twenty-five or thirty of the Institute faculty, I tossed convention aside and told Baroda to make an American specialty (with a recipe, he turned out satisfactory brownies) and Indian food, picoras, savory bits of dough rolled around herbs and fried for an instant. Baroda insisted on adding a cake. I was dubious, but it turned out to be the British classic, pound cake, and a big hit.

The Indians were delighted, for they never got Indian food at American parties and from then on Americans brought their guests to my house for an introduction to Indian food, to curries and picoras, which I adore.

My household, like my furnishings, was to follow an Indian pattern. I added sweeper and bearer to Baroda who, under the caste work-system, never opened a door or scrubbed a floor, and, as I looked at the neglected land out back, I decided to have a gardener on my domestic staff. An odd, old fellow worked next door, looking as if he had grown from the soil. My neighbor had inherited him from former incumbents and told me he was a landmark at the Institute. Though she did not like him, she hesitated to turn him off and asked if I would like to hire him.

That is how Buknu came into my life and he shall be part of it until one of us dies. He banished weeds and grew flowers —roses, zinnias, peonies, snapdragons, sweet peas—to delight my eyes and vegetables that would have delighted my palate if I had not seen what fertilizer he used. (Those which were cooked I ate.) And each day he brought votary offerings from his crops to me in hand-woven baskets, still-lifes he created of growing things.

One morning I asked him about some curious objects, almost transparent and gleaming like silk, that hung from trees back of the bungalow. They were, he told me, cobra shells.

"And where do the cobras live?" I asked him, trying to keep my voice steady.

"Right there. Under the bamboo trees."

When I stopped shaking, I made my way across the grass, scrutinizing each step ahead. "Do you know," I told my neighbor, "that we have cobras living between us? And they hang their shells on my bamboo trees every night?"

My neighbor was wise in the ways of India.

"Buy a mongoose," she suggested without nervousness.

"I don't know how to buy a mongoose," I exclaimed.

It seems that, in the hierarchy of caste, cooks buy mongooses. She sent hers for one.

The mongoose was full of charm, but showed no inclination whatever to stalk cobras and pierce their throats with his pretty, sharp teeth. Instead he turned into a beguiling house pet. I did not feel any safer with him than without him, so I went off to see the Department of Sanitation at the Institute.

"I have cobras," I announced, feeling very brave because I had not fainted or had hysterics or anything. "They live under the bamboos I pass every time I come to see Dr. Koshy."

"But you have a mongoose, haven't you?" said the man.

"Yes, a darling," I said, "but he doesn't seem interested in the cobras."

"Well," the expert explained, "cobras won't come out during the day when the mongoose is awake. After he's asleep, you're probably asleep, too. I shouldn't worry. A cobra is afraid of a mongoose and he can smell one."

After that the mongoose, the cobras, and I were perfectly contented inhabiting in harmony the same plot of ground.

My only battle in setting up housekeeping in Allahabad was over the matter of the common kitchen fuel. I simply could not bear the thought of eating what had been cooked over burning cow dung.

This cost me cash and endless trouble. To get coal I had to have a permit. The coal was incredibly costly and tended to crumble to dust as soon as it got hot. To ignite it was a major battle. I do not know which is scarcer in India, matches, paper, or kindling—in a country deforested centuries ago by a population which has exploded steadily through those centuries, all forms of wood are hard come by.

Then as I grew to know the villages where the cow dung fuel is fashioned, I lost my prejudice. I watched the old women knead it with their hands and dry it on the walls, to build new walls and huts or to make bricks to burn. The sun had already drawn off all offense. There was no odor. Baroda was at last allowed to use cow dung in his wonderful stove and my household settled down in peace.

I am a housekeeping woman only peripherally, but I do like my home to be pleasant as I admit I like my clothes to be gay. A career and a goal do not necessarily blunt the femi-

nine instincts. But first, as always, was the work I had come
to do.

The most important place in my bungalow was the veranda. This was my classroom. I had three strips of matting
for my trainees to sit on and a low stool for me. Since paper
to write on was as scarce as paper to burn, I set up a blackboard. These were my workshop and my tools.

When I started, everything was unsettled: how long I would
be there and exactly what I would do. The only thing I knew
for sure was that my pupils were to be seventy-two highly
educated MAs and BAs who were wholly untrained for the
work they would be sent out to do. What and how they were
to teach the village illiterates was up to me.

Dr. Koshy and I talked so long during our first conference
that I asked for a desk in his office. I wanted to tap the store-
house of his resources, the knowledge he combined in his head
of both Western education and Eastern custom.

Together we threshed out the problem a dozen times. We
agreed on an over-all aim: to give these teachers an approach
based on empathy strong enough to penetrate tradition. But as
to method, we ended up where we started. This was a pioneer
effort. I was to proceed on my own, by trial and error.

Child of the West, little sister of China, and for so many
years wife to a man who had found such wisdom in the faiths
and intellects of the East and taught me so much, I faced my
trainees on the first morning with trepidation. There were
forty grown men and three women looking at me expectantly.

I drew a deep breath. "We are," I began, "starting something new in India."

3

"Let us think," I begged my pupils, "what we will do in an India without Gandhi but an India where Gandhi's spirit still walks among us. I am religious and I think you are, Hindus, Moslems, Christians, Sikhs, Parsees, Buddhists. That is good. To work in the villages of India we must be dedicated, and dedication comes from religion. Are we capable, like Gandhi, of harmonizing to work together? How shall we start? With an hour of meditation?"

The response was from the heart.

"How shall we begin?" I asked them. "With the Gandhian prayers and the excerpts he made from five religions and repeat them every day?"

They decided among them that another way was better for us. The theme for meditation was to come from me and they would form a small committee to meet each day and decide whether to have a Hindu chant, a Moslem prayer from the Koran, a Christian hymn, a reading from the Granth Sahib of the Sikhs, or quotations from Zend-Avesta or Buddha.

No working day since that February 13, 1953, when we joined together in faith and hope on the veranda of my half-bungalow, has passed without that hour of meditation.

If we started each morning in a mood of peace and of occasional exaltation, we rolled up our sleeves afterward to tackle the hard problems that faced us. I found that many of my savants had been born in villages and were reluctant to discuss any "new" approach to what they knew so well. They said reasonably that, though they had been educated at city universities, they were bred in villages and saw little sense in *studying* them.

"You have been educated away from the village," I answered. "By no effort of will can you turn yourselves back into the villagers you were. Besides, the villages you grew up in have changed. Gandhi made them change. Freedom has penetrated the village, though not yet material benefits. Gandhi spoke the word that means most to all Indians, *renunciation*, and you made him your father, your confessor, your leader. Then he changed you so that today there are new villages and we must go to them with a new approach."

Small things brought my own conviction home to me. On my trips between Allahabad and New Delhi in a little Austin, I found the bullock carts plodding down the exact center of the road. I must drive around them, forcing my car onto the rutty shoulders of the road. In the old days, British buses had priority and the bullock carts gave way humbly to any car. Now even when the drivers slept soundly on their mounds of produce, the animals had been retrained so that they refused to budge from the smooth middle. Nobody could make them.

I told my students this as a parable, and they understood. It was a new India. Bishop Fisher, I told them, had said: Gandhi put a ramrod down the back of every outcaste. Today they stand straight like other men. It was to these free people that we were trying to bring literacy and progress in a practical way.

Take stoves before taking books. I hated the time-honored stoves of India for more than personal reasons. Those who had to sit for years beside them, with stinging eyes and clogged nostrils, often ended up stone blind or with choked lungs. At the Institute they hoped to replace these stoves with electrical equipment. But the poverty of the villages was such that it would take two more generations before the villagers could cook with electricity. Twenty householders must sign contracts guaranteeing monthly payments before the poles began to

march over their land. In the meantime, we could teach them
to use chimneys.

And to build platforms around the wells so that standing
water would not seep in and contaminate them.

And to dig latrines.

How proud they are of such innovations! I was invited to
be guest of honor at the inauguration of a latrine, a truly
great day in the life of one village. (It would have meant
more, I regret to say, if the man who had contributed the
materials and land had not cherished it as a showpiece. The
rest of the villagers who had labored to build it went back to
using the fields.)

As for teaching them to read and do sums, we had to find
out how to make it possible for people without any rudiments
of learning, who worked hard all day and lived in the dark at
night. Over and over as I looked for simple, practical solu-
tions, I felt my Bohn's hand reach out to me and his voice
speak through mine.

"We must free them first from the moneylenders," I said.
"What system of accounting do the moneylenders use?"

They used a system which might be said to be the original
abacus, only the moneylender—instead of making it of wood
as the Chinese did—put it on paper. Moneylenders had to
be literate—and thus fooled and cheated the brother who
used paper only to plant his thumbprint. We would teach
them the moneylenders' system, however archaic it was.

Each morning after meditation we worked on charts of the
Hindi language. It was Gandhi's wish to make Hindi India's
national language. I got in touch with the National Institute
in New Delhi, which sent me a list of two thousand words
compiled in the villages as those most frequently used, words
like salt, and the names of vegetables and fruits, the common
household words and those needed to express human relationships. Tagore had made flipbooks for new literates and we
studied these. I wrote to England for another word list used
by British government institutes. From all of these we made
up our own.

Some of our group fanned out to study what the village people wanted most to know. Indians are proud and to give adults nursery tales to learn by would insult their intelligence as well as their pride. It was not to read about the Three Bears and Goldilocks or their Indian equivalents that work-worn men and women would give their night hours. We wanted to prepare books for them in simple language on adult subjects. As we expected, their first interests were agriculture and religion. Next, to our amazement, came the movies. People who had never seen one and scarcely hoped to see one before they died wanted to read about them, plots and stars.

I wrote the very first book, using our new word list: *We, the Government.* Then the problem was to get others written for our special purposes.

There was now too much to do! The weeks passed, the staff grew—alone I could not do it all, however tireless I found myself in pursuing these new goals—and a pattern was hammered out with love and thought on my veranda. At the Institute we were still referred to as "this new thing that has come up" but we no longer felt new. Because of long-term commitments and involvements elsewhere, our people came and went—from Betty Mooney, my right hand in the early days, to Dick Cortwright, a valuable lieutenant who later returned to America to study further. For three months Margaret Lee Runbeck was with us and this gifted and engaging author, with her fair skin, the kind so many people in California seem to have, as if they had drunk an excess of good milk all their lives, wrote our second book. So many of them helped, and I loved them all and thanked God for them. What they did was not for money, heaven knows. There was little of that.

We experimented with all sorts of teaching aids, puppets, and flannelgraphs, and began to evolve our own work kits. We read the books already available for "new literates" and found that fewer than half of them passed the test of readability, holding the mind's interest while not exceeding the written vocabulary for grown-up students. In the end I designed a tin trunk to hold fifty books. Our Tin Trunk Libraries, painted bright red, black, and white, went out into villages transported on the backs of bicycles. Later we made up Literacy Kits, with blackboard, chalk, eraser, slates, slate pencils, colored charts of the alphabet, basic books and a Coleman-type kerosene lamp made in India, which gave the brightest light ever seen in these villages. With a Literacy Kit, one of our teachers was equipped to teach twenty-five students at a time.

While our work grew and spread, I did not dare stop to think of the British estimate that before partition there were 762,000 villages, all in need of what we were doing. I remembered my Bohn waking up from a feverish nightmare and crying out to me in despair: "We have preached to them, the millions in India who long for a better life, but what have we done to help them help themselves? Nothing!" But he never used the vastness of India's problems as an excuse for doing less than he could. I have met many do-gooders, so called, in my life who weep constantly over the magnitude of the world's sorrows, treat the world as a personal wailing wall against which they can proclaim their virtue in the light of their despair. Virtue, they believe, will never triumph. It always seemed to me only a little less self-indulgent to be like this than to wear rosy blinders, refusing to see beyond the little protective walls you build around yourself. There are those who insist that nothing can be done, so why try, or that the poverty-stricken and underprivileged really prefer to remain so. Do what you can, old darling, I seemed to hear Bohn say. Build what you may and then leave what you have built behind you.

Our work in Allahabad never stopped, even over holidays. In fact we all resented any time lost. When the heat came down upon us, hard and destroying for those of us who were not bred and baked in its yearly ovens, we knew we had to go to a hill station. We needed a rest badly, and planned to leave in mid-April.

Five Indians who were doing social work in the villages came to see me in early April and asked if I would hold a conference with them in May, during their brief vacations. I knew that the heat would be 110 degrees in the shade in Allahabad, yet each of these men was looking after ten villages, making a total of fifty, and I could not close the door on them. I would be the happiest woman in the world, I told them, to offer a course in May, but I was one of those foreigners who could not support the heat. "We will come wherever you are and pay our own fares," they offered.

I had heard of an abandoned barracks at Landaur, sixty-five hundred feet above the plains, and I wrote a brigadier general of the Indian Army to ask for the use of the idle buildings. He agreed and so we did not have to stop teaching when the weather forced us to seek high ground.

Two Indians who had joined us in those early days became the pillars of my strength.

A. R. Siddiqi arrived as a trainee on the veranda of my half-bungalow. His specialty was dairying on a scientific basis, which he taught at Bihar until the government, for lack of funds, closed his department. At Allahabad, where his father lived, he heard about us and came to classes. In the course of teaching teachers we had learned to spot quickly those who were inspiring. Siddiqi had infinite innate tact and good humor. When there was trouble in the villages, he was the man we sent. His ways were winsome and he could charm doubters the way fakirs charm snakes. With his merry nature and pearly teeth, he converted many a villager into a firm supporter and his smile carried us through difficult hours.

E. C. Shaw was my other mainstay. He had worked in the villages for a Methodist mission and I liked him immediately because whenever he showed me one of "his" villages, he pointed out first what the villagers themselves had done, platforms for wells, roads, latrines. And he was a handyman himself, who could do everything he helped others do.

We three marched together in step and understanding, and when our troubled time came, we operated as a unified triumvirate.

It was a shock to us all when we discovered that the Institute still thought of our program as "temporary." I suppose I had foreseen an eventual cut-off point in the Institute's hospitality, but I still do not know why it came when it did. Perhaps we got too big, a separate entity too vital to be housed under the same roof with them. We had to move when the tenuous tie was cut and I became uncertain of the future.

For the interim I rented a little house. It was inadequate, as the half-bungalow had long since become inadequate, and I tried to option a tract of land next door to the Institute. In some ways the property was admirable for my purposes, well stocked with buildings which had once been a mission for lepers, jointly owned and administered by various churches and then abandoned. Alas, before I could collect enough to make a down payment, the Institute purchased it for its own needs.

We were close to homeless and one night I went to bed in a state of worried distress that we should have no future. When I awoke it was with my heart as high as the first day in Allahabad when I had bounded from bed saying to myself, "I have a half-bungalow!" Now I said, "I have a house, and we will make do with that."

Early in 1954 I left for America to find some money. All my life since the fire at Bao Lin I had been a beggar. It was not hard for me any more to raid pocketbooks in a good cause. It took some doing this time but the able trustees of an organization called World Literacy, Inc., accepted my proposals and underwrote the budget of forty-five thousand dollars I presented. I came back to India raring to keep going.

We were now thirty or forty strong and we had that one small house on a back road. The boys dug a well. We bought tents and whitewashed an old garage, painted it outside, and added a lean-to to make a veranda for classes. We were all going to have to live together, so Buknu made us a garden with a teahouse in the center for social, out-of-doors companionship. Shaw helped with everything, working like a Trojan with his know-how, and Siddiqi made everything gay as he supervised the renovations done with next to no money. Our mood was golden.

The lease ran for a year and the word *temporary* was real to us now. We stayed on good terms in spite of crowding and discomfort, but it was foolhardy to think of continuing on such a makeshift basis. I found a third home, in the heart of town, which none of us liked. It made us urbanites when we wanted to be only with country folks, but the houses were fine, across from the University, and the property of a generous maharajah. There was plenty of room for us and for thirty trainees, a half-house for me, small and delightful. We were comfortable, but not happy.

The lusty vitality of our program needed a perfect base on which to grow. The heart of any city was not the place for us, although I enjoyed the intellectual and social life. When I visited Lucknow, in the north of India, the governor urged me to consider moving bag, kits, and staff to his part of the country. But I had cried out when apprised that I must prepare for dispossession by the Institute, "I can't work any place else!" and I was still clinging to the familiar nest. My wings were growing stronger, though, and perhaps were strong enough for me to fly away. Gandhi's plea was for a concept, not a place, and it did not matter where the center was.

Meditating, I took stock and realized that I had very little money and an enormous dream and that I was, for all my vigor, at an age where I must exercise caution. I did not have seventy more years to spend.

In a state of indecision, seeking to find out where I belonged in the grand plan which I believe affects us all, I decided to go to New Delhi. If answer there was, it lay there.

At three-thirty in the morning Shaw and Siddiqi drank coffee with me and wished me Godspeed. My secretary and I set out in the predawn in the rattling little Austin. All the pieces of its engine seemed to roll around under the hood as the pieces of my mind rattled about in my head while we jounced over the rutted roads.

We were the only moving object on a long, lonely stretch of road when a tire blew out. Before Vincent could get the jack in place, people had arrived from nowhere to help him. When anything happens, this is the way in India. If help was needed, help came, from some hidden village somewhere or from the seemingly empty fields. I thought of the eternal willingness to help in this country. The deep spiritual roots. The generosity.

A little farther along, we were stopped by a great tree, one of the rare trees left in India. Its roots had been loosened by the deluge of rain that was still falling and it had crashed across the road. Other people were forced to pull up, too, and we talked together. I suggested that we borrow saws to cut off the branches and ropes to haul the trunk from the road. The whole population of the nearest village turned out, in spite of pouring rain. In the end they swiveled the tree trunk so that it lay parallel to the road instead of athwart it.

Soaked and tired, but grateful, we moved on again. You cannot help these warm, helpful people unless you love them enough, Welthy, I said to myself. Do you love them enough? You can scarcely make the slightest dent in the poverty and ignorance of a land so overpopulated and undereducated. They have an instinctive sense of brotherhood, the Indians, but you are not truly one of them. You have always known that you were not one of them, that they must do what needs to be done for themselves. Are you sure you can help? Would it perhaps be better to go home, to go back to the life you were living? After all, there are still places you have not been. There are things you want to learn. There are things you want to talk about and tell about, and you can always talk about India, too, when you find an audience. Perhaps you should leave this monumental task in India to the eager and young, to the inexperienced who will learn, to the people whose country it is. Are you sure you are right to be here?

I leaned back and relaxed in spite of the jolts from the car. My next step would be irrevocable. I must think and decide. Should I follow the way my widowhood had taken during the fourteen years since my Fred died, a useful, suitable way, full of new things and people, very proper to fill a grab bag of interests like mine? Was I on the wrong track in setting myself up as a Hercules to tackle the most Augean of stables?

Already in my life I had circumnavigated the globe six times. What about a seventh, an eighth? And betimes home to my comfortable New York apartment and my friends, to lectures before eager audiences, to talk on the radio and appear on the new TV medium which I enjoyed. It was a way of life that suited my temperament, my essential loneliness without Bohn, my catlike curiosity which grew rather than diminished with each new country I visited, and my love of gab. How pleasant to be paid for doing what you most enjoyed: traveling and talking about it!

In my heart I called to my Bohn, who always seemed to come when I needed him most if I waited for him quietly enough.

In 1947 I had gone all around this "shrunken" world again, seen Gandhi for the last time, and gone on to a changed China in the throes of a new and vital struggle for cohesion and freedom. When I came back, I pondered the importance in the post-World War II world of all that lay east of Suez.

I asked one group of college women, wonderful women, really interested in the world, how much they knew of history, literature, religion, philosophy, poetry, art, music, or even manners in the East? All of them answered that they knew little or nothing.

I had felt again then a sense of mission. This was more than half the world and I was fortunate enough to know the two largest Oriental countries well. Empathy is different from sympathy. It takes time plus sympathy to develop empathy. Prejudices, blind and manifold, were the biggest stumbling block.

Such small things made up "cultivation" in one country and were "barbaric" in another. At an expense of aching fingers and hours of effort, I could eat with chopsticks like a native and thus was a "nice" woman in China. In India I

used the thumb and two fingers of my right hand, seeing to
it that no food went beyond the knuckle, and keeping my left
hand idle in my lap. ("You eat with your FINGERS?" "But of
course, they think we are very dirty people to eat with knives
and forks that other people have used. You wash your own
hands, but who washes your silver?")

For two years I had stayed in the U.S. and spoken of China
and India. When the latter great subcontinent gained her
brand-new freedom, I was filled with excitement and good
will toward her. Yet I remembered that when I spoke to many
of the educators of India, who would lead the new India, they
had put universal literacy low on the scale of what must be
done. It would come "in time." The children would be gradually introduced to school.

But can they wait, the new Indians, I wondered? There
were those who did not think so and I agreed with them. A
child may change a family's attitude—in time—but India's
attitudes were five thousand years old. It was the adults who
needed to learn, and quickly, if India was to be a successful
democracy.

Then I had come back to India in 1952, not sure what there
was for me to do, to see and taste its new freedom. And Dr.
Mosher had sent for me. . . .

Now I was riding along the road to New Delhi, deciding
whether or not to stay. What would Bohn have said? "Take
it easy, old darling. You have plenty of other things to do!"
or "Go to it, Han. It's your job"? Madame Curie once asked
her Pierre, "How could one of us go on if one should be
taken?" Pierre thought for a moment and then said, "Whatever happens, even if one has to go on like a body without a
soul, one must work just the same." Of course. But I would
work hard whether I went or stayed. Did I want to start from
scratch again, as I had started in Bao Lin after the fire when
I was still under thirty? To go through the infinitely painful
process of acquiring land in the land-hungry, crowded Orient,
to build from its foundations a place to do my work?

As if my Bohn had called it to my mind, I remembered a

brush with a small, black astrologer in Cairo. I had admired his green cap, which meant he had been to Mecca, and his long striped gown. In absurd but sufficient English, he had offered to read my fate in the Egyptian stars. I followed his instructions to face the sun and concentrate on the balanced forces of nature, on the invisible stars. He made notes, frowning intently, and then he grinned from ear to ear. "You will live long life," he shouted at me happily. "Ninety-three— MAYbe ninety-four." Then, in triumph, running the last words together like a blessing, "and you will have only four days sick in ALLYOURLIFE!"

I reckoned that he did not count a broken knee or busted elbow as sick. No more had I. I'd had my "four days sick" in Calcutta after the Congress. So, as of this trip to New Delhi, I was left with twenty, MAYbe twenty-one good healthy years. I chuckled and seemed to hear an echo in Bohn's resonant baritone. Time enough to build—and to take it easy, too—after I had built.

My hat had settled over one eye. My face was caked with dust. My mind was made up. I was going to stay.

4

New Delhi was the center of government and publishing. There were many efforts being made to plan the education of India and to print her textbooks. Vast bureaucracies were at work—and mine was just another project to be processed. My reputation was established and a bit of red carpet or a cup of tea graced my reception by those in authority. In time, I could unravel all the tangled tape and do what I had come to do, but I might find myself in competition with publishers of books, with government-sponsored plans and projects. I decided to change my terrain, to go back to Lucknow. The governor of the state of Uttar Pradesh, Dr. K. M. Munshi, had urged us to come and establish our center near his capital, and had offered to help us to find land.

Land around Lucknow was no more readily available than anywhere else in the teeming country, but it was cheap. I began to commute to Lucknow from Allahabad, rising at three in the morning before the bullocks were out in immovable force, to take the hundred-forty-five-mile trip. Vincent had relinquished the wheel of the ancient Austin to Babu Lal, chauffeur, mechanic, and protector. That car was his wife and mistress and never has a woman been more tenderly guarded and cherished. Siddiqi went with me, a winsome bargainer who knew more of the mind of cunning peasants who owned most of the land than they knew themselves. By 8 A.M. we were established at the Royal Hotel, from which we conducted our search operations.

Governor Munshi was determined not to let us betake ourselves to any other part of the country. Obligingly he sought to please us. Near Lucknow he and his wife had sponsored and built a memorial center to the poet-patriot, Sarojini Naidu, where orphans of Indian army men were trained to be self-sufficient. Adjoining land was available.

The head man at the Sarojini Naidu Center, a Punjabi, waved to the fields back of the houses that made up the Center. "All you can use, and we should be delighted to sell land to you cheap."

"But where," I asked, "would our entrance be?"

"Oh, it would be simple to run a road back to you, with a gate at your entrance," he answered.

So we would again be under the auspices and perhaps the shadow of another institute whose objectives were basically unrelated to ours, and we would not even have direct access to the main road. I make many mistakes, but seldom the same one twice.

In the end Siddiqi and I boiled it down to two choices. There was a tract of ten acres, my minimum requirement, just at the six-mile marker outside Lucknow on the Kanpur Road —and there were fifty acres of rich, pleasant land for sale five miles farther out.

The larger acreage had more to offer, amplitude and good earth, but I had carefully followed the line of light poles that stretched from the city. The poles did not march as far as this land. It behooved us to have electricity. We represented light and modernity. Besides, as a housekeeper, I did not want myself and my staff saddled with the responsibility for cleaning the lanterns in which we burned our midnight oil. Still, the land was splendid and I could get it for about the same price as the worn ten acres that lay within the reach of the poles.

C. B. Gupta was Minister of Supplies for the state, a man known as a friend and protector of the people, dedicated to the well-being of Lucknow. Though he had a drive for personal power and a love of appointing his friends to office, this fascinating character lived simply and austerely in the way of Gandhi. I went to him with my dilemma.

"By all means the fifty acres," he advised.

"What about electricity?" I asked. "I can't possibly afford a power plant of my own and then an engineer's salary forever after."

"I'll put in the poles myself," he offered, "all the way out to you."

I thanked him most warmly and said I must think it over.

Meditation was for me a well-developed mental discipline, applicable as readily to practical problems as to spiritual ones. Back at the hotel I meditated.

All the political reverses and changes I had watched over my years seemed to rise in my mind. Warning signals flashed. "Welthy, you've been talking to a politician. Politicians come into office and are thrown out of office. This worthy man has already been in and out in the past. What would happen to you if with all his good will he did not have the time in office to get your electric poles in for you?"

That settled it. It was to be ten acres.

The land was a patchwork of minute holdings, many allotted to the agent, Mr. Gurnani, with whom we dealt. Once a week, month after month, we trailed up to Lucknow to negotiate. Babu Lal waited in the car for us wherever we were. In the sunshade at the top of the windshield he kept a book or newspaper and while he waited he read. He was a living advertisement of our wares. Siddiqi acted as agent, seeing to it that each peasant was satisfied to allow Gurnani to sell to us. In every case we saw that the individual owners had a signed statement guaranteeing that they would be paid off when we got the land. It took a year.

In the spring of 1956, when the land was ours, I meditated again.

"Welthy, Fred said the greatest mistake missionaries made was to lock up the deeds to their missions, hospitals, asylums for lepers, schools, colleges, universities, and even small orphanages in safe-deposit boxes in New York City. When China was taken over by the Communists they found that all the mission institutions belonged to Americans; they must have felt that the missions believed Chinese Christians were not to be trusted with ownership. This is no way to earn respect—for Christians or Americans or missions."

Then I called on Bohn, meditating deeply. "What would you have done, my wise and dear husband, in my shoes?" The answer came as if direct from him, sure and heartwarming: form a board of Indians and turn over the deed to them.

When I was invited to the All-India Adult Education Association I went straight to Dr. Armanatha Jha, one of the finest educators in the country, and told him I wanted a counterpart to World Literacy in the U.S. I wanted a committee of Indians to direct the operation in India.

"I will be your first chairman," he offered, and until his death he headed the India Literacy Board, which cooperated with World Literacy as our directors. The deed is in the board's hands, truly a gift from America to an independent India. Few "home office" strings are attached. The cooperation between India Literacy Board and World Literacy, now World Education, have made our mission what it is.

In the spring, we began to move from Allahabad to Lucknow and in June I made my last before-dawn journey. We had no buildings on our land, but we had temporary quarters less than a mile away: one house for trainees, one for classrooms, a bit of a one for me, one for Shaw, Siddiqi, and the other staff members—and plenty of grass on which to spread out.

I went to New Delhi in the hopes that the government would give us plans for our new buildings. Draftsmen were assigned to draw up a set. Very pretty plans they were, but based on Western concepts. Streets pointed north, south, east and west, with little village houses lined up along them. It did not speak to me of India and our work, but it did clarify my ideas of what I did not want.

My friends are everlastingly helpful when I am in a jam, which I very often am. Dear Dr. Rajan, a brilliant, American-trained Madrasi, looked at the plans I did not like and listened to me.

"The man you want, Welthy," he said, "is an English

Quaker with an Indian wife. He has a hospital in the hills and he won't come down. But he's a great architect, and he loves India. You go to him."

This was the first time I had heard of Laurie Baker and his wife, who was a medical doctor and woman of new India. The man had given up his career in England, his rising reputation in his own field, to dedicate his life to India as an act of contrition because he felt that his country had wronged India, which he loved. This was his religion, this his penance.

I wired and asked if he would receive a total stranger. His answer was MOST WELCOME.

It was sure to be a rough trip, but I had Siddiqi and Babu Lal with me and departed confidently. The first night we stayed in a little shack called a hotel at Bareilly and the second at another even smaller place in Pilibhit. The third day we came to the village of Ghat and the Sarda River. The bridge was down and the car could go no farther. Suspended across the rushing, raging river that had risen to destroy the vehicular bridge was a temporary walkway with a slippery rope railing. There was nothing to do but cross on it—or go back.

"Babu Lal, can you stay here, sleep in the car, and find some way to eat until we get back?"

He had already reconnoitered the situation and showed me a shanty, a sort of roadside store, where a man sat on the floor cooking his meal. The man's family lived nearby and would bring Babu Lal what he needed. He would not, under any circumstances, let the car out of his sight.

Peasants on the river bank were glad to make a little money carrying our suitcases and bedding, and we followed them across the bridge. It sagged and bounced under my weight. I did not dare look down at the sweeping, dangerous water. Clinging to the improvised railing, I set one foot ahead of the other and prayed.

My knees were shaking so much I had to rest on the other side. By then it was seven in the evening and I was dead tired.

Since my broken knee had been spliced back together with a silver screw, long walks had become a problem, but there was no other way to reach the town from which a bus would take us the last few miles. We set out, but two miles along I said to Siddiqi, "Rashid, I can't go any farther. I'm going to unroll my bedding and lay it down on these stones and sleep."

Siddiqi said seriously, "Let me carry you."

"Don't be preposterous," I retorted crossly. "I weigh as much as you do. More!" He grinned enchantingly. Rashid is thin as a beanpole.

A troop of ponies came by, wee, poor creatures with heads so small and manes so large and bushy their faces were buried. Each one rolled under the weight of two bulky bags of grain as they plodded by. Siddiqi asked the drivers in turn to take me on a pony but, after looking me up and down, each one shook his head. Siddiqi's blandishments, vocal and financial, increased with desperation until the very last man succumbed.

Between them, he and Rashid lifted me onto the pony's bony swayback. I pushed my skirts shamelessly up over my aching knees so I could straddle the bags of grain. The poor beast threatened to collapse under the strain, as step by agonizing step we went up a long hill through the gathering dusk, Siddiqi lighting the way with my flashlight.

We reached town just as the bus to Pithoragarh rattled out of the darkness. I had to be lifted up again, the step was so high, to the seat beside the driver, and room was made for Siddiqi somewhere in its crowded interior.

When we arrived very late at the crossroads which was our destination, there was our host himself, waiting for us. This kindly man said comfortingly, "See, I have brought a *dandi* for you." Never did this poor excuse for a sedan chair look so luxurious, and I made the last stage of the trip sitting majestically relaxed while the bearers swayed rhythmically upward with me aboard and Mr. Baker, with Rashid, walked behind. I called to my new friend, "Where do you live, Mr. Baker?" He pointed to a dazzling star and said, "There!"

His enchanting house was indeed on the very top of the high hill just under the star. Dr. Kuni, his wife, beautiful and a highly trained scientist who was physician in the hospital Baker had built and which he ran for her, immediately sensed my utter fatigue. She put me to bed in the guest house her husband had recently finished building, most of it with his own hands, and told me gently, "Sleep, sleep."

I awoke to a mountain morning in India, indescribably refreshed. The clean air and white snow, the smell of coffee, delighted my senses. Over breakfast, I began to know my hosts.

"How did this romance come about?" I asked eagerly, all aglow when it came to love. "And why do you hide your light up here where only the stars can see you, Mr. Baker?"

"After working in China, I came to India and drew the plans for the missions to lepers, including most of the churches. I got exceeding weary of having my designs sent to New York so that New Yorkers could decide that they knew better than I did what kind of buildings and accommodations the lepers of India needed," he said, wrinkling the nose in his humorous face. "So I married Kuni instead!"

That was all I got out of Laurie Baker. I myself looked over his marvelous hospital and pharmacy, run much as Dr. Schweitzer runs his. Families bring their patients and cook their food in the fireplaces Laurie has put in each room, for it is cold in these hills. I saw one patient arrive in a sedan chair which had been carried for sixteen days through the mountains. His leg was broken into splinters. Dr. Kuni took him in and made him walk again.

For three days I sat talking with Laurie while Kuni tended the patients. No one had ever understood as he did. His imagination vaulted over mine, translating dream into sketches as he sat without speaking, his hands constantly moving. As I talked he blocked in, scribbled out, added, subtracted, and covered endless sheets of tracing paper.

Dormitories, administration building, an open-air theater

primarily for puppets who speak to the people in their own terms, a place for me, a place for Dr. Koshy, a place for us all. The form that enclosed the buildings was roughly an oval, with streets flowing freely, curving and meandering. A wall in front would serve two purposes—enclose our peace and tell our purpose. The murals would be of villagers and teachers, Hindi charts, puppets, men, women, and children learning with their teachers, all sitting cross-legged on the ground, and, as a summation, a turbaned man reading. The gate in it would be wide, so that the wall would shut no one off. Through it would be visible the flag of India flown from a staff planted in a flower bed.

Then I said, "I must have a house of prayer for all people." Laurie Baker had been to China and knew what I meant when I said, "A thatched roof, curving upward like a pagoda roof to culminate in a finger toward God." "Circular," I added, "with glass walls—and in the center, inside, a pool of quiet water." His plan was more beautiful than my dream, and the house of prayer was to be set in the heart of the village.

At the end of a week, when his sketches were almost completed, I brought up the question of fee. My diffidence was matched by his amazement. It had not occurred to him that we should pay. It was for India. Of course I sent him money later, a pittance compared to what he deserved. He accepted it, but only for his hospital.

I was so happy when I set off back down that mountain with my sketches that I jogged along like a girl. At the end of the bus line I walked briskly the miles from the town to the river and, such strength had I drawn from the hills and from being with the Bakers, I crossed the perilous bridge without a quiver.

Babu Lal was waiting faithfully, guarding his beloved Austin. He turned it around and the three of us headed for Lucknow with singing hearts. Laurie Baker would send on blueprints and specifications to carry out the graceful plans, and meantime we had a job to do. Selecting a contractor was almost as complicated and delicate a matter as buying land.

We would have him start with the portals. Even while we were still operating from temporary quarters, our gateway would be symbol of the future. Inscribed above the wide opening would be these words, in Hindi and English:

Saksharta Niketan

Literacy House

5

On September 13, 1956, I turned the first clod of earth on our land, just to the right of our gate. Here would rise our administration building and our outdoor theater. Laurie Baker had arched a wing between the main structure and the library, giving it the shape of an E. Brick benches under the sky would seat an audience of three hundred thin Indians (almost all Indians are thin) in front of the covered stage. We planned a gala opening when the building was completed, a demonstration of our plans and purposes.

Of course our normal work went right on from our bustling temporary quarters. Teachers were trained in short, intensive courses and went forth into the villages. Our traveling libraries in a field work van given us by the women of Greenwich, Connecticut, radiated for thousands of miles. We commissioned books and, as soon as they were written, published and distributed them everywhere to new literates. To my infinite delight, CARE agreed to finance our Literacy Kits and we stepped up production. Our fortnightly newspaper, *Ujala*, later to become a weekly, went with them so that villagers could keep up with the news as soon as they learned to read.

As soon as the first single interior room was completed, I moved in where I could supervise the work. That is how it happened that my first days and nights at Literacy Village were spent in the ladies' rest room.

The furnishings, as of that time, consisted of a commode. I put a gaily colored screen around it and added a cot and a desk. The sweepers, who were used to this problem, dealt with

267

the sewage disposal. For the future, we should have a septic tank.

To my distress, I discovered that one person who knew less about septic tanks than I did was our carefully selected contractor, Mr. Khanna. I began inveigling experts out to Literacy House to explain the principles of drainage to him and his foreman. As in China, I had to become in effect my own contractor, with Khanna as straw-boss.

For a temporary dining hall, we had a trestle table of boards laid between two pillars of the veranda. On it I put an oil stove. My cook lived at home and came by day to fix our meals, washing the vegetables in buckets of water lugged from the well. It was very satisfactory.

Along with the workmen, my secretary arrived each morning and between us we kept abreast of the endless paperwork such a project entailed. The Literacy House staff members and accountants came often to consult me on the work they were doing, and drop-in visitors were already taking up a good deal of time. Still my interest centered on the blueprints kept spread on a big table.

To make a dream come true is nearly always fantastically difficult. Practical people abhor dreams in the making, only approving them when they become practical realities. Our concept was stirring and Laurie Baker's plans exquisite, with an absolute minimum of straight walls and no rectangular buildings at all. The circular House of Prayer for All Peoples was the heart of the matter, setting the rhythm of slow curves. "You just can't build in circles and with all those curly walls," said our voluntary advisers, shaking their heads.

I was undisturbed by this predictable attitude until a young man was hired and sent to me as an assistant. He was energetic and intelligent and I looked forward to unloading most of the responsibility for building onto his youthful shoulders. But he had to believe in the plans. Instead he took one look and said firmly, "I will have no part in putting such buildings up!" I thought his resistance would crumble as he came to understand them, but when he began to tell Khanna to "pay no attention to her" because he was eventually going to run the show anyway and intended to build as he liked, there was nothing to do but ask for his recall. He had an odd misconception of his job—which was to cooperate with me! I missed the young man, a splendid fellow in his way, and was forced back on my own, blessing the knowledge accumulated as resident contractor for Bao Lin.

One drastic and irretrievable error, too costly to rectify, had been committed before I had moved onto the grounds. Our property runs for six hundred feet along Kanpur Road. The gate, naturally, should have been centered exactly three hundred feet from each boundary. Instead it was set up sixty feet to the south of center and we were forced to swing the whole village closer to our lot line than is esthetically pleasing or actually safe. Until we have more land, we must make do with the shift. It means that thieves come in the night over the near boundary and sometimes steal from us despite our watchmen.

Of course no amount of care could eliminate all mistakes, but I was determined to prevent further disasters. Though I kept in close touch with the work going on from our temporary Literacy House, my main absorptions were with concrete and wires, windows and pipes, roofs and tiling, and I spent thousands of hours bent over the blueprints, measuring and translating from quarter inches into feet until my head reeled.

In a system essential to India, as it was in China, I was the overseer of the overseer and of an assistant overseer who oversaw the contractor. Seers and overseen, we were a necessary chain to production. We had the dream and I modified it only to conciliate two powerful influences: climate and cash. We had too much of one and not enough of the other.

Ventilation was vital and certain original concepts had to be adapted to allow an air-flow through the buildings close to the ceiling so that heat should not build up under the roofs. Floors became my mania. They must be of cement for coolness, for cleanliness, to take the hard wear and keep maintenance to a minimum. Cement has more variety than you may think. In Calcutta, Fred and I had first-class cement floors, lovely dark red ones, smooth, easy to wipe up after dust storms, and handsome combined with carpets. Such glossy, colorful floors were beyond my budget and I sternly banished my happy memories of the bishop's apartment. Ours at Literacy Village—growing so rapidly into a multiple of literacy houses!—must be made from ordinary cement. They were rough, but from the first we kept them immaculate. Simple cotton rugs called *duris*, hand-woven and cushiony, would cover them for the trainees to sit on and set up their six-inch-high portable desks.

We learned together, all of us, on the job. Mr. Khanna mastered the art of septic tanks and was so pleased that he acceded cheerfully when I insisted at times that we do more tearing down than building up. When our designs were not realized, we tore out wires, we tore out floors, we tore out windows and started over—but for every two steps backward we took three forward.

A second room erected in front of the ladies' room turned itself into a kind of waiting room for callers and associates. Eventually it served the same purpose for the young women who came to live in the dormitory, so suited was it to this un-planned use. For a short time I considered living in it. The proportions were delightful and the design attractive, but it was too open and exposed. I retreated to my own smaller room to deal with important matters and slept in it at night when the watchman and I were the only people on the grounds.

It hardly seemed possible, but somehow all our activity cul-minated in a great burst of creative determination—and by late spring 1957, the Administration Building, with its arched theater and its library on the far side, was completed.

I tried once, in America, to describe our theater, and a young girl commented admiringly, "You mean you've got a drive-in!" For one happy moment I had a vision of the slow and unwieldy Indian bullock carts streaming in the gate and parking before our puppets, but all I could do was to shake my head.

Invitations to our opening, our *tamasha*, went out two weeks in advance after we had checked to make sure what day and hour were convenient for our two patrons and friends, Governor Munshi and Supply Minister Gupta. Justices of the courts, heads and department heads of universities and colleges, our friends in Delhi and Allahabad, and other friends all over India were invited. From the response to the R.S.V.P. on the invitations we knew that we should have a crowd. But in India people are also very likely to arrive without bothering to say they will.

The day came. The skies were clear and a breeze blew. I was up at dawn and sat on the steps of my own little house-to-be meditating on this milestone. It had not been easy. The staff had held together loyally and the New York office had backed us to the hilt, but we had had little help from outside. Yet Literacy Village was opening its gate to the public, to India, to the world.

I looked around. In spite of the debris and confusion of building in progress so much had been accomplished. Our front gates were in the wrong place, but they were graceful and strong. The murals on the walls were vital and beautiful, painted by a brilliant young Swiss artist sent to us by Laurie Baker, who had worked for room and board with the lusty good will of the young. Our money had come in driblets but, like poor folks everywhere, we made do, and barbed wire was all we could afford to protect the rest of our land from marauders, men and animals. Some day, I vowed, a low, curving brick wall would supplant the barbed wire.

Our soil was sour and alkaline, but somehow Buknu, the ageless man whom I had uprooted from Allahabad and planted in Lucknow, had wrought a magic with the fertilizer he loved and with his dark, gnarled hands. Neighboring cows actually skinned their hides trying to get through to the young, misty, greener grass in our compound and flowers bloomed around the staff which flew the flag of India. In a vase, I always had a bouquet delightfully arranged by Buknu. Spindly trees were trying to root in the poor soil and several of them might flourish. Sometimes villagers have only one great neem tree from which they clip tiny ends of branches to rub their teeth shining white and under whose shade they gather. We hoped our neem trees would grow tall.

The building, the proud Administration Building, was truly a dream come true.

That morning, all of us who belonged to Literacy Village went together into one of the classrooms for the shared meditation essential to us. The theme I chose was that life goes forward on the steppingstones of the past and of our ideals. What was to come we could learn. What we had was the dedication in our minds and hearts.

Refreshed, we set to work. A table was on the stage, covered with a homespun cloth in a thousand colors, which I had given the Village, and in its center was a vase of dahlias produced from our starved acres. Chairs were arranged for the guests of honor, Governor and Mrs. Munshi and Mr. Gupta among them. Over the theater seats of brick topped with cement went a *shamiana*. This Indian awning makes its appearance, supported by poles, to shelter all rituals, ceremonies, and outdoor conferences against sun and rain. Delicious designs are appliquéd on its under side. It is a joy to look up from your seat beneath a *shamiana*.

Our exhibition was ready. There were photographs of trainees, of adult classes in the villages. Copies of the first books we had commissioned tailored to the needs of new literates were on display, and a small, proud sign noted that their sales had exceeded ninety-three thousand. The editorial staff would be seated at their desks when our guests arrived, to demonstrate how forthcoming books were to be prepared and how our news magazine, *Ujala* (Light), was edited. (I hoped the Ford Foundation would help me establish a school of writing, which they later did.) In our library was our greatest extravagance, a luxury on which I had insisted as a necessity. All my life in the East, in China and India, I had seen the destruction wrought by termites. For our precious shelves of books I had held out for prohibitively expensive steel stacks.

Here were the seven hundred carefully selected books on education sent us by the Asia Foundation, a brand-new set of the *Encyclopaedia Britannica,* begged for us from the publishers by Mrs. Nellis of Detroit, the *Book of Knowledge* contributed by the Grolier Society through Walter Ross of Kansas City. (The sorority he founded, Beta Sigma Phi, has also become one of our benefactors.)

And at the great back door of the library, like the door of a storage warehouse, stood a pick-up truck ready to load from the stacks one of our tin trunk libraries.

Everything was ready, and I felt that we had made not too modest a beginning in our work.

Our guests began arriving at two o'clock. They came in cars and in tongas, on bicycles and in buses (which had begun to make regular stops at Literacy Village), and on foot. We sent out a hurry call for more chairs and mats. When the governor arrived a few minutes before the appointed hour of three he found not only us waiting to receive him but also a huge, happy crowd.

Each official guest had his own guide to lead him through our displays and I myself went ahead with the governor. Later I realized that talk begun in Hindi had rapidly lapsed into English—India's educated people speak it so beautifully and some of them find it more natural to their tongues than their own language.

When we took our places on the platform, I was happy that Mrs. Munshi was with me, symptomatic of the new India; Gandhi had said, "To call women the weaker sex is libel." Women were taking their place in all the social movements of the country beside their men. Some of them had gone from purdah into parliament in their lifetimes.

Our trainees lined up and sang a song of new literacy to the music of the old "Banda Mataram," the first national anthem. Then there were speeches (aren't there always speeches?) and next the puppets. With puppets it is possible to be acid, daring, and good-tempered and to underline a moral in a gay Aesopian way without offense.

We had chosen a playlet about the dowry system. The puppets cheerfully ridiculed the man who sells all his lands so that he can give his daughter a fancy wedding. If this is not his first daughter but his fourth he is probably already in life slavery to the moneylender. All the puppet men, women, and children in the village had a fine day of it—and then the poor puppet father was left to spend the rest of his life paying for the party. With laughter, we taught that seventeenth-century customs can become travesties and tragedies in a twentieth-century world. In this case, the governor of Uttar Pradesh laughed more heartily than anyone else and clapped his approval.

Near my own little unfinished house we had a second *shamiana* and under it served Indian tea and salty delicious picoras and Bengali sweets. It is not polite to ask high officials to sit on the ground, so we had rented folding chairs quite indistinguishable from the folding chairs my mother and my mother's friends rented for entertainments in Rome, New York.

After tea, Governor and Mrs. Munshi made a ceremonial exit and, without prompting, the staff instinctively formed a line to bid them farewell. Then, as dusk fell, our other guests departed.

Weary and happy, I walked back in the dark to my room. What I thought about was a day in Allahabad, four years earlier. Our work had just begun. One night I went into a village school and talked with the twenty-five villagers who turned up every evening after their hard day's work to learn.

"Who would like to tell me why he came to the school and continues to come?" I asked.

A smiling young fellow who had a newspaper in front of him beside his slate and pencil jumped to his feet, but shyly did not speak.

"Can you read a newspaper now?" I asked.

"Yes," he said. "Thank you."

"Could you read when this school opened in August?"

"Not a word, dear Madame," he answered.

"But now you read the newspapers?"

"Every day, Madame."

"And what do you find in them?" I asked.

"America is going to send rockets to the moon," he said.

"Would you like to go to the moon?" I asked joking.

"Oh no, thank you, Madame," he replied seriously. "I want to stay here in this school."

6

On my eightieth birthday, I was in New York working from the offices of World Education, Inc., our new name for World Literacy, of which I am now president. I was leaving in a few days for a trip all across the country to talk about Literacy Village in a hundred communities and then was going back to India. The tang of fall, nowhere so beautiful as in the northeastern U.S. where I was born, was in the air.

Messages poured in from a thousand friends, young and old, a few even older than I myself became that day. Many were personal friends and many more friends of the work I do. Among the telegrams was a special message from Chester Bowles, former U.S. Ambassador to India, one from Prime Minister Nehru, and one from the Dalai Lama, who had appointed me official consultant on education to the Tibetans in India who went into exile when the Communists took over. I had good wishes from young Vice-President Nixon and from young Senator Kennedy, one of whom would be our next President.

A "surprise" party in my honor was being given by the children of the U.N. at noon and that night a party for close friends and associates would include some members of my own Chinese family. My heart was overflowing.

As I dressed for the day, choosing a hat with a certain care not justified by its sobriety or my calendar age, I lifted my voice in song. Not in a song, but song, phrases from old hymns I loved, from operas studied so long ago, from oratorios and, oddly harmonious, atonal wavering Chinese phrases and a few bars of new India's favorite anthem. Then I sat down for a

276

minute before embarking on the strenuous schedule of the day to compose my soul and meditate, to speak to Bohn.

I am not sure that he observes anniversaries, which seem so important to us on earth. Still it was an occasion and perhaps he was closer than usual. I seemed to hear him say, "Still going strong, are you, old darling?"

Not me, I thought, but all the things we have stood for, you and I. And whether I add ten more to this fourscore of my years or not, it will be as Olive Schreiner wrote from Africa: "Where I lie down worn out, other men will stand young and fresh. By the steps that I have cut they will climb; by the stairs that I have built they will mount. They will never know the name of the man who made them. At the clumsy work they will laugh; when the stones roll they will curse me. But they will mount, and on my work; they will climb, and by my stair. And no man liveth to himself and no man dieth to himself."

India *is* a key country in this world of 1960, I told Bohn, just as you said it would be, the key to the East, to coexistence between East and West. China and Russia have more land and China more people, but huge, teeming India is an independent republic. If it stays that way, if democracy takes deep root in its worn and ancient soil, how fortunate for the world, how important for the future.

How vital this country of India is to the U.S. and to Western civilization and to all religion, I mused. Not in the narrow religious sense, but as Fred Fisher believed in it, as it is represented by our House of Prayer at Literacy Village. Gandhi said, "Mine is not a religion of the prison house. It has room for the least among God's creatures, but it is proof against insolent pride of race, religion, or color."

As if counting up accomplishments on a day of reckoning, I reminded myself that already five thousand teachers had gone forth from Literacy Village and taught over a million and a half people in India to read. Then I paused to say a blessing for all the people who had helped.

We had had help from everywhere, from our government

and from the Indian government, from wonderful, rich American foundations and organizations and from the people of the United States without number—in their unparalleled generosity.

I thought of the day when I was in a New York taxi headed downtown to see a publisher about helping with a book. I exclaimed to the pleasant young man at the wheel that it was a joy to be alive on such a day. The driver turned square around, endangering our lives, to say, "My God, woman, I like to hear somebody say that!" We talked all the way downtown and I told him what I did. "My God, do enough of that and there won't be any more wars," he said and I declared I hoped not. The meter rang up $1.75 and I handed him two dollar bills. "Keep it," he said. "Keep it all. Use it for me!" "Wait, I'll give you a receipt for tax deductibility," I said, but he waved and drove off with a grin.

We Americans may be called ugly and anti-Americanism may be a recurrent sentiment in many a country, but one trait has always saved us from hatred. Unique unto us is this generosity, personal generosity. Let need arise and appeal be made, we open our hearts and reach in our pockets. It's a frontier generosity, the kind that makes all other men neighbors if they are in trouble.

Of course there is never enough money to do all I want to do, never will be. But I will go on pleading for what I know will be usefully spent. I shall ask for Point Four money for expansion and for foundation grants to pay those dedicated volunteers who are always so willing to come if we can transport and maintain them. I'll ask for sums to pay for books, supplies, and trained workers. I am grateful, with all my heart, for this aid and happy that those in power over such powerful sums have the imagination to realize that our work is vital.

My deepest gratitude, though, goes to the people, all sorts and kinds and ages of people who give of their own. To those who offer $350 to "adopt a village," for this provides a teacher's salary for a year. To those who support a work supervisor who looks after ten villages for $750, or who build a staff house at a cost of $2500. For $25 they put tin trunk libraries with 50 books into villages and for $10 make a man somebody.

Ten dollars? That's what it takes to start a man or woman reading in India. I went one night to watch a teacher as he showed a gaunt, middle-aged villager how to write his name. Taking the pencil and slate, the man laboriously copied out the four letters, *Rama*. Then he pointed to it with a flourish. "That's me! Once I was nobody. Now I am somebody!"

The taxi driver's two dollars added to the collection of nickels from a bunch of Chicago schoolchildren who opened their sticky hands to release them into mine, to a five-dollar check from a retired schoolmarm in Utah, and on the other side of the world a human being learned to read.

How exciting it is to be alive, I thought on this morning of my birthday, and to know what that mystic Oriental poet meant when he wrote the lines that shine with wisdom and hope for the future:

It is better to light one candle than to curse the darkness.

DATE DUE

DISPLAY			